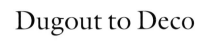

Dugout to Deco

Dugout to Deco

Building in West Texas, 1880 ★ 1930

Elizabeth Skidmore Sasser

Texas Tech University Press

11 March 1994

For Mike McCarroll

Happy 33rd Anniversary.

Kindest wishes always.

Elizabeth Sasser

This book was set in 11 on 14 Galliard and printed on acid-free paper that meets the guidelines for permanence and durability of the Committee on Production Guidelines for Book Longevity of the Council on Library Resources. ∞

Jacket and book design by Barbara Whitehead

Printed in Hong Kong through Palace Press

Library of Congress Cataloging-in-Publication Data

Sasser, Elizabeth Skidmore, 1919–
    Dugout to deco : building in West Texas, 1880–1930 / Elizabeth Skidmore Sasser.
        p. cm.
    Includes bibliographical references and index.
    ISBN 0-89672-324-0 (cloth). — ISBN 0-89672-325-9 (paper). — ISBN 0-89672-328-3 (limited ed.)
        1. Vernacular architecture—Texas, West—History—19th century. 2. Vernacular architecture—Texas, West—History—20th century. I. Title.
NA730.T52W488 1993
720'.9764—dc20   93-19438
                                                              CIP

93 94 95 96 97 98 99 00 01 02 / 10 9 8 7 6 5 4 3 2 1

Texas Tech University Press

Lubbock, Texas 79409-1037 USA

To my daughter, Lisa, and to

my husband, Tom. Also in memory

of Shaman, a brave and noble

dog who shared our travels.

Contents

Illustrations

Photography by Thomas and Elizabeth Sasser

Foreword

IT WILL COME as a pleasant surprise to many—even those who have lived in West Texas and studied or practiced architecture there—that West Texas architecture can be defined and has its own identity. The region has been described before, of course, but usually in "cowboy" terms, and the writing that has attempted to capture its mood or get some sense of the place has often fallen short of the mark.

West Texas takes awhile. It becomes clear to those who visit for any length of time that unlike places with interesting topography and scenery, areas that are more densely populated and photogenic, West Texas is just too vast, flat, and, during the extremes of weather, too harsh and forboding. Every traveler knows that the popular vacation spots high on the travel agency's list, are frequently so hyped and so effectively marketed that they quickly pale when experienced. This process is reversed in West Texas. What seems at first an endless expanse to be crossed on the way to the ski slopes and points West or to the large cities of South and East Texas, the land, when given time and a closer look, slowly reveals itself.

On a purely visual basis, access to West Texas is a gradual experience. Traveling north, south, or west, you go through no mountain passes, only diminishing trees and a sudden climb to the top of the Caprock announces a confrontation with a new land. My own introduction to West Texas came as a young student on my way to Lubbock's Texas Tech University from the East. I drove "up on West Texas" at the edge of the Caprock near Wichita Falls, and at that point West Texas took on topographical character. The architecture, however, did not appear to possess dominant or particularly aesthetic characteristics. Until this book it has been basically lost or overlooked as a subject for study or appreciation.

To know the architecture of the region marked off by Dr. Elizabeth Sasser in this volume would require a search of hundreds of miles. *Dugout to Deco* makes this search possible. This book is a clear case of the needed task finding the right person. No one but Betsy Sasser could have or would have written it, and it is important for this reason. It is the right book on architecture because it is about what makes architecture happen and about architecture as a part of the history of West Texas. It is the right book on Texas history because it has included architecture and its building processes as an integral part of the development of our society.

The photographs are what all good pictures should be—clear: they have the right number of the right things with none of the mannerisms and stale techniques that often plague professional photography of architecture.

What the book does not do, thankfully, is attempt to make the tired, redundant, and unsupportable case for Texas architecture. Our architectural heritage is far richer than that, and while there are influences from the very early native and Spanish cultures, architecture in Texas, as in America generally, is imported. The strongest influences on the building of the people who first came here had more to do with the weather and survival than the ideas of design and refinement brought mostly by way of the Eastern seaboard and Europe. Truly American architecture is surely the skyscraper and the shopping mall, and they did not originate in Texas. We have them as well as examples of all the styles and trends that have become typical of American architectural development. Dr. Sasser has simply rounded them up in their West Texas existence.

Dr. Sasser is one of the nation's leading authorities on architectural art and architecture. She has been for years the soul of the College of Architecture at Texas Tech University. She has instilled in her students and others who have read her many articles a lasting sense of history as the fundamental and unavoidable bedrock of architecture, its study, practice, and enjoyment. She brings to this book all of the scholarship, charm, and wit typical of her work. Reading *Dugout to Deco* is not unlike attending her classes, and through it she has laid out the architecture of West Texas before us in a way not only rare but necessary for the understanding of architecture's role in our lives.

Architects, who will generally agree that our profession often fails to convey the necessity of architecture beyond mere building, will want everyone to read this book. The Texana buffs and the historians need to read it, and those involved in the preservation and conservation of West Texas's fine buildings have a new tool and text. There is now access to a subject long neglected. The architecture of West Texas has been connected to that of our state and nation, and now the literature of architecture is more complete.

Richard Payne

Introduction to the Author

I BELIEVE THAT one of the most worthwhile human pursuits is teaching. Elizabeth Skidmore Sasser may be the teacher who has led me most firmly to this belief. Perhaps it is because of her unbounded enthusiasm for her subject, her genuine care and respect for students, or some unique, mystical combination of capabilities. Whatever the reasons, with Betsy Sasser, learning is simply more satisfying, more dynamic, and more fun than with any other teacher I know.

Now she has written a book about a subject for which she has a special and longstanding enthusiasm: the rush of change in West Texas from the open prairie to an established and specific architectural culture in the fifty years between 1880 and 1930.

In *Dugout to Deco,* she ebulliently chronicles the fast-tracked development of this unique stretch of mid-America from mesquite to *moderne.* As a native West Texan, I take new satisfaction and pride in my own springing ground and its history viewed through Sasser's remarkable time-lapse lens.

Information remembered becomes knowledge, and knowledge steeped and nurtured may become wisdom. Maybe wisdom is what we need most—the wisdom to celebrate and conserve a heritage that this book proves worthy of reverence.

After four decades in the classroom, Betsy Sasser is currently free to practice her magic at large. Now, through this handsome and most readable book, one of the very best teachers continues to teach.

Paul Stevenson Oles

Preface

I do not require of you . . .
to form great and curious considerations in your understanding:
I require of you no more than to look.
[Santa] Teresa

IN WEST TEXAS, if the subject is architecture, to *look* is to discover ignored and half-forgotten shelters and buildings, often bypassed by progress, whose walls contain the not so long ago memories of a pioneering society and of its rapid transformation. There are very few places in the United States where so much has been compressed into such a short span of time as the fifty years between 1880 and 1930, the span that defines the scope of this book. Only a decade or two before 1880, the Staked Plains belonged to the buffalo and hunting parties of Indians. By 1880, the bison had been dispatched to bone yards by the hundreds of thousands and the native Americans had been confined on reservations. In the next ten years, there were other endings: the closing of the open range, the passing of free grass, and the last cattle drives churning dust over unfenced land.

But there were also beginnings: the railroads that earlier had helped to establish settlement patterns in the East and South and the farmlands of the middle west, were pushing farther westward bringing Texas's western frontier mill-cut lumber, windmills, and barbed wire to encourage the migration of farmers, ranchers, and tradesmen looking for homesteads and a better life for their families. As in other parts of the country, towns grew up along the tracks and county governments were watched over from courthouse domes by Justice with scales in her hand and eyes unbound—blindness was dangerous where the sky was constantly scanned for blue northers, black clouds of dust, and tornado funnels. The first homes were tents and wagons. The arid climate, the intense summer heat and winter chill, the lack of trees for shade or lumber, dictated ingenious solutions for more permanent housing. The dugout, cut into the earth or into a low hill, was one answer. Insulation was assured but not neat housekeeping. Within ten years on the High Plains most of the dugouts had been replaced by box-and-strip houses (the West Texas term that will be used throughout the book for what is commonly called *board-and-batten*). The simple buildings were nailed together with mill-cut lumber shipped (once rails were laid), from sawmills in the eastern woodlands. The Queen Anne style quickly relieved the plainness with a serving of wooden gingerbread as well as towers with spires that pushed up like hatpins. By 1915, a barrage of "isms" introduced West Texans to classicism and the Renaissance, with California Mission influence waiting in the wings, together with an overdose of Tudor Revival. At the same time, cities played host to tall office buildings of reinforced concrete.

Unlike older and more established parts of the country where the first building efforts were torn down and replaced, in West Texas dugouts and box-and-strip stores and houses continued to coexist in the company of Queen Anne and, farther south along the Rio Grande, adobe haciendas. During the 1920s, eclectic borrowings gained in popularity adding to the melting pot Spanish Colonial Revival, as many of the architects who traveled to Spain in the 1920s called the Spanish Renaissance style that they introduced into their work when they returned to the United States. Moorish details, also appeared together with the post–World War I newcomer, *art moderne,* or Art Deco as it is now known. As the twenty-first century moves closer, the continuing presence of buildings reflecting the evolution from function to fashion and back again in a short fifty years is as remarkable as it is rare.

Jim Corder in his account *Lost in West Texas* laments the lack of coffee-table books that reveal the strange loneliness of the West Texas landscape. He notes, the "picture books of recent years . . . . leave a hole in Texas that stretches southward and eastward from the Caprock down to I-20 and over to Dallas and Fort Worth. They show pictures of East Texas, of the coast, of the Hill Country (everyone has to show pictures of the Hill Country) . . . . maybe a shot of Palo Duro Canyon" (p. 95). The same omissions occur in books on Texas architecture. Guides to Texas homes praise correctly the Landergin-Harrington house in Amarillo, the Kell house in Wichita Falls, and Lubbock's Ranching Heritage Center, but then there is a silence as deep as the polar ice cap. El Paso is consigned to oblivion with a few sentences about the missions along the Rio Grande. Laredo might as well be a suburb of Mexico City, and Uvalde, Ozona, and Dalhart are less familiar than the geography of Oz.

The visual texture of Texas architecture is like a patchwork quilt from which large patches are missing. Perhaps *Dugout to Deco* inspired by love of the country and travel throughout a good portion of West Texas, will help to complete the quilt. For the purposes of this book, West Texas is the Panhandle west of a flexible line extending from Wichita Falls to Laredo with a spur to Fort Worth. This deviation is justified by that city's claim to be "where the West begins." The boundaries in the far west are defined by the state line. The southern extremities touch the Rio Grande and are anchored by El Paso and Laredo . More than thirty-five hundred miles were covered in less than a year. There are no architectural guidebooks to this region. Historic markers, state and national, are evidences of public concern and civic pride. Everywhere there are unmarked discoveries that could cause the degree of excitement usually reserved for unearthing an intact skeleton of a brontosaur or a sword blade lost by Coronado.

It should be pointed out immediately that the object of these travels was not a search for beautiful architecture, though there are beautiful examples included among the illustrations. The purpose was to locate and photograph shelters that reflected the life-styles and desires of people who successfully endured difficult and austere living conditions from which they were able to move with amazing speed to more spacious and comfortable homes. The subjects are also barns and outhouses, courthouses and jails, stores and railroad stations, churches, hotels, and opera houses. Forts, which have been covered thoroughly in a number of studies, were considered beyond the scope of this book.

Dugout to Deco is not specifically about architects and the development of architectural offices, a subject which deserves a study in its own right. While Jenney, Adler, and Sullivan were revolutionizing tall office buildings in Chicago and young Frank Lloyd Wright was spreading the gospel of the Prairie house in West Texas, settlers were living, getting an education, and worshiping in vernacular buildings, the work of unnamed carpenters and contractors. Courthouses and municipal buildings, symbols of civic pride and civility, demanded the trained hands of architects from Fort Worth or Dallas or Austin. There is, however, an exception to the lack of emphasis on individuals. That exception is Henry C. Trost who practiced in El Paso from 1903 until his death in 1933. Only recently rescued from an undeserved limbo by June Marie and Lloyd Engelbrecht's fine biography, Trost was a participant in virtually every architectural style crowded into the first three decades of the twentieth century. He accepted each new development, including the influence of Buddhist temples in Bhutan, with vigor, enthusiasm, and the ability to lift each "ism" from any semblance of dull and mindless copyism into a personal statement of uncompromising excellence and originality. By choosing examples from Trost's work a comprehensive view of three decades of stylistic changes can be observed freed of triviality and possessing significant design qualities.

It would be a mistake to expect *Dugout to Deco* to function as a conventional history of architecture stressing names and dates and plans and cross-sections. (Interiors have been left unexplored. Spaces for living and the furniture cherished within them are too important to be squeezed into a few paragraphs.) Neither is it about the preservation, restoration, or rehabilitation of historic architecture. It is a book in praise of West Texas, its people, and the buildings in which they lived, played, worked, and worshiped. It is a tribute to the nameless builders and the later architects whose vision was translated into three-dimensional structures that continue to give reality to the pioneering spirit, the indomitable will, and the sense of humor that colors almost every story told by those who were there in the beginning.

The photographs selected to illustrate the qualities of West Texas building, both its unvarnished forthrightness and its aesthetic values that are rarely corrupted by self-consciousness, reflect, in some cases, building types typical of a period; others illustrate a particular function. Some examples give pleasure because they are unusual and unexpected.

Details of a few buildings are included without a view of the entire structure. The justification for this is that ornament speaks directly about craftsmanship and, in the days before machine production, a molding or bracket was marked by the tools of the craft, that is, the hand of the craftsman. Remove the ornament from a building and that building would, in many instances, present a mirror image of a dozen others. Ornament and color contain clues to the tastes of the owners of late nineteenth- and early twentieth-century architecture. Some preferred plainness and restraint while their neighbors reveled in an orgy of bric-a-brac.

There are fine buildings that have been omitted from *Dugout to Deco* because of lack of space or the problem of repetition. For every example included there are dozens of equally interesting ones worthy of inclusion. If the readers' favorites are not present, it will indicate the innumerable homes, churches, offices, schools, even dollhouses and carousels, waiting to be brought to the public's attention. This is the challenge that lies ahead for those who set out on journeys *to look* and to perceive the architectural heritage hidden in the thousands of miles of West Texas. It promises to be a splendid adventure.

Acknowledgments

WRITING THE TEXT of *Dugout to Deco* and photographing remarkable and often unexpected buildings along some six thousand miles introduced my husband and cophotographer, Tom Sasser, and me (and our traveling companion, Shaman, a German shepherd) to many men and women who were interested in the project and encouraging and helpful. We wish to thank particularly "Butch" Dickerson, mayor of Quanah; one of the last residents of Sanco, now almost a ghost town, who drove up in a pick-up and told us about the history of the site; Don McCune, park superintendent at the Magoffin House in El Paso, and the knowledgeable young woman who gave us a personal tour of the home; Gerald Smith, a resident of Silverton, who called from his pick-up and arranged for us to drive off the beaten path to visit and photograph an almost undisturbed dugout built by the grandfather of the present owner of the ranch, Charles Wayne Mayfield. Mr. Mayfield graciously left a televised Southwest Conference football game to give us a tour. This was the last stop on our photographic journeys during which we had been looking without success for a dugout in situ. The episode seemed an omen of approval from the pioneers with whose lives we had become deeply involved.

Special appreciation belongs to friends that we have known and valued for many years: Louise Arnold's friendship and interest were instrumental in making this book a reality; Nelda Thompson provided encouragement; Curry Holden and Frances Holden (author of *Lamshead After Interwoven*) made a visit to Lambshead Ranch near Albany possible and created the opportunity to see a portion of the ranch with its legendary owner, Watt Matthews; Sue and Emily Rickels gave us a tour of Laredo and introduced us to Gloria Canseco from whom we learned a great deal about the city on the border as well as about a preservation project in progress along the Rio Grande; Fred and Nancy Griffin provided information about El Paso and about the recently restored train station; Dudley and Virginia Thompson shared their enthusiasm and pleasure in the subject and photographed Tom and myself for the flap of the book jacket; Craig Alan Drone offered very useful information from his architectural thesis on the station at San Angelo; and John Lott shared his knowledge of the KCM & O rail line.

I thank the chambers of commerce that we visited for information and city maps, especially Ann Stelzer of the Post Chamber of Commerce for information on the Santa Fe station in Post. Our gratitude also belongs to museums from one end of West Texas to the other. The Southwest Collection on the Texas Tech University campus, the XIT Museum in Dalhart, the Panhandle Plains Museum in Canyon, and the Museum of the Llano Estacado in Plainview have been generous in contributing the expertise of their staffs and their resources.

Above all, my gratitude and thanks for the generosity and faith in the book belong to the CH Foundation and the Helen Jones Foundation in honor of the sisters Christine DeVitt and Helen DeVitt Jones. Thanks go to the Ranching Heritage Center at Texas Tech University and to Gary Edson, director of the Museum of Texas Tech University and its Ranching Heritage Center, for permission to photograph—often at off-beat hours in order to catch the proper light—buildings preserved on the Ranch site.

I am indebted to those who have read the manuscript of *Dugout to Deco* and who offered valuable suggestions and their deeply appreciated support: Jim Steely, director of the National Register Programs, Texas Historical Commission; Charles Harper, FAIA, architect and former mayor of Wichita Falls; Steve Oles, FAIA, architect and author of books on architectural delineation, most recently *Drawing on the Future*; to Richard Payne, FAIA, architect and architectural photographer for such books as *Historic Galveston;* our daughter, Lisa Sasser, AIA, Assistant Chief Historical Architect for the National Park Service, Washington, D.C.

Last, but by no means least, my thanks go to Judith Keeling, the able and patient editor associated with the Texas Tech University Press who has believed in this book and guided its progress from beginning to end. My thanks also belong to Marilyn, Carole, and Fran of the University Press who assisted *Dugout to Deco* through its long, sometimes frustrating, development.

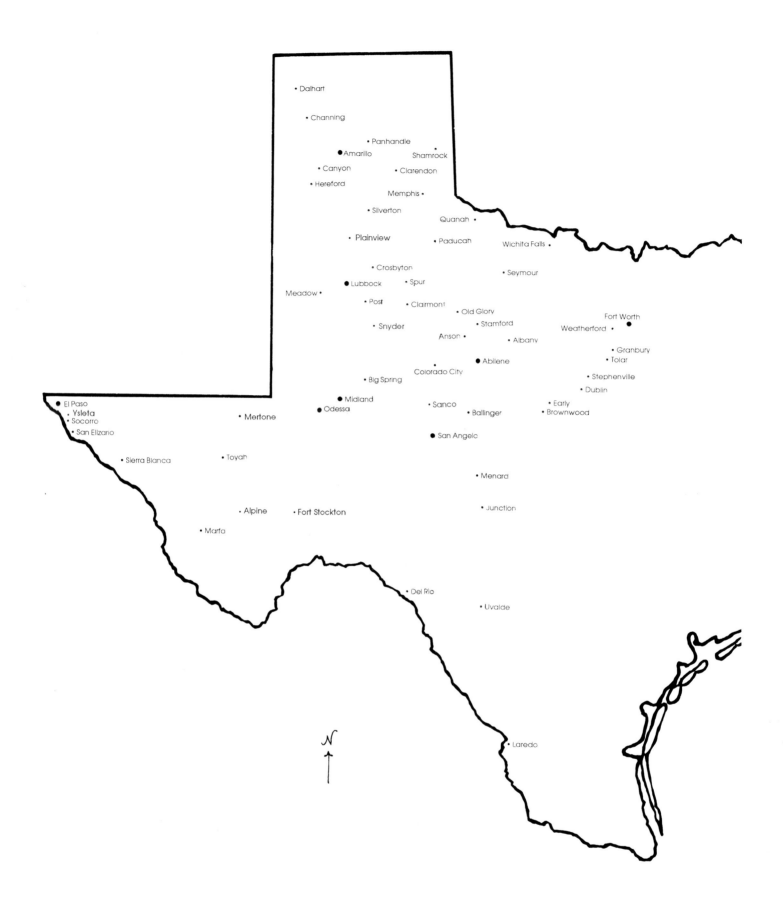

• Dalhart

• Channing

• Panhandle
● Amarillo   Shamrock •
• Canyon   • Clarendon
• Hereford
                Memphis •
        • Silverton
                        Quanah •
        • Plainview   • Paducah   Wichita Falls •

                • Crosbyton   • Seymour
        ● Lubbock   • Spur
Meadow •
        • Post   • Clairmont
                        • Old Glory
        • Snyder   • Stamford   Fort Worth
                Anson •   • Albany   Weatherford • ●
                                                    • Granbury
                                        ● Abilene   • Tolar
                        Colorado City •   • Stephenville
                                                • Dublin
        • Big Spring
                ● Midland   • Early
El Paso ●   • Sanco   • Brownwood
• Ysleta   ● Odessa   • Ballinger
• Socorro
• San Elizario   • Mertone   ● San Angelo

        • Sierra Blanca   • Toyah
                                        • Menard

                    • Alpine   • Fort Stockton   • Junction
                • Marfa

                                        • Del Rio
                                            • Uvalde

                            N
                            ↑

                                    • Laredo

Renderbrook-Spade blacksmith shop (1917), Ranching Heritage
Center, the Museum of Texas Tech University, Lubbock

I
In the Beginning, the Open Range

The sun up-sprang,

Its light swept the plain like a sea

Of golden water, and the blue-gray dome

That soared above the settler's shack

Was lighted into a magical splendor.

Hamlin Garland, *Prairie Songs*

THIS BOOK IS about the buildings that developed on the arid plains of West Texas between 1880 and 1930. From covered wagon to skyscraper, architecture metamorphosed in the blink of an eye compared with the slow progression usually associated with historical sequence. The land, which in a fifty year period attracted cattlemen, cowboys, sheep men, farmers, women and children, businessmen, teachers, doctors, preachers, lawyers, oilmen, real estate entrepreneurs, and an occasional outlaw, will be defined by a line fifty miles or so east of the 100th meridian, reaching north to Oklahoma, sending out a spur to Fort Worth, and then running west again to the New Mexican border and south to the Rio Grande. The first part of this narrative describes the mid-1870s when the ranchers and cowboys, drawn by free grass and the open range, began the trek to the Panhandle and South Plains. They pioneered a new frontier and helped create the myth of the American West. During the short years before the frontier was finally closed at the beginning of the twentieth century, the cattlemen did not invent a great architecture but gave new dimension to the idea of form dictated by function as a way of maintaining life under dangerous, difficult, and lonely conditions.

According to the U.S. Census of 1870, there was not a single U.S. citizen located permanently in the vast spread of the Texas Panhandle. Five years later the population of West Texas was estimated to be one hundred persons per one thousand square miles. In 1876, a law was passed creating fifty-four counties in Northwest Texas. During this same year, Charles Goodnight drove Texas's first herd of shorthorn cattle to Palo Duro Canyon south of present-day Amarillo. Here he established the JA Ranch, using the initials of John Adair, his English partner, to form the Goodnight brand. At the end of the next four years, the population on the South Plains had increased to 3,175 diverse human beings.

In the 1870s, the West Texas landscape looked little different from the scene that unfolded in April 1541 before the eyes of Coronado and the party he led east from New Mexico in search of gold and the dream of Quivira. Coronado and his conqistadores traveled along the southern drainage of the Canadian River, moving toward the Texas Panhandle. There they were confronted by cliffs rising like the walls of an impregnable fortress. They called the flat land spreading out from the sheer rock walls Llano Estacado, the "stockaded" or "palisaded" plains. This was later mis-translated into "staked plains" by Anglo-Americans who, in what Bolton called "an engaging folk tale," told of stakes driven in the ground to avoid getting lost in the waves of grass. Swinging southward from the Canadian River, the Spanish caravan moved in a leisurely way over the great expanses of featureless land where nothing could be seen but "cattle and sky." A chronicler of the expedition wrote:

> The country where these animals [the buffalo] roamed was so level and bare that whenever one looked at them one could see the sky between their legs, so that at a distance they looked like trimmed pine tree trunks with the foliage joining at the top. When a bull stood alone he resembled four such pines. And however close to them one might be, when looking across their backs one could not see the ground on the other side. . . . This was because the earth was so round, for, wherever a man stood, it seemed as if he were on the top, and saw the sky around him within a crossbow shot. . . . There are no trees except along the streams found in some barrancas, which are so concealed that one does not see them until he is at their very edge.

Castañeda noted, "The grass grows very tall near the lakes [the playas of contemporary times], but away from them it is very short." Another member of the party observed, "Traveling in these plains is like voyaging at sea." The description resembles the flat lands of Castro, Hale, Swisher, and Lubbock counties over which Coronado's expedition is believed to have traveled.

In the last decade of the twentieth century, the tableland of the South Plains is just as flat as it was when the Spaniards first rode across it, but the surging herds of buffalo are gone and the fields are covered by a snow of white cotton. But in 1873, when Rollie Burns encountered buffalo grazing in Roberts County, he found that herds might be a mile or two wide. He recalled:

> During the two days we watched these shaggy beasts, I heard men talking and making guesses as to the number of buffalo. The lowest estimate was five hundred thousand, and the others reached

from that to one million. I later read a book by Charles Siringo where he saw, in 1877, one million buffaloes at the big lake near where the stock pens at Amarillo were later located. In 1873 the buffalo hunters had not yet come into the country, and we little dreamed as we watched the herd pass that these huge beasts would soon all fall at the crack of the professional hunter's gun.

In the mid-1870s two events were inextricably linked: the extermination of the buffalo and the end of the Indians' freedom to roam the Llano Estacado. In the seventeenth century, the relations between the Spanish in New Mexico and the Indians were generally amicable, largely because of the Indians' desire for trade goods. New Mexican traders became known as Comancheros, from the name of their most privileged customers, the Comanches.

By the middle of the nineteenth century, as Anglo settlers migrated to Central Texas to raise cattle, the peaceful balance took a warlike turn. The Comancheros began to incite the Indians to conduct raids for cattle and horses against the newcomers. These raiding parties became especially vicious during the Civil War years, when men had gone off to join the army and forts were left unmanned. Horses and cattle were plundered and women and children were often captured. After the war, the return of the men who had been mustered out of the army helped to drive the marauders north to the Llano Estacado. There the Indians' fury was further aroused by the arrival of the professional buffalo hunters together with a few homesteaders and cattlemen. The intervention of the Army in 1874 and the establishment of Fort Elliott on the Sweetwater effectively ended the Indian rampage as well as the influence of the Comancheros. The so-called Red River War of 1874–1875 in the Panhandle forced the return of the Indians to the reservations, leaving the buffalo hunters to clear the land for cattlemen and settlers.

The date 1880 marks the opening of what has been called "the new frontier." Evidence of this approaching event was stamped on West Texas history in 1875 by the appearance of Charles Goodnight's JA brand at Palo Duro Canyon, signaling the first permanent ranch in the Panhandle. A year later Thomas S. Bugbee drove a herd of longhorns from Kansas to Hutchinson County where he established the Circle Quarter T brand. In 1882, he sold his holdings and bought a ranch near Old Clarendon, a town referred to by perverse cowhands as Saints' Roost, because the property was bought with the understanding that liquor would never flow in that moral community. Gradually cattle brands became as numerous as the constellations in the night sky: the Four Sixes, the Frying Pan, the Lazy F, the Matador Flying V, the Rocking Chair, the LX, the Spade, the Circle S, and the IOA, to mention only a few. Early in the winter of 1877, Major George Littlefield founded the LIT, using the first three initials of his name.

The XIT Ranch was the largest of the Panhandle ranches. Three million acres of land acquired in 1884 stretched over large sections of Dallam, Hartley, Oldham, Deaf Smith, Parmer, Bailey, Hockley, Lamb, and Castro counties. The property was held in the public domain and reserved for building a state Capitol; thus, the immense spread was received in exchange for the recipients' promise to replace the old state house that had burned in 1881. It was stipulated that the new Capitol had to be "larger than that of any other state—and at least one foot higher than the United States Capitol in Washington." The venture materialized under an Illinois group who adopted the title the Capitol Syndicate. In 1885, the first herd of twenty-five hundred longhorns arrived at the ranch. The money provided by the syndicate for the Capitol at Austin from the sale of 3,050,000 acres was approximately $3,224,593.45, that is, at approximately $1.06 per acre. This was less than a bargain, inasmuch as since unwatered land in West Texas was selling for about 27 cents an acre. It is not an exaggeration to call the XIT's acquisition the "biggest land swap" in Texas' history. The result was one of the finest state Capitols in the country.

If *big* is an adjective that comes to mind when the Lone Star state is mentioned, T. R. Fehrenbach cites an appropriate noun. He writes, "Say *Texas* anywhere, and people answer *cowboy.*" Before moving to the High Plains of West Texas, the cowboy and cattleman had their beginnings in the Nueces Valley. In 1842, when the Mexicans abandoned their Texas lands and moved south across the Rio Grande, they left behind, lean, durable, and usually disgruntled cattle, imposing creatures

often with a span of as much as eight feet from the tip of one horn to the opposite tip. Cattle represented the first requirement for a would-be rancher. The next necessities were grass for grazing and a source of water. The third need was the cowboy, as a wise old veteran of the cattle trails defined the species—"a man with guts and a horse." The horse made up the fourth and, perhaps, most important part of the evolving western scene. The art of working a herd "from the top," rather than on foot, was a piece of the legacy inherited from the Mexican vaqueros. Cowpunchers on foot had no hope of managing herds of five thousand bellowing beasts. Men on horseback could control the waves of moving flesh. The horse was not thought of as a way of getting from here to there but as man's most valuable asset and possession. "A six-shooter and a fast horse meant the difference between life and death," Colonel Dodge wrote in 1877.

Guns were a protection against wolves, rattlers, and rustlers. The horse lifted a man above others who were content to grub the soil with a spade or hoe. The horse increased the cowboy's speed in the pursuit of cattle or outlaws. The pistol contributed a feeling of power and worth. In the saddle with holstered pistol, the cowboy was an equal among equals. Round-ups and trail drives cemented the cooperation with a group of peers, but the need for swift individual judgment and the ability to act alone was never ignored.

In the 1870s and 1880s freedom was in the air; the open range of West Texas offered almost unlimited land that belonged to the public domain. There were free grass and free water. Driving herds across unfenced country was hard work, but the cattle were fattened by grazing on the rich grass as they slowly wound their way to the railroads bound for the stockyards of the Midwest. There was little incentive to bother with filing for legal ownership of the land. The brief period of the open range was described by Walter Prescott Webb as "one of the outstanding phenomena in American history. . . . The cattlemen spread the institution of ranching over the empire of grass. During the period and for ten years after [until 1891], men, cattle, and horses held almost undisputed possession of the plains."

Matador half-dugout (1889), Ranching Heritage Center, the Museum of Texas Tech University, Lubbock

AT LEAST in the beginning, the ranch owner supervised his cowboys from a saddle, not from an office. When ranch buildings became necessary, the first considerations were functional: the availability of grass and water; a spring or a stream that would not run rainless during the dry months; a few trees for shade and some protection from winter blizzards. Charles Goodnight, like many others, built a dugout as his first living quarters. He is said to have used poles from an abandoned Comanche campground for the rafters. Located on the floor of Palo Duro Canyon, there was not a neighbor within a hundred miles—the distance to Fort Elliott. It was 250 miles from a railroad or a supply base.

The term *dugout* suggests the method of construction used for this primitive type of shelter. A Texas cowboy named John Young recalled the building of such a one-room shack: "We dug an open-topped rectangular

Mayfield dugout (1889), near Silverton

Las Escabardas (1886), Ranching Heritage Center, the Museum of Texas Tech University, Lubbock

hole into the South side of a slope near water. Thus the back wall and a part of each of the two side walls were formed by the ground. The remainder were made of logs chinked with mud. The flat roof [of dirt-covered logs] butted against the hillside, but a line of mounded earth prevented water from running off the slopes onto it.

Rollie Burns, quoted earlier, described a slightly different method of construction used by an old bachelor on the South Plains near Estacado: "His dugout was made in the conventional way. A hole was excavated about four feet deep. The walls were built up about three feet with sod. A ridgepole was put across the center, and smaller poles cross-ways. On these were placed brush and a layer of sod, and then a layer of earth." That this design had problems is made clear by Burns's next remark. He added, "The rain caused the roof to cave [fall] on John while he was asleep. . . . The ridgepole had struck him over the heart and caved in his chest." That this was was not unusual is confirmed by Everett Dick in his study of dugouts and sod houses. He wrote, "When the roof was well soaked its weight was immense. The rafters sank deeper and deeper . . . until occasionally the roof caved in . . . burying people underneath the ruins."

In spite of objections to living like a prairie dog and the occasional dangers, dugouts prevailed as a practical solution on the prairies until more permanent living quarters could be built. In addition, the dugout was not expensive. North of Texas in frontier Nebraska, Elder Oscar Babcock, a Seventh-day Baptist minister gave an itemized record of the cost of a fourteen-foot-square dugout built in 1872. The cost was as follows:

One window (8″ × 10″ glass)	$1.25
18 feet of lumber for front door	.54
[in West Texas a blanket was usually hung over the opening]	
Latch and hanging (no lock)	.50
3 lbs. nails to go through roof	.19 ½
Length of pipe to go through roof	.30
Total	$ 2.78 ½

Two dugouts moved from their original locations and rebuilt as they might have appeared in the 1890s are in an outdoor setting at the Texas Tech University Ranching Heritage Center in Lubbock. The half-dugout was originally from the Matador Ranch in northern Dickens County. (See page 5.) The protective embankment from which it was scooped has been recreated. A single room with a typical earthen floor has been framed above the ground level with branches cut from cottonwood trees. Inside and out, chinks were secured against the weather by daubing them with clay. When possible, the dugout door faced southeast to avoid the winter's blustering northers and to catch a breath of summer breeze ruffling the stifling heat.

From the Long S Ranch there is a two-story dugout that illustrates the evolutionary process that began with an underground room shoveled deep into the flat ground. An upper level of box-and-strip construction was built in 1912 to be used as a sleeping loft for cowboys riding the line on Colonel Slaughter's Silver Lake Ranch.

In Briscoe County an original dugout remains largely undisturbed. Excellently preserved, the Mayfield dugout stands close to the rim of a canyon near Silverton. It was built in 1889 by the grandfather of Charles Wayne Mayfield, the owner of the ranch. The earthen floor is defined by fieldstone walls. Three massive beams brought up from the canyon bottom support the main roof. The central one is held in position by a sturdy vertical post. Cedar branches were placed over the beams and then covered with brush and sod. The doorway faced south, and two small windows, boarded up in recent years, admitted light. It is nearly a century since it was a home for the pioneering family, but it still has an atmosphere of warmth and protection. (See page 5.)

The dugout, customarily the first living quarters on a ranch, was followed by a more permanent home. On the Goodnight land, the dugout was abandoned in a short time for "a comfortable house [made] from the canyon timber, without the use of a single nail."

Without a neighbor in a hundred-mile radius and two hundred fifty miles from a railroad or a supply base, Goodnight, for a short time, had the Texas plains entirely to himself. In May 1877, however, Molly Goodnight traveled with John Adair, Goodnight's English partner, and Mrs. Adair to what was then called the Home Ranch in the canyon. The Adairs left after a few weeks, but Mrs. Goodnight stayed on, as someone observed, "the only Eve in a vast Eden."

There is an account of the Goodnight living quarters written in 1885 by a reporter sent to the Panhandle for the *Galveston News*. His assessment suggests the rapidity with which settlers moved from dugout to fully developed ranching complex. The newsman wrote:

> The improvements at the main headquarters of the Palo Duro ranch are better than those of most of the other Panhandle ranches. . . . The main house is a commodious two-story wooden structure of large logs and planks. The mess-house is a large and very substantial structure. . . . Near to this house is a dairy, where the butter is made and stored during the summer in sufficient quantities to last headquarters during the entire year. . . . A short distance from this house is the poultry yard and house where the largest and finest breed of fowls are kept. They supply eggs by the gross for this village. . . . Across the street is the large blacksmith shop, where wagons are mended and horses shod. . . Adjoining this structure is the tin shop, where all the tinware used on the ranch . . . is manufactured from the best and heaviest quality of tin. The water at this farm is strong with gypsum, very unpalatable to the stranger, and in warm weather can discount a double dose of Epsom salts.

The JA ranching headquarters was typical of, though grander than, the usual ranch accommodations. The choice of materials depended upon those locally available. For example, the headquarters of the Frying Pan Ranch, in the western half of Potter County, was of adobe. An old photograph shows a few straggling flowers on the earthen roof where some wild seeds drifted and took root. When fieldstone was available, it was combined with wood. Las Escarbadas, headquarters for one of the eight divisions of the XIT Ranch (see page 6), was a long stone building covered by a pitched roof with a chimney at each end. It was built in 1886 in Deaf Smith County near Hereford but now is on display at the Ranching Heritage Center.

A typical layout for a ranch in the days before fencing consisted of a headquarters, a bunkhouse for the cowboys (referred to as the "mess house" by the Galveston "explorer," as newspaper reporters were called), a meat and milk house (see page 8), a barn with an open shed attached, a blacksmith shop, a hitching bar, and two or more corrals.

In some parts of Texas, the corrals were called "round pens." (See page 9.) The absence of square corners kept animals from injuring themselves if they were crowded into corner spaces. The elimination of corners also made it easier to pursue and rope a steer or horse. The circular plan was defined by posts set firmly in the ground and connected by horizontal wooden rails. The rails were lashed to the verticals with strips of green raw-

JA milk and meat cooler (1880), Ranching Heritage Center, the Museum of Texas Tech University, the Museum of Texas Tech University, Lubbock

hide. As the rawhide dried, it contracted, making the structural elements of the corral rigid and unyielding under the strongest pressures. Connecting two corrals there usually was a fenced passage, called in the vernacular a "shoot." It served its purpose when full-grown cattle were branded. Fifteen or twenty beasts would be crowded in the shoot to prevent dangerous struggling and kicking when the red-hot iron was applied.

In the barn were stored oats and baled hay not grown on the ranch but bought at a considerable expense as a supplement to the usual diet of buffalo grass. These were for the horses that pulled wagons, and for the so-called kept-up ponies. Kept-up horses were the saddle ponies always on call for immediate crises. Such unexpected events had a habit of occurring at night when it could be

difficult to rope one of the regular ranch stock. These privileged horses were sometimes assigned stalls in the barn during the winter months. (See page 10.)

A blacksmith's shop was a necessary part of the ranching operation. The Renderbrook-Spade smithy (see page 1) now at the Ranching Heritage Center in Lubbock, dates from 1917, but it is typical of the earlier blacksmith's quarters.

Bunkhouses seem to have been uniform in their bare bones survival standards and their unmistakable odors. The usual building materials were cottonwood logs, when they were at hand, or weatherboard. At the Ranching Heritage Center, the bunkhouse came from land purchased for the JY Ranch by Robert Benjamin Masterson. (See page 10.) It dates before 1887 and was originally in eastern King County near Benjamin. The

Corral, Ranching Heritage Center, the Museum of Texas Tech University, Lubbock

Barn, Watt Matthews Ranch (twentieth century), Lambshead near Albany

Masterson JY bunkhouse (c. 1887), Ranching Heritage Center, the Museum of Texas Tech University, Lubbock

Chuck wagon, Ranching Heritage Center, the Museum of Texas Tech University, Lubbock

Masterson bunkhouse was built of local stone without mortar. It has a single chimney and a porch in front to give shade on a hot afternoon or protection from rain or snow. The floors of bunkhouses were usually of packed earth. The furnishings were meager. When cowboys came in from their duties, they spread blanket rolls on the floor or on link-spring cots. Pages from mail-order catalogs, magazines, and old newspapers were pasted on walls and ceilings as insulation against dust and wind. Culture and aesthetics were not priorities. One story is told of a cowboy suffering from loneliness and boredom while spending a winter alone in a shack papered with news sheets and farm journals. He read the north, south, east, and west walls and was just starting to read the ceiling when he was mercifully called back to headquarters.

Men living in the bunkhouse or lonely dugout on the range sometimes had an unexpected companion—not the faithful dog who could not be trusted to keep quiet at strategic times while rounding up a stray steer and who was often a mistaken target for coyote hunters but the cat. The cat protected food supplies from mice. "It was no rare thing," Rollins wrote, "to see a man riding cross-country and solemnly holding on his saddle horn a cat bound ranchward to guard filled flour sacks." According to Rollins, during the 1880s there was a fixed price for felines. This was always ten dollars. The amount may seem to reflect badly upon a cat's worth until it is remembered that ten dollars was a large portion of a cowboy's monthly pay.

Jim Christian, a literate line rider for the JA Ranch in the Panhandle, reported, "When I went into winter camp, I always took plenty of novels and tobacco, and usually a cat. . . . A cat and a briar pipe were lots of company when a fellow spent months shut off from the world." He had good words for his pony, too. Christian said, "The hoot of the owl and the howl of the coyote were music to my ears through the long night. My comrade was my horse. A fellow could spend lots of time petting [and] currying . . . a horse."

Except during the winter months, the cowboy did not spend much time in the bunkhouse. Out on the plains or on the trail, his requirements changed. Range "architecture" began with the chuck wagon and included the clothes the cowboy wore. The chuck wagon (see page 10) was the oasis of the desert: the delivery truck, trailer home, ambulance, and coffee bar of the nineteenth century. It was the product of frontier ingenuity and Charles Goodnight. In 1866, the father of West Texas ranching rebuilt a surplus Army wagon, which he chose because of its extremely durable iron axles. For his trail crew's convenience, on one side, he secured a barrel that would hold enough water for two days. On the opposite side, he balanced the weight with a heavy toolbox. Over the wagon he placed bent ribs or bows across which canvas could be stretched to give protection from rain and shade from the sun. The innovation that decided the course of chuck wagon design as long as these kitchens on wheels were used, was the chuck box. It had two features. Installed on the rear of the wagon "facing aft," the cupboard had a lid that was let down and propped on a swinging leg to form a substantial work table. (See page 13.) Lighting at night was furnished by a lantern on top of the chuck box and by the adjacent camp fire. The box has been compared with a Victorian desk filled with drawers and pigeonholes. The larger shelves just above the table surface contained the coffee pot and a bottle of medicinal whisky to be prescribed only by the cook (and often *to* the cook). Another shelf held such indispensable ingredients as salt, lard, and baking soda. Still another held the sourdough keg, molasses, and matches. Vinegar, chewing tobacco, and rolling tobacco were not forgotten. The drawers contained flour, sugar, pinto beans, dried fruit, and eating utensils. There was one compartment known as the "possible drawer" that had those items needed to treat every possible calamity: castor oil, calomel, bandages, needle and thread, a razor and strop. Down below the table was storage for skillets, dutch ovens, and pot hooks. Bulk food stuffs were placed in the wagon bed—green coffee beans, onions, potatoes, dried apples, along with grain for the work team of four horses or four mules responsible for pulling the chuck wagon. Guns and ammunition, slickers, bedrolls, kerosene, axle grease, an extra wagon wheel, salt pork, and raw beef were also loaded aboard. The wagon designed to Goodnight's specifications met with such general approval that it was standardized and produced by the major wagon builders, including the Studebaker Company, famous in the early 1950s for some of the most handsome automobiles ever built. Studebaker sold chuck wagons for between seventy-five and one-hundred dollars. In

The Log of a Cowboy, Andy Adams added another function performed by the chuck wagon. While on the trail, he explained, "At every noon and night camp we strung a rope from the end of the wagon tongue back to stakes driven in the ground or held by a man forming a triangular corral. Thus in a few minutes under any conditions, we could construct a temporary corral for catching a change of mounts, or for a wrangler to hobble untrustworthy horses."

And so on the western frontier, form and function were coalescing. Two or three decades before Frank Lloyd Wright advocated the practicality of built-in desks and tables and cabinets, Charles Goodnight was already putting this concept into practice. Of these pioneers, John A. Kouwenhoven, explorer of the vernacular arts in America said: "The men and women who built a civilization in the American wilderness had to relearn a truth which many of their European contemporaries had been able to get along without: the truth of function. They had to become familiar with the nature of materials and the use of tools."

Nowhere has function been better illustrated than by the manner in which the open range was brought under control by the ingenious solutions to problems offered by the cattlemen and cowboys. A part of the inventive application of form dictated by function was present in the cowboys regalia. This familiar apparel copied by movie heroes and the drugstore breed was never considered for its picturesque or symbolic possibilities, it was chosen for one purpose only—it suited the needs of the work performed. Architecturally speaking, the hat provided an improvised roof over its owner's shoulders as a protection from sun, rain, and snow. Removed from the head and rolled up, it was a cushion for napping. It was a bucket for carrying water to extinguish a campfire and sometimes a drinking cup. The hat, removed and swung from left to right, was a way of signaling to companions out of earshot.

The vest was a small-scale replica of the chuck wagon, or a portable chest of drawers. Rollins points out that the vest "was worn not as a piece of clothing, but solely because its outside pockets gave handy storage" for such necessities as matches, tobacco papers, a bag of Bull Durham tobacco, and "natural curiosities"—a gold nugget, a piece of crystal, an elk's tooth, or Indian arrowheads.

The bandana or kerchief was a curtain separating the cowboy from threats of nature. Loosely tied with a square knot, it had nothing to do with chic. When pulled up around nose and mouth, it protected the wearer from dust kicked up on the trail or at the round-up. It was also a defense against frost and chill.

Chaps, sometimes referred to as "skeleton overalls," were the leather barriers shielding a rider's legs from cacti, sagebrush, bark, thorns, and bruises from contact with a fence or a steer. When the weather required, the cowpuncher was encased in a long raincoat of yellow oilskin. During fair weather the slicker was rolled and laid across the rear of the saddle behind the cantle where a fastening of two thongs held it in place. In the folds of the oilcloth a frying pan was inserted together with rations for the journey. According to Rollins the edible supplies consisted of "some flour, bacon, coffee, salt, and as a substitute for yeast, either a bottle of sourdough or a can of baking powder." At night the slicker was unrolled to become a tent cloth, especially welcome on wet evenings.

The saddle itself was valued almost as much as an ancestral home might have been in a gentler society. Properly broken in, it was a moving chair during the day. It made roping possible unlike the thin saddle of easterners, which was contemptuously dubbed the English "postage-stamp." The western saddle enabled a cowboy to mount a moving horse rapidly or lean from his mount to pick up an object on the ground. It made night herding less arduous since the rider could catch forty winks without dismounting. Finally, the stock-saddle was the universal pillow of the sleeping cowboy whether in the bunkhouse or on the trail.

The comforts of life on the open range were few. The extremes of climate on the High Plains were met with ingenuity and good nature. Those early precursors of the Mies van der Rohe philosophy of "less is more" were survivors. Their legacy of hard work, inventiveness, and the ability to make-do without fretting for the frivolous amenities was passed on to the next generation of settlers. The relation of form to function would continue to dominate the buildings inhabited by the next wave of men and women who came to West Texas— the generation who saw the land enclosed with barbed wire and who built the windmills silhouetted against the vast sky.

Chuck wagon, Ranching Heritage
Center, the Museum of Texas Tech
University, Lubbock

2

Windmills, Barbed Wire, and Rails

There are, indeed, few merrier spectacles than that of windmills

bickering together in a fresh breeze . . .

their halting alacrity of movement, [their] uncouth

gesticulation; their air, gigantically human, as if a

creature half alive, put a spirit of romance into the

tamest landscape.

Robert Louis Stevenson

I hear the whistle of the locomotive . . .

Whenever that music comes, it has its sequel.

It is the voice of the

civilization of the Nineteenth Century saying,

"Here I am."

Ralph Waldo Emerson

Ropes station (early 1900s), Ranching Heritage Center, the Museum of Texas Tech University, Lubbock

IN THE DECADE BETWEEN 1880 and 1890, the Texas Panhandle was transformed by the Industrial Revolution and harnessed by people who possessed the uncanny ability to see and solve problems, turning the solutions into an improved life for settlers and profit for themselves.

For homesteaders, gambling on their chances of success in a land described in 1854 by the U.S. Boundary Commission as a "barren plain without water or timber producing only a few stunted shrubs insufficient to sustain animal life," there were four aces waiting to be played. These were well digging equipment, windmills, barbed wire, and railroads. Used in tandem to revolutionize the vacant lands of West Texas, these inventions brought about the end of the open range, the cattle drive, and the longhorn whose image was imprinted in early ranching history and commemorated in the paintings of Frank Reaugh. (See page 16.) From the earliest migration of cattlemen to the Llano Estacado, the needs were always for good pasture and an adequate supply of water. It did not take long before the grasslands along the rivers or plots with easy access to springs were exhausted. When the farmers began to move into the wide open spaces, they also required land for grazing and a dependable source of water for their fields and livestock with enough left over for a vegetable garden and a few flowers. Sections with easily available water were usually the first claimed, and the days of tapping underground water sources for irrigation were still in the future. The families, who traveled by wagon and later by train from farms in the Midwest or from the exhausted farmlands of northern Georgia, Tennessee, Alabama, and Mississippi, must have remembered the wells that were dug at their former homes. They found, however, that the problem of well digging in West Texas was different. In the East and South, water was close to the surface of the ground. If shovels and pickaxes penetrated no more than ten or twenty feet, a water supply was usually waiting. Under such conditions hands and a rope could be relied on to draw up "the old oaken bucket" filled to the brim. On the Texas High Plains the ground was hard and solidly packed. Although there were excellent supplies of water, these were far beneath the ground. Mechanical equipment was needed to reach the necessary depths. It was the industrial establishment in the East that provided the means for freeing

Sketches of cattle by Frank Reaugh, courtesy of the Southwest Collection, Texas Tech University, Lubbock

(Top) Eclipse windmill, Ranching Heritage Center, the Museum of Texas Tech University, Lubbock

(Opposite) Walpole windmill, Ranching Heritage Center, the Museum of Texas Tech University, Lubbock

the water. The device that came to the rescue has been described as "a mechanical drill which could make a hole six inches in diameter and sink . . . as deep as 400 - 500 feet straight through the upper 15 feet of 'Rim Rock' covering the Plains."

In 1882, such well-drilling machinery was introduced to Carson County in the Texas Panhandle by Colonel B. B. Groom of the Diamond F Ranch. The drills used were horse-driven. The technique had not as yet been refined, but when the first wells were drilled this did not keep neighbors from gathering and looking on with a mixture of skepticism and interest. One of those immediately attracted by the process was Charles Goodnight. In 1883, he requested that Groom supervise the drilling of an experimental well on his Palo Duro spread. The approval of Goodnight was all that was needed to thrust the business of well digging into a success story soon shared by windmill manufacturers.

Since raising water by hand was impossible in West Texas, a well was useless without the mechanical means to draw water to the surface in sufficient quantities to provide for the ranchers' large herds as well as the farmers' growing number of blooded livestock. The windmill was waiting. It was another product of eastern ingenuity and an invention that could be modified by westerners to fit their own needs. The mills' wheels were turned by wind, which was not in short supply on the West Texas plains. The wheels might remain idle in Indiana or Ohio waiting for a breeze, but out on the plains, the great circles turned day and night lifting water to fill stock tanks and wooden storage barrels. The American windmill was another triumph of function adapting form to its needs.

The process of raising water and building a windmill in the early 1900s in West Texas has been vividly described by George Hancock. His reminiscences in *Go-Devils, Flies and Blackeyed Peas* capture the gritty homeliness and strengths developed in the pioneering communities on the South Plains. He wrote:

The plains would have never been settled had it not been for the windmills. When someone started a new homestead, the first thing to do was to establish a little fire protection. They would plow three or four rounds around a couple of acres or so, then burn the grass off. Next came the well

driller. . . . The wells were drilled with the "spudder," a steel shaft about twenty feet long hanging to a steel cable. It plunged up and down literally beating a hole in the ground. . . . The mill tower was built laying on the ground and the mechanism, including the wheel and fan (tail), were added before it was raised. It was pulled up with a homemade scaffold and a block and tackle. It was then bolted to four cedar posts set deep in the ground. If the driller was still there, he would pick it up and set it with the drilling derrick. He usually set the pipe and foot valve along with the sucker rod before he left. If everything was working right and a little wind was blowing, a stream about the size of your finger would come out the pipe and you were ready to start building a new home.

Hancock continued:

People who could not afford an overhead tank, which was most of them, pumped the water from the windmill into a 55 gallon wooden tank. Water was carried from the barrel in buckets to the kitchen (the reason most mills were close to the house). An overflow pipe from the barrel led to the milk trough and from there to the stock tub or tank, or sometimes, to a small earthen pond. The trough could be any size, but was usually a foot wide and six or eight feet long and one foot deep. The overflow pipe was set to keep about two inches of water in the trough. The sides were opened or screened and there was a lid on it. By draping a cloth over the containers with the edges in the water, we had the same effect as a water cooled air conditioner. The hotter and dryer the day, the cooler the food, provided the wind blew. Otherwise too bad. . . . The country schools all had a windmill with a barrel and one drinking cup for everybody.

The windmill on ranches and farms cannot be separated from its counterpart along the new railroads. Trains depended on windmills built close to the tracks for the supply of water, usually heated to steam by coal (often imported from Thurber, which is marked today by a single great smokestack), needed to propel them through small West Texas towns. Thus, the railroads provided an example of the windmills' efficient performance.

Trains also shipped windmills to farmers and ranchers at a low price because the mills were designed to be knocked down for efficient packing and for easy reassembly that could be accomplished without skilled mechanics or specialized tools. Like so many other designs created to efficiently fit their purpose, the windmill was beautiful. Even historians have grown poetic at the thought of the wind-catching wheels; Walter Prescott Webb quotes John J. Ingalls who spoke of those "'vivacious disks [that] disturb the monotony of the sky.'"

Today windmills and stock tanks are often thought of not as they actually look but as they appear in paintings and drawings by Peter Hurd and hundreds of other western artists. To a traveler in the early 1900s the windmill on the horizon of the West Texas flatlands meant more than a subject for a lithograph or watercolor. It meant that somewhere in that empty landscape there was another soul, a kitchen stove with coffee simmering in a pot, a handshake, an exchange of gossip and observations about the weather. The windmill was above all a humanizing invention as well as a life saving one for thirsty livestock and people. (See page 17.)

A SUBJECT OF DISCUSSION might be, Which came first on the South Plains the windmill or barbed wire? As usual Goodnight played a part in the answer. In 1883, Goodnight installed a windmill on his Palo Duro Ranch. During 1884–1885, he led the vanguard by stretching barbed wire across his Tule property. Goodnight's barbed wire was brought to West Texas by freighters who profited on the return trip east by carrying loads of buffalo bones to be ground up as fertilizer.

The story of the invention of barbed wire is as thorny as its subject. A variety of claims was filed to protect inventors' rights. J. F. Glidden, however, is the candidate most deserving of a large portion of the credit. The invention was "mothered" when the Gliddens were living on a farm in De Kalb, Illinois. Mrs. Glidden's favorite flower bed was a favored meeting ground for the neighborhood dogs. To deter the canine vandals, Mr. Glidden strung wire around the endangered plants. The smooth wire was useless; so in desperation, he tried making barbs of short pieces of wire and attaching them to the smooth lengths of fencing. This worked like a charm, and barbed wire was on its way to win the West for the farmers against the protests of cowboys and cattlemen. Another account traces barbed wire's origin to the thorn hedges used in the British Isles to dissuade cattle from trespassing. Whatever the case may be, Glidden applied for a patent on 27 October 1873; after the application was amended the patent was granted the next year. The new concept in fencing was first manufactured by the American Steel and Wire Company.

The importance of barbed, or "bobbed," wire in the development of West Texas cannot be exaggerated. In his writing, Webb emphasized, "Without barbed wire the Plains' homestead could never have been protected from the grazing herds and therefore could not have been possible as an agricultural unit." In the beginning, barbed wire fencing resulted in bloodshed and not just that of an unlucky horse or steer. Many of the cowmen hated the farmers, or "nesters," as they were called, for fencing off the open range land and cutting it up into pastures and fields. Barbed wire prevented unobstructed grazing on the abundant grass and blocked the paths of the cattle, whose guides looked for the shortest distance between two points. When the cattle ranchers found themselves hemmed in and forced to take "a crooked route," their wire cutters demolished the fences as quickly as they were strung. In the end the cutters capitulated, influenced by men like Goodnight who had the foresight and wisdom to accept the inevitable and to understand the advantages fencing offered. On unfenced land, crews of cowboys had the job of constantly riding the line, patrolling the ranch's borders to prevent their cattle from straying and to keep out herds with neighbors' brands. Barbed wire offered a way of reducing the number of men needed in the isolated line camps. The nature of barbed wire provided solutions to other difficult problems. With the lack of trees in West Texas, lumber for traditional fencing had to be shipped to the Plains at a considerable expense. All that barbed wire required was well-spaced posts. The wire fencing withstood the "northers" drifting down from Canada, and snow did not collect against the lines of wire. Like the compact units to which windmill parts were reduced for shipping, rolled barbed wire was easily portable. Of all of the advantages offered by barbed wire, the most valuable one was the opportunity to improve breeding stock. J. Evetts Haley wrote in his biography of Goodnight that "no one factor in the West so affected the grading of cattle as did wire, for with the

Barbed wire

enclosed ranges each man had exclusive use of the fine sires he placed with his cows." It was inevitable that stock farms would replace many of the great ranches. The day of the lean and magnificent longhorn was at an end.

What had barbed wire to do with everyday life and architecture? The farmer brought with him and his family the desire for a more settled way of existence than that willingly endured by the early cowmen. Property rights were contained by fences. Women were less apt to have to make do with shanties or dugouts; if they did, it was for a shorter time. Loneliness caused by the distances between one household and another was palliated, if not cured, by barbed wire. During the early days, telephone lines were erected on the posts of barbed wire fences, and geographically isolated neighbors were able to take comfort in other human voices. When barbed wire carried companionship by way of the telephone box, it was a stabilizing force contributing to permanence. A shelter became a home—a place to entertain and a place where there might be a piano or organ, books, lace curtains, and flowers from the garden.

BUILDING WAS no longer controlled by the resources at hand. Materials were delivered by train instead of by the slow freight wagons. Sawmills ushered in the day of the box–and–strip farmhouse. Train tracks across the Panhandle brought the beginnings of towns and county seats. As the urban population increased, business was stimulated. Railroad stations, courthouses, hotels, banks, office buildings, churches, and schools all demanded designs to fit their varied functions. The appearance of building types associated with or symbolic of particular purposes began to replace the emphasis on pure function. This diversity in architecture was to a large extent fostered by the railroads.

The first transcontinental railroad, the Union, Pacific, and Central, united the nation "from sea to shining sea" in 1869, but it was eighteen years before railroads came to the Texas Panhandle. The first railroad to cross the land recently inhabited by buffalo was the Fort Worth and Denver City. As the name suggests, it had its beginning in "Cowtown." Its rails edged through Wichita Falls, Quanah, Childress, and Clarendon, leaving Old Mobeetie and Old Clarendon to become ghost towns. The tracks moved on toward the future site of Amarillo, a settlement spurred into existence as a result of the railroad's expected route.

The story of Amarillo's early development is typical of the relation between the railroads and the growth of towns along the routes, and it illustrates how the coming of the trains influenced the development of West Texas. When rumors of the approach of a railway line were spread, real estate speculators and hopeful settlers rushed to acquire property at a strategic location. Land near the present city of Amarillo was first offered for sale on 29 May 1888 at a site close to a railroad construction workers' camp. The crews of workmen had already been joined by men and women lured by the predictions of an important new town. In order to be first on the spot, first to get the best buy, many were willing to wait in impermanent and ramshackle tents made from hides and flapping cloths or to inhabit the everpresent covered wagons. This raggle-taggle camp was called Ragtown.

More affluent factions were just as eagerly waiting to contend for the lion's share of the land that seemed likely to become the seat of Potter County. One of the contenders was Colonel James T. Berry. Berry was a pioneer in the real estate business and one who had had a hand in developing Abilene, Texas. The large tract of land that he purchased had little to distinguish it in terms of either beauty or climate. The expanse of severely plain prairie was watered by Wild Horse Lake, as it is now called. Trail drivers had paused there as they pushed up clouds of dust on the way to Dodge City. Its appeal lay in the news of the advancing rail line. Through shrewd maneuvering, Berry's holding was voted the future site of the county's government. A newspaper, *The Pioneer*, observed that "the child which was born to the Free County of Potter," was to be christened Oneida. The article further enlightened its readers with the information that the "election . . . passed off in fine order and good feeling, which marks everything in the Panhandle." Shortly after the votes were counted, Oneida was dropped like a sour dough biscuit for the more fanciful Spanish title Amarillo, meaning "yellow," the name of several creeks in the area. With these preliminaries settled, some lumber for building was hauled by wagon from Tascosa and Clarendon. Many of Ragtown's residents, correctly suspicious, as time would prove, chose to remain in their tents. Wood for heating came from a few trees growing along the banks of the Canadian River, though some preferred to gather buffalo and cow chips out on the plains. Water was brought from Amarillo Creek, while the women went to Wild Horse Lake to do the family washing. It was not long before the problem of water was satisfactorily solved thanks to the new drilling techniques and to the installation of windmills.

At this point, the officials of the Fort Worth and Denver City Railway decided to move their stock pens one mile west of the planned development. Even before the name *Amarillo* was placed on a map, it had become a shipping center for enormous herds. One resident remembered as a child walking with her father to see "a solid mass of cattle spreading to the north, south, east, and west, by count fifty thousand head of them." She described with nostalgia the "beautiful, quiet autumn evening and the gold of the setting sun which cast a glow over the cattle as they milled about bawling softly."

As fate would have it, the town guided by Berry's skill as a developer took a sudden detour. The change in the location of the stockyards may have played a part, but Berry's plans were thwarted by H. B. Sanborn, who owned the neighboring Frying Pan Ranch. Sanborn had looked on with little enthusiasm as Berry's development flourished. Not only was the projected county seat not on Sanborn's land, but he was not even given the opportunity to obtain an interest in the venture. To counter this, on 19 June 1888, Sanborn bought a spread adjoining Berry's property. Having taken this step, he promptly announced his intention to build a town on his newly acquired acreage. At the same time he pointed out how unfortunate it was that Berry's Amarillo was dangerously located on a draw that was subject to flooding when it rained. Sanborn was helped in this enterprise by his ranching partner, none other than J. F. Glidden, the inventor of barbed wire. As apprehension began to mount in the minds of those who had bought home sites from Berry, Sanborn considerately offered an exchange of lots enabling those interested to move to his projected town. Some residents stubbornly refused to change locations; when this occurred, Sanborn bought their houses, loaded the structures on skids and shifted them over to his own property. By 1890, only the courthouse remained in "Old Town." This made little difference, since in 1889, Sanborn had already arranged for another courthouse to be built in "his" Amarillo. In June 1899 the new building was hailed by *American Breeder Magazine* as "one of the most attractive courthouses . . . a magnificent brick structure, spacious, and well arranged, and it is worth the very reasonable cost, $38,000." Another strong point in its favor was the fact that the bricks from which it was built were made locally.

Sanborn had also promised to construct a fine hotel. This was opened for business in April 1889. The importance of an attractive hotel near the railroad cannot be overestimated. The first Pullman car had appeared in 1872, but many attracted by the land recently made available wished to stop for a few days to become acquainted with the advantages presented for farming or ranching and to investigate the quality of life in the towns sprouting like cottonwood trees in an arroyo. A hotel could make a memorable first impression, stressing the amenities offered by a young city rising out of the dust and flat landscape. Sanborn, well aware of this method of attracting new residents, did not hesitate to spend forty thousand dollars (two thousand dollars more than

for the courthouse) on his two-story frame hotel with forty rooms. It was located on the southwest corner of Third and Polk streets, close to the train station. It was named, without benefit of flights of imagination, The Amarillo and painted the ubiquitous yellow.

When an enlargement of the hotel's facilities became necessary, Sanborn proposed to move the Tremont Hotel from "Old Town." Sometime late in the fall of 1889, B. B. Haydon was employed to relocate the Tremont at the so-called Glidden and Sanborn addition. Old timers recalled that this was accomplished by putting skids under the building with a heavy rope extending from the hotel two or three hundred feet to a capstan or revolving cylinder manned by a yellow mare by the name of Queen. The horse was driven around and around to wind up the rope, in this way drawing up the building. The move, however, was delayed on the way to the new location by severe winter weather. Finally late in the spring, it was set down close to The Amarillo Hotel to become a twenty-five–room annex. The parklike area "with a fountain between the buildings" was enclosed by an iron fence "to keep the cattle and hogs out."

The importance attached to a hotel located close to a train station was also demonstrated at Dalhart. The yellow brick Commercial Hotel was constructed in 1903, south of the Rock Island and Fort Worth/Denver tracks. It was surpassed six years later by the De Sota, designed in the popular mission style. Opening in 1910, the De Sota was intended to attract those who were "more worldly and more discriminating in their tastes." Its appeal is described by John C. Dawson in his book *High Plains Yesterday*. He wrote that by that time

hot water and baths could not only be available, every room could and would have a full bathroom—hot water, commode, bathtub, and all. And every room would have a telephone—an amenity rarely found in that day. Every door on every room would be of solid walnut. The door fixtures would be of solid brass . . . There would be bellhops promptly available at the guests' beck and call. There would be a horse-drawn hack, manned by a uniformed driver, which would meet every incoming train and carry guests and their baggage to the hotel and return them to the depot at the time

Felton Opera House (1908), Dalhart

of their departure. The dining room (equipped with fine linen table cloths and napkins and impressive silverware), would accommodate up to forty-eight people at twelve pure walnut tables.

Entertainment was harder to provide than silverware and hot baths. This void was filled in many of the new communities by an opera house. Dalhart's Felton Opera was opened in 1908. The brick building looked very much like any other place of business. It was two stories high, and its first floor was intended as rental property—culture was fine, but turning a profit was better. Access to the second floor was by means of two stairways, a narrow stair leading from Main Street and a grander one entered from Second Street. John Dawson remembered:

Both stairways led to a hallway running the length of the building and from this, one entered a room, also extending the length of the building, at the front of which was a stage with huge canvas curtains that could be lowered or raised by means of man-operated pulleys. In front of the stage was an orchestra pit. Balconies ran along both walls

and here, as well as near the stage below the balconies, were boxes where the more opulent and discriminating could see and be seen better. The chairs available for the audience were movable, so the place could be converted into a ballroom.

Before the railroad, it would have been difficult to arrange for traveling companies of actors or musicians to stop on the sparsely populated Llano Estacado. Once rails were laid, train transportation provided not only a large part of the audience but also the entertainment, whose cultural values might be questionable. Consider the ad announcing a double bill of *Canal Boat Sal* and *A Quiet Boarding House* to be performed at the Felton Opera House. If intellectual fare was lacking, at least polite behavior was encouraged with the warning, "Spitting tobacco juice on the floor is strictly forbidden!"

Who were these guests for whom entertainment and lavish accommodations were provided in an as yet unsettled land? After the bonanza years of the cattle industry, it was the farmer and his family who looked toward the west for land and a cultural environment to combat the raw frontier. They were turned away from the settled life in the Midwest by the rising prices of productive agricultural acres and attracted to cheap land and closely knit communities. Between 1890 and the entry of the United States into the first World War, more and more men and women were drawn to West Texas. Jan Blodgett observed in her thoughtful study *Land of Bright Promise* that "by 1890 changes in the cattle industry" and a growing demand for land for farmers caused the owners of the vast XIT Ranch to decide that the time had come "to open up 80,000 acres of their holdings to colonization by farmers." Other ranchers followed suit. Land agents were eager to find buyers among farm families. There was an equally short supply of skilled laborers and businessmen, doctors, and lawyers in the settlements putting down roots in the Texas Panhandle and South Plains. Dr. W. C. Holden has explained that "no sooner had sufficient people arrived to organize a county, than they began to take steps to encourage other people to come. They wanted neighbors, they craved the things which are made possible by community life such as social life, schools and churches." Prosperity depended upon the growth of the population. This led to a wave of boosterism, nourished by

White Deer station (early 1900s), Meadow

civic pride and the promise of profit. Speculators and owners of large sections of land joined by members of commercial clubs, the railroad managers, and local newspaper editors played an important role in encouraging new families to move to West Texas.

Clarenden's *Northwest Texas* (1878) became the Panhandle's first recorded newspaper. A requirement, according to one source, for a successful news sheet was "a 'shirt-tail' full of type, a simple handpress, an editor with a large amount of courage and a dedication and determination to help develop his adopted community into the 'Metropolis of the Plains' or the 'Paradise of the Panhandle.'" Such idyllic allusions, designed to attract new residents, are amusing. Readers were urged to "settle in the Garden Spot that is the South Plains of Texas—Crosbyton is the place." Hereford's Commercial Club conducted advertising campaigns in the early 1900s boasting of homes with "beautiful Kentucky Blue Grass lawns," new sidewalks, one hundred automobiles, no saloons or "disreputable joints . . . and seven religious denominations."

The railroads' propaganda was equally enticing. The Missouri-Pacific gave its blessing to the opening of the Fort Worth and Denver City line, which, it promised, would bring optimistic buyers to "the chosen land," where "perpetual sunshine would kiss the trees." Then, with an uncanny flare for prophecy, it added that vines would bear "luscious fruits" to be "compressed into ruddy wine to be sent to the four points of the compass to gladden the hearts of all mankind." Could this be the same land that less than fifty years earlier Joseph Gregg, in *Commerce of the Future* (1844), had described as "steppes . . . only fitted for the haunts of mustangs, the buffalo, the antelope, and their migratory lord, the prairie Indian?" Maps of the same period labeled the territory including the Texas Panhandle simply as "The Great Desert." By 1881, L. P. Brockett, author of *Our Western Empire*, treated the Panhandle with greater tolerance. Tipping his hat to the "mezquite," he assured those who read his book that "where these lands are broken up and plowed deeply, the roots of the mezquite aid in bringing up the moisture from below and the rainfall increases year after year." With a respect for honesty, he admitted that the Panhandle "is not well watered, and sections of it are not watered at all except by wells. Its rainfall is very small [and] . . . the pasture, though scanty, is nutritious where water can be obtained." In spite of an occasional warning of the difficulties to come, the land hungry looked at the readily available acres and listened to the sales pitch of local boosters and the promotional campaigns of the railroads that would transport them to their future.

THE FIRST POINT of contact offered the would-be immigrants, even before they entered the oasis of the hotel or discovered the cultural advantages of an opera house, was the railroad station. The stations that appeared along the tracks laid through the small towns on the South Plains had been given an architectural expression a half century earlier in the Northeast. In the beginning, railroad stations turned for their design to tollhouses built at intervals along an expanding system of roads. These collection points for payment were often houses with an extended roof beneath which carriages and passengers could find protection from rain or snow. Following this example, early stations adopted a houselike appearance with an extended roof, or porte cochere. Although many changes took place, it was the covered platform that would continue to set the station apart from other buildings.

The relation of station and house was maintained, particularly in rural New England and the mid-Atlantic states. This pattern may be traced, in part, to the availability of do-it-yourself books on architecture that suggested to the builders, thumbing through the pages, that house styles could be easily adapted to the construction of small railway stations. In the middle of the nineteenth century, the growth of cities and industry fostered nostalgic and romantic visions of country living. A cottage in the country was looked upon as an ideal retreat. Andrew Jackson Downing's best seller, *Victorian Cottage Residences,* praised the Swiss chalet "with its drooping, shadowy eaves," and it was soon adopted by many American farmhouses. Gothic Revival architecture was considered equally appropriate for humble cottages or the mansions of the wealthiest citizens. It would certainly provide solutions for the design of stations along the rail lines. It was Richard Upjohn who inadvertently developed a solution. In the

1852 edition of his *Rural Architecture,* there was a drawing of a country church in the Gothic manner, which was sheathed in vertical boards. Here was an example of Gothic verticality brought about by simple and inexpensive means, and it furnished an excellent prototype for the country station. Better still, the wooden construction, which combined the popular features of the chalet and the Gothic style, was not difficult to construct. When the railroad moved west forty years later, not only had wood been accepted as a useful building material for stations in small towns, but a detail borrowed from Tudor England had been added—the oriel window. It differed in design from the prototype; in the station the window projected at the ground level whereas the Tudor use indicated a bay at the upper level. (See page 14.) Translated into the American bay facing the tracks, it allowed the stationmaster to see the platform and to have an unobstructed view of trains approaching from both directions. In warm weather, it served as a ticket window. Both Upjohn's Gothic and Downing's Swiss chalet encouraged the use of overhanging eaves upheld by brackets or supports. These vergeboards, or decorative gable trimmings, were easily cut with a jigsaw from a thin plank. Displaying a typical mid–twentieth century aversion, Lawrence Grow referred to the process as "torturing" wood with "the turning lathe" that "led to a multiplicity of . . . creations too amorphous to be alluded to by any designation other than 'gingerbread.'" Although many country stations in the east were liberally treated to a trim of wooden crochet, jigsaw gingerbread was not an indulgence of which West Texas stations were guilty.

Two typical and well-preserved stations on the South Plains are the Ropes Station, formerly at Ropesville but now at the Ranching Heritage Center at Texas Tech University, and a station rescued and moved from its original location at White Deer to a small park close to the railroad tracks at Meadow. (See page 23.) Both of these are painted yellow, indicating by the color that they were built to serve the Santa Fe Railway. Like most railroad stations, those in small towns were built from standardized plans drawn up by designers employed by the railroad lines. A foreman was usually sent to the location where a small station was to be constructed to supervise local workmen. (In the case of more important building projects, the railroad's own bridge-and-building crews ["B&B gangs"] were transported to the site.) In contrast to the earlier wooden station houses in the east and south, West Texas stations varied from the standard design. The usual features were retained, that is, the projecting bay and the gabled roof with a chimney indicating an iron pot belly stove in the sparsely furnished waiting room, but the extended roof protecting the platform, which came to be regarded as a signature of the station, was frequently omitted. It might be assumed that the sunny weather in a semiarid land made the sheltering roof less necessary, but even more to the point, strong winds could easily lift the roof and blow it down on the track.

Not all stations in West Texas were of the simple wooden type associated with the Ropes and White Deer examples. A notable example, entirely different in material and appearance, was constructed at Post in 1911 at the time tracks were being laid by the Pecos and Northern Texas Railway Company for the "parent operator," Santa Fe. The architect was Louis Curtiss from Kansas City. He had gone to Paris to study at the Ecole des Beaux-Arts, but upon his return to the United States, he developed a highly personal vocabulary of forms. In 1906, Curtiss was employed as an architect by both the Fred Harvey System and by the Santa Fe Railroad. His design for the station at Post, faced with white terra cotta, remains refreshingly contemporary. (See page 26.) Curtiss seems to have been influenced by two sources. One was the work of the young Frank Lloyd Wright, who, during the first decade of the twentieth century, was revolutionizing domestic architecture with his Prairie houses built in the suburbs of Chicago. A feature introduced by Wright was the use of projecting moldings to accent the horizontal bands with which he divided the exterior walls. Curtiss also chose slightly projecting horizontal moldings to give unity to his composition. At the Post station, these caused crisp shadows to alleviate the monotony of the station's light tile surface. Curtiss must have been aware of the power of sunlight in the Southwest to produce vigorous patterns of dark and light that in architectural design often erase the thin line between architecture and sculpture.

Wright's influence shows again on the east side of the station where attached pedestals were added as bases for plant urns. The urns were still in existence twenty years ago. Although the decorative planters have disappeared

from Post, urns are still present at another Curtiss station built during the same period at nearby Snyder. (See page 26.) The designs were closely related to those used by Wright at the recently restored Dana-Thomas House in Springfield, Illinois. As Brendan Gill has phrased it, "Frank Lloyd Wright found it hard to resist adding . . . urns to his designs, [and] other architects followed his practice leading to an epidemic of urnomania throughout the Middle West." And occasionally in West Texas!

The second source apparent in Curtiss's Post station is associated with the Santa Fe's route through the Southwest. A clear indication of the architect's knowledge of early New Mexico architecture was established by a 1909 adaptation of a Spanish mission design for the El Ortiz Hotel in Lamy, New Mexico. At Post the influence was more subtle. The massive walls are a reminder of pueblo apartments and the dramatic role of light and dark shadows on the adobe. On the upper part of the west facade of the station a horizontal band, centered by the Santa Fe logo—an Indian symbol of the sun circle quartered by a cross—connects projecting piers decorated with panels of sculptured relief. The design also suggests a familiarity with the awakening interest in Mexican archaeology. (See page 20.) Is this reference to an ancient civilization fanciful? A possible answer is contained in an inscription found on the wall of what was once Curtiss's luxurious Kansas City apartment. It reads, "I will go into the desert and dwell among ruins. I will interrogate ancient monuments amid the waste places of vanished empires."

In contrast to the exotic elements present at Post, a station built at San Angelo in 1909 for the Kansas City, Mexico, and Orient Line was as American as apple pie. (See page 27.) It was the offshoot of a grand plan for a rail line to run from Kansas City through Oklahoma and Texas to the Mexican border and then on to Topolobampo, a port on the Gulf of California. In 1900, at a banquet in Kansas City, the concept for the KCM&O was unfolded by a brilliant planner and businessman, Arthur E. Stilwell. The news of Stilwell's project spread rapidly to Texas towns through which the rails would be laid. San Angelo, hoping to occupy a site on a branch line traveling to San Antonio, jubilantly responded by presenting the right-of-way through Tom Green County and adding a one hundred thousand dollar cash

Detail, Santa Fe station (1911), Post

Santa Fe station (1911), Snyder

Santa Fe station, Post

Station, Kansas City, Mexico, and Orient Line (1909–1910), San Angelo

bonus. Long before the arrival of the trains, the railroad's engineering department had begun drawing up the plans for the San Angelo station. Albert T. Camfield was responsible for several design proposals; of these about thirteen sheets of drawings survive. On 7 May 1907, the design was accepted for a two story brick structure, roofed with red Spanish tile, The ground plan was to measure 35 feet by 112 feet. The lower floor was divided into waiting rooms, including a ladies' parlor, and a gentlemen's smoking room; a passenger ticket office, a hall, and toilets; a baggage room; and, at the extreme northeast end, an American Express office. The second floor was intended for office space. Completed in 1910, the station was described as "the prettiest of the Texas division."

The red brick structure, following convention, was surrounded by a platform in this instance covered by a roofed porch. On the sides, the porch roofs were carried on wooden posts, but facing the track, five cast-iron columns were used as supports. (See page 29.) Low arches spanned the columns, suggesting the loggias common in Italianate stations in the eastern United States. Three dormer windows looked out from the tile-covered hipped roof, but the most distinctive feature of the station was a tower facing the tracks. It projected through the eave of the main roof line, but unlike the tall towers in many other parts of the country, it rose only slightly higher than the roof ridge. The tower was capped by a pyramidal roof on which a twenty-foot

gold-painted flagpole, ending with a gold leaf–covered ball, was mounted. The stars and stripes were intended to float from the heights as a patriotic landmark. A large block of artificial stone inscribed with "KCM & O RY of Texas" was placed over the flat arched windows. Today the name block has been painted over with the later designation, "Santa Fe." The KCM & O passed to that railroad in the late 1920s.

Craig Drone in his study of the San Angelo station calls it "one of the finest examples of an almost purely functional design, very utilitarian in its character with little ornamentation." He assigns it to a category known as the Railroad Style, an indication of the impact railways and their station houses have had on architectural terminology. The definition of Railroad Style is not precise. It is usually applied to stations displaying an Italian Renaissance influence. A typical station of this type is described as one in which "the eye is led from one-story wings [on either end of the rectangular plan] up to the two-story main block and finally to the tower, so the building seems to grow up from the site." With a handsome fully developed tower, the station in El Paso is one of the best examples in West Texas. (See page 28.) Carroll Meeks has observed that in the simple directness of such stations there was the "undeveloped possibility of producing a truly American railroad style, straightforward and appropriate to an unsophisticated country, but like so many other American false starts this one too died young, smothered by newer fashions imported from the other side of the Atlantic." This arrested development is preserved in the dignity, simplicity, and functionality found in El Paso and in the more modest character of the station at San Angelo. Both possessed the proper character for West Texas, where frills were less valued than a pair of good, sturdy boots.

The train station has been called an "image of the community, representing at a glance something about its size, affluence, livelihood, and social range," even its civic pride. Unlike the landing at which a steamboat dropped anchor or the modern airport inconveniently located miles from a traveler's destination, the station at which passengers riding the rails were deposited was located in the midst of a town, where clues to the interests of the inhabitants were clearly visible. As West Texas grew, the station site was close to sprawling stockyards or overshadowed by grain elevators; the dome of a courthouse and box-and-strip storefronts often could be seen edging along a still unpaved street.

If newcomers were eager to pick up impressions of rapid growth and industry conveyed by the view from the station, they, in turn, were as eagerly viewed by the inhabitants of the town. The station was a gathering place filled with hustle and bustle, with puffing steam and bells and whistles. Children came to the station to watch for the trains and to put their ears to the track to listen for the hum indicating the approaching engine long before it was visible. The station was a place to exchange news and gossip, to wait for the mail and the latest headlines. The newspapers and magazines brought by the trains as well as the telegraph wires, which accompanied the expanding rails, helped eliminate provincialism and brought all parts of the country closer together.

The railroad helped to close the gap between the frontier and the Eastern seaboard. Architecture began to change as new styles moved west. Transport by rail made materials—lumber and brick and stone—more easily accessible. Cheap transportation allowed experienced craftsmen to move where buildings were under construction and jobs were waiting. The facade of West Texas was being prepared for twentieth-century alterations.

Railroad station (1890s), El Paso

(Detail, opposite) Station, Kansas City, Mexico and Orient Line (1909–1910), San Angelo

3

Box-and-Strip:
West Texas Vernacular

[The settlers seem to have had] the ease, civility,

and charm of the Old South with, however, an added

energy and industriousness infused into them by

the higher altitude and aridity of the High Plains.

Moreover, these people had to have rare qualities of

optimism and self confidence and a high degree of

individualism and desire to be beholden to no man

for their survival. After all they came of their own

free will, giving up the people and the means of

livelihood to which they had become accustomed, in

order to take a gambling chance of finding a better

life in this new and undeveloped land.

John C. Dawson, *High Plains Yesterdays*

Bairfield School (1890), Ranching Heritage Center, the Museum of Texas Tech University, Lubbock

IN WEST TEXAS, the transition from wagon, tent, or dugout to a simple wooden house of box-and-strip construction happened quickly. On the treeless prairies, the first requirement for building permanently was a source for cut lumber. The railroads connecting the new towns in the Texas Panhandle brought wood shipped from the sawmills located in the eastern woodlands. The "boxed" buildings that resulted were a form of vernacular, or folk, architecture. The term *vernacular* is in no sense derogatory; it describes buildings constructed by men without formal architectural training—"architecture without architects" to use a phrase coined by Bernard Rudofsky. (In the United States, the first school of architecture did not become a reality until a program was developed at the Massachusetts Institute of Technology in 1865. Before that time those wishing professional training in architecture hastened to Paris to take the entrance exams, offered only in French, that would allow them to enroll in the famous Ecole des Beaux-Arts.) The buildings associated with vernacular architecture are first and foremost functional. The primary considerations are the needs of people living in specific environments and the adaptation of available materials to meet these needs. In some civilizations the building skills and the structures that take shape are passed from generation to generation with only minor modifications.

The process of years of trial and error does not apply to the box-and-strip methods of construction used in West Texas. A new technique of wood framing was first developed in Chicago during the 1830s. It had been customary for heavy timbers to be mortised and tenoned together or held in place with wooden pegs. John Deodat Taylor changed the concept radically with the development of a skeletal structure assembled from light sticks nailed in place. None of this could have taken place without nail-making machinery, which since the early 1800s, had been mass producing inexpensive nails of uniform quality. Taylor's rapid and expedient method of construction called for two-inch vertical boards of varying widths to be closely spaced and nailed on a light frame. The vertical boards were continuous from the foundation to the roof. The cladding, or outer surface, was made up of horizontal strips laid flush using a shiplap joint. Carpenters and contractors looked at Taylor's structure with amusement, expecting the results to

snap in the lightest wind or blow away. They derisively called the process "balloon framing." The label was so apt that it quickly outlived the original sneer and became a part of the architectural vocabulary. Balloon framing spread like wildfire throughout the growing cities of the Middle West. Board-and-batten, or *box-and-strip*, as it was called in West Texas, was a spin off from the balloon frame. (Because of the preference of West Texas for *box-and-strip* rather than board-and-batten, the former will be used throughout the text. For further definition of terms, see the Glossary.)

There were some differences. In box-and-strip buildings, floors were considered separate units. At each level the vertical studs were only one story. The cladding, which gives box-and-strip construction its distinctive appearance, is made up of vertical planks, or boards, with narrow strips, or battens, nailed over the space between the wider verticals, thus sealing the cracks and helping secure the interior from dust or cold winds. No insulating material was used. The builders who seized upon the new way of using mill-cut lumber were usually anonymous. The simplicity of the method was eagerly accepted by carpenters and farmers and pioneers moving west.

A farmer and neighbor of Ralph Waldo Emerson inadvertently made a strong case for the balloon frame by offering a criticism of brick and stone used in farm buildings. He pointed out that masonry was "not so cheap, not so dry, and not so fit for us. Our roads are always changing their directions, and after a man has built at great cost a stone house, a new road is opened, and he finds himself a mile or two from the highway. Then our people are not stationary, like those of the old countries, but always alert to better themselves and will remove from town as a new market opens or a better farm is to be had, and [so they] do not want to spend too much on their buildings."

This willingness to follow the main chance might have been written a few decades later about Old Mobeetie, Tascosa, and many other Panhandle towns whose rapid growth had been nailed together by "boxed" buildings. Bypassed by the railroad, the dirge was sounded by train whistles blowing in the far distance. The *Pioneer* announced the exodus of Tascosa's population with a succession of dreary items. On 17 August 1889, the paper regretted that "Mrs. John Ryan and the little ones took

Box-and-strip house (1903), Ranching Heritage Center, the Museum of Texas Tech University, Lubbock

the train Tuesday night for Amarillo, where they joined Mr. Ryan and where they will make their home for the present." A few months later, it was reported, "Ira Rinehart is preparing to pack up his goods . . . and ship to Texline where he will open a grocery." The restless spirit and the need to find new opportunities left Old Tascosa behind to molder in dust and decay.

The "greener fields" were apt to be merely dustier, but the robust spirit and optimism of West Texas settlers defied the hardships to be endured before the rewards, often meager at best, could be tallied. No one has summed up the intangible covenant between the West Texan, the flat land, and the endless sky better than A. C. Greene, who wrote:

> There was something about the enormous wildness. . . . Something that pulls the eyes across the land, sweeping the vision gently upward (even today), sending it to the horizon . . . lifting it to a pile of high cumulus clouds, into the thin, blue sky that seems to draw everything beneath it upward—man and moisture alike—taking man out

of himself toward something more vital and bigger than his comparison with other men.

It surrounds him and isolates him in West Texas. . . . It makes him reach out and touch untouchable things, this wildness; to travel down a corridor of clouds that will reach some ultimate door in the horizon—and this is no pretty metaphor, for in the open country the clouds hang high and flat before you, achieving a three-dimensional synthesis with the horizon until, to a man on the ground, they are forming the ceiling of an immense passageway to that point in perspective where they meet the land.

It was the landscape of the sky, the never-ending path to the rim of the earth where the empty bowl overhead seemed to touch the ground, the freedom from encircling mountains that must have strengthened the settlers' will to survive the winds and dust, the rainless summers, and the heavy line of clouds marking the advance of winter's "blue northers."

Detail, box-and-strip house (1903), Ranching Heritage Center, the Museum of Texas Tech University, Lubbock

Eyes were also drawn toward and teased by the mirages skipping across the flat landscape. Mary Hampton Clack, who lived close to Abilene, remembered seeing "what appeared to be a blue lake of water rippling in the sunlight." A year later she saw the "young city of Abilene inverted above the tops of the mesquite trees which grew in the vicinity. Some of these buildings," she wrote, "were visible in the air, no part of which could be seen from below. However their images appeared to be reflected in water; they were upside down." Perhaps those who witnessed the mirages from dugout doors may have hoped they were in the presence of signs that predicted another sort of miracle—the escape from dirt floors, dust sifting from the ceiling, and the unwelcome visitation of scorpions and snakes to a box-and-strip home with at least two rooms and a lean-to kitchen.

A box-and-strip house built between 1903 and 1904 was moved during the 1970s from Martin County to the Ranching Heritage Center at Texas Tech University. The simple rectangular structure, with a lean-to added at the rear, is an excellent example of "boxed" construction roofed with shingles. (See page 33.) The floors are lifted on wooden posts (cedar was preferred when it was available), but fieldstone supports were also common. By keeping the floors from contact with the ground, wood decay resulting from the occasional hard rains that pelted down and turned the flat land into shallow lakes was kept at a minimum. The walls are built from vertical boards spaced as closely together as possible and nailed at top and bottom to horizontals called "nailers." The gaps between the wider wall boards are covered by one-by-four strips to seal the interior as tightly as possible. Along with the cut lumber shipped from the sawmills in East Texas, window casings, cornices, doors, and door frames were also sent by rail to the growing towns and farms. In spite of the improvement over living beneath the ground, conditions were far from ideal. Lacking wall insulation, box-and-strip houses were no match for winds and "dusters" On the morning after a night snow, patterns of white lines were often traced over the blankets and quilts.

If slender finances permitted, the interior walls might be hung with canvas. An old timer in King County, however, did not find much to praise in this treatment. He recalled, "Mother took the thin canvas that ceiled the living room and kitchen down and emptied the sand out and washed the canvas and stretched it again, because it kept out wasps and dirt dobbers in summer and a portion of the cold in winter, then she had to take it down again when it snowed because the heat from the stove caused the snow that sifted in through the roof to melt and drip. One morning [the canvas] caught fire on top and Dad had to climb up on the roof and put the fire out in his underwear."

Another commonly applied wall treatment seems to have had more positive results. Miss Tommie Clack's memories of her girlhood included this snippit of information: "I remember reading off the 'wallpaper' in our new ranch house, reading newspapers which were pasted to the wall to help keep out the wind. It was great fun picking out letters from the *Taylor County News* stuck to the wall. . . . Later we had regular wallpaper, which cost 10 cents a roll, 15 cents for a double roll. Pioneers rarely threw anything away. They found new uses for it. Scraps of leftover wallpaper were used to line quilt boxes or were placed in the safe where dishes were stacked."

Miss Tommie also remembered how hard glass for windows was to acquire. She wrote, "The first windows in our new home were made of panes about eight inches by eleven inches—small panes which, if broken, could be replaced at less cost." Windows in the early days of Lubbock, according to Seymour Connor, were usually standard four-light constructions that were only rarely fitted with weighted sash. They were sometimes mounted horizontally to slide open rather than to be raised. This poses the question, Why? The windows shipped to the new towns on the South Plains were standardized, and it seems likely that they were intended for higher rooms than those found in box-and-strip structures. Under such circumstances the horizontal installations were both logical and expedient.

Glenda Riley has written about the lives of women living on the frontier. She discovered the importance of curtains. Covering a window, often glassless, in a familiar way helped to temper the severe environment and "seemed to be a particular mark of civilization to thousands of plainswomen who took pride in having [curtains] hanging at the few windows they had." It was not important that these were often made from newspaper, muslin, cheesecloth, or old sheets. Some sturdy souls even sacrificed dresses trimmed with lace for this symbol of a gentler life-style.

A lack of insulation against heat and cold was made worse by the fact that even "the best of wooden windows became loose in the dry climate and tended to seep sand during the windy season." The front porch provided some relief from the sun. Making a primitive evaporative air-conditioner was an accomplishment of Ross Edwards, who fixed a "bed sheet over the window" of a "little old boxed and stripped room." Then, all that was necessary to complete this "first class cooling arrangement was carrying enough water to keep the sheet wet."

Cistern, Ranching Heritage Center, the Museum of Texas Tech University, Lubbock

The water was undoubtedly carried from the cistern, an important feature of every home. (See page 35.) It caught the rain channeled from the roof through gutters and spouts and allowed the lady of the house to do the washing with soft water. In dry months, water was either hauled in by wagon or brought from the windmill to the tubs sitting on the outside wash bench. The water had to be heated to a boil in an iron pot placed over a fire in the backyard. A little lye was added to soften the water: "Clothes were piled into the pot of boiling water and continuously 'punched' with a broom handle. They were then transferred to the first tub of warm water and scrubbed on the rub board with a generous application of lye soap and elbow grease until all evidence of dirt was gone. There were usually three tubs involved, the scrubbing tub, the rinsing tub, and the second rinse tub," which would have a small amount of bluing in it to whiten the wash. The clean clothes were placed on a clothesline or spread on a barbed wire fence to be dried by the sun and wind. If a dust storm came up suddenly, the result was a disaster and rewashing was the only recourse. The ordeal of the weekly wash seems to have stood out more sharply than encounters with Bonnie and Clyde or rattlesnakes among the aggravations indelibly imprinted on the minds of the women who were bringing up their young families in box-and-strip homes.

The uncomplicated and economical method of constructing boxed buildings allowed almost every farmer, storekeeper, or mechanic to provide for his own shelter.

(Opposite) Potton House (1901), hipped roof with crest, Big Spring

Pyramidal roof (early 1900s), Crosbyton

It had the added advantage of flexibility. The box-and-strip house at the Ranching Heritage Center is an example of the one-story, side-gabled roof type with a porch across the front. (See page 35.) Simpler and possibly earlier in development was the square box with a roof pitched from the four sides to terminate in a peak, or pyramidal hipped form. The equilateral hipped roof of the square plan required more complex roof framing, but was less expensive to build because fewer timbers with a long span were needed. (Interestingly, Joe Pickle in his book on the first twenty-five years in Howard County says such a house was "described loosely as a bungalow.") A hipped roof might form a flat line at the top along which an elaborate metal cresting was placed (See page 37), or the pyramid might end in a flat platform edged with a balustrade (see page 38), as in the Square House Museum in Panhandle. Both the side-gabled roofs and the pyramidal roof types could be easily adapted to cover two story houses. A third house plan was L-shaped. This house type had a gabled front with a wing extending at right angles. A porch usually stretched across the wing. (See page 38.) Most houses had lean-tos added at the rear.

The Harrell House, now at the Ranching Heritage Center, was begun in 1883. It represents a progression of additions relating the story of two decades of building. The house was originally located on Deep Creek, a tributary of the Colorado River near Snyder in Scurry County. Building first resulted in one room with walls of sandstone slabs laid in mud mortar. The stone came from a nearby gully; the mud was brought from the creek banks. (See page 39.) When the property changed hands in 1897 and a new addition was begun, lumber still had to be freighted to the site. (See page 40.) Two years later, a double fireplace was put in place and a wing with a long porch was built across the front of the house. This resulted in a T-shaped plan using box-and-strip construction.

A house of similar vintage, near Anson, was the boyhood home of David L. Caffey. Like the farms around it, he wrote, it "had its own personality—its own face, its wrinkles, and its idiosyncrasies:"

The house was 'L' shaped, with a covered porch and scroll trim along the front and a breezeway between the two main sections. [My mother and

House with L-shaped plan (1890s) at 315 Bridge Street, Granbury

Square House Museum (1887), Panhandle

father] occupied the big front room, with the girls across the open breezeway and the dining room and kitchen behind. A fireplace and a wood stove provided uneven pockets of warmth in the winter months. The boys' room was at the very back end of the long row of rooms running . . . north from the main front room.

The old house was built on posts on a foundation of the kind known as "post and pier." That is, several massive posts were sunken into the ground and sawed off level and a platform floor was built on them with no underpinnings involved, so the person might stand out east of the house and see the sun setting underneath it in the west. . . . This kind of construction had its advantages and disadvantages. On the one hand, it left a shaded and easily accessible space where certain food supplies might be kept cool on occasion. It also provided handy storage for ladders, cane poles, and other odd items . . . but it was a nuisance in other ways. Hens often tried to protect their eggs by laying them up under the house.

Caffey recollected the time when a rattlesnake was discovered in the cool darkness beneath the house.

Without hesitation, a neighbor who was on the spot drew his gun and blew the snake to smithereens. The trouble was, the shot also passed through the space under the house and out on the opposite side, killing four chickens who were scratching around in the backyard.

On the west side of the Caffey house, a door jutting up above ground level led down a flight of steps to an underground room that served multiple purposes, including a storm cellar. The link between dugout and storm cellar is obvious. As tornadoes rampaged like runaway trains over the prairies, a family must have felt secure in a shelter dug into a hillside or piled with earth. When the box-and-strip house was completed, if the dugout was preserved, it became a root cellar, a place to keep canned jellies and fruits, a cool room for milk and cream, a "guest" room for stray travelers, or a space for hired hands. Most of all, it was a safe haven if storm clouds threatened. When the northern sky turned black, mothers all across the flat land would "gather up" the kids and "herd" them to safety.

There was another "necessary," the "outhouse." A one or two holer was customary. Hardly of sufficient merit for box-and-strip construction, it was nailed together with planks and placed over a pit excavated for the refuse. Jim Corder provided a sympathetic glimpse

Harrell House (begun in 1883), Ranching Heritage Center, the Museum of Texas Tech University, Lubbock

at this lost past when he paid the following homage to the outmoded commode of the back lot. He said,

> The outhouses I have known best were structures ordinarily of wood, about five feet square, or less, standing some six feet high in front, the roof slanting downward to a rear wall of maybe four and one-half feet. The two sides were sometimes decorated with designs cut into the wood, the crescent moon and the diamond being the most widely favored figures. [In Ohio, if the younger members of a family were feeling frisky, it was common to dump a bucket of water through the crescent on a sitting target, in the process dampening the Sears Roebuck catalog.] In some instances, the door was so decorated rather than the walls, and in a few instances, both sides and door were adorned, though the discriminating thought that made entirely too busy an effect. The outhouses of my memory were almost all of the gray-brown achieved by weathering on unpainted wood. Some few, to be sure, were painted, but it seemed an affectation, and I recall that if, on Halloween night, the choice presented itself to a group of boys between a painted and weathered outhouse, there was no contest as to which got toppled over.

If the barn and other farm buildings at Caffey's home place followed the usual custom, they continued the box-and-strip tradition. At the Ranching Heritage Center, most of the ranch buildings are examples of this simple, swift, and durable form of construction. The U Lazy S Carriage House, originally located ten miles south of Post in Garza County, was built about 1900 for John B. Slaughter. It is a two-story harness, saddle and carriage house walled with boards and battens and covered by a shed roof. The central part of the enclosure was reserved for the carriages. On one end, there was a room for saddles and harness. At the opposite, end a storage area for livestock feed was located.

In the background, the large red 6666 barn stands against the sky with a grand functionality that is awesome. In strong sunlight, the shadow patterns made by the boards and battens are as bold as those of a Japanese woodcut. (See page 42.) The blacksmith shop is of the same construction and color as the barn. A window on

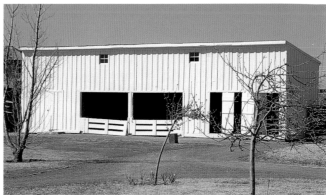

U Lazy S carriage house (1906), Ranching Heritage Center, the Museum of Texas Tech University, Lubbock

(Top) Outhouse, Baylor County Historical Museum, Seymour

(Opposite) Harrell House (begun in 1883), Ranching Heritage Center, the Museum of Texas Tech University, Lubbock

a gabled side of the building has a hinged cover that when propped open acts as an awning. This device was also adopted in some box-and-strip houses.

6666 barn with cotton gin in the background, Ranching Heritage Center, the Museum of Texas Tech University, Lubbock

Box-and-strip was as practical in towns as it was useful on farms and ranches. When speed and the enclosure of the most space with the least material were important, light wood framing offered the answer. Caffey described adolescent Abilene as "a precarious and unstable mix of elements from the the raw frontier. . . . The town had banks, churches, schools, and an opera house. . . . At the same time, there was little . . . to indicate grace or permanence. Most of the houses and a good many of the businesses were yet of plain and hasty construction, *boxed and stripped in the simplest fashion* [italics mine]. They reflected little attention to looks and not a great deal more to comfort."

In the 1890s, Lubbock, the self-proclaimed "hub" of the South Plains could have shared the same description. As an inducement to buy land and settle in the new Lubbock County seat, the Nicolette Hotel was one of the first buildings constructed. It was a square, two-story frame structure with an attic covered by a pyramidal roof from which dormer windows projected. It was soon joined by the jail and courthouse in that order.

On 11 May 1891, bids were accepted for a jail to be placed on the northeast corner of the square. This was Lubbock's first public building. The importance given jail architecture in the towns of West Texas is interesting. Often the jailhouse was the most solidly built ar-

chitectural accomplishment. The jails at Silverton (see page 43) and Clairemont (see page 43) were surrounded by such heavily rusticated stone walls, they could have withstood an assault by Pancho Villa and his gang. Whether Lubbock expected nothing but law-abiding citizens or couldn't afford the financial requirements of stone, the jail was a boxed structure. In the period after it was completed, it served as a temporary school.

The first session of classes organized by Miss Minnie Tubbs closed with a ceremony faithfully reported by the Lubbock *Leader*. A society notice informed the eager public that "the exercises began at noon and consumed the evening in nice recitations by all the scholars." The account continued, "Space forbids us making special mention, but will say that one and all did exceedingly well. At night a sumptuous supper was set, and all made themselves at home—at the table." After the installation of the cells, the jail could no longer be used as a focus for a community gathering, unless a hanging was in progress.

Civic functions passed from the jail to the courthouse once it was built. The specifications for Lubbock County's first courthouse were settled three days after the bid for the jail was accepted. The requirements stated that the building should be forty-eight feet wide, fifty-six feet long, and twenty-four feet high. An acceptable cost must fall between eight thousand and twelve thousand dollars. Plans were submitted to the architectural firm of Gill, Woodward, and Gill of Dallas, who accepted the proposed price of twelve thousand dollars. Materials were hauled from the nearest rail points, Amarillo and Colorado City. The result was a two-story wooden structure with projections at the four corners, giving the illusion of towers. Each "tower" was capped by a pyramidal roof that led the eye to a larger pyramid covering the central block of the building. From it a cupola rose. The courthouse was ready for occupancy at the beginning of 1892. Unfortunately, the wooden structure was not able to withstand high winds. A severe dust storm whipped through Lubbock in 1896, bringing about the cupola's downfall and twisting and warping the courthouse walls. The walls were resquared, but the cupola was not considered worth the effort.

From the beginning, the courthouse was the center of various activities. The literary society was organized and met there. Church congregations were welcomed, and an organ was installed in a second-floor room for church services and community singing. On Saturday night, the courthouse played host to dances attended by people who came from miles around. In many communities, this was an accepted function. Mrs. Nonnie Rogers, who began married life in a dugout, remembered enthusiastically all-day rides to Clairemont for all-night dances. She wrote, "We'd dance all night and go home at sunrise. The steps of the courthouse seemed awfully steep going down into the light of the rising sun."

By the last years of the 1890s, numerous enterprises had grown up around Lubbock's main square: two hotels, a growing number of mercantile establishments, a blacksmith shop, a barber shop, a grain store, a livery stable, two land firms, six lawyers' offices, and two *daguerreans,* a term that appears to refer to photographers. Makers of daguerreotypes must have been nearly obsolete at the turn of the century.

Across the South Plains, if there were no permanent photographic "studios" in a town, an itinerant photographer would periodically arrive on the scene, stretch his tent and for several weeks record for posterity the faces of the inhabitants. For children the ordeal of having a picture taken meant combing their hair and dressing up in their Sunday best with black-ribbed hose over

Clairemont jail (c. 1893)

(Top) Silverton jail (1894)

Store (1920s), Old Glory

(Opposite) St. Paul's on the Plains (1913–1914), Lubbock

the knees and polished high-top shoes. One participant in a group picture with four siblings said, "The photographer told us to look for the bird to come out of the contraption he used to take the picture. We looked, but if it ever came out, we failed to see it and we talked about it for days wondering if there really was a bird in it, and what could have happened to it."

A business that made a rapid exit from Lubbock was the "saloon and liquor emporium." Two sources of local pressure ensured this enterprise was short-lived: the manager of the nearby IOA ranch who feared temptation might cause his cowboys to slip over fences and sprint to town and the organized church groups who did not regard the proximity of hard liquor as an uplifting influence for the citizens.

Needless to say, the business district was entrenched in box-and-strip stores and offices. The storefronts rose above the lower roofs, producing an appearance of height and importance. The high boards above the entrance provided space for advertising and the owner's name.

B OX-AND-STRIP served another purpose in West Texas. Inexpensive and easy to build, the method of construction was adopted for schools. Although the importance of education was recognized, the accommodations for students and their teachers did not adequately support this recognition. Miss Tommie Clack contributed first-hand information about the early beginnings of education in Taylor County. During the last decades of the nineteenth century, she taught in a one-room frame school building in a settlement near Abilene called *Colony Hill*. This was a subscription school, financed in part by parents who paid tuition for each of their children. In Abilene in 1881, the payment was one dollar per child for four weeks. Terms lasted half a year and a teacher's salary was about thirty dollars a month. The dedicated, or distracted teacher was expected to teach grades one through nine with one or two pupils at each level. Miss Tommy explained, "While older children recited, the younger ones amused themselves by writing on the blackboard, by drawing on paper, or by modelling horned frogs or other figures from clay which the teacher furnished."

The one-room schoolhouse at the Ranching Heritage Center in Lubbock was moved to its present location from Clarendon. (See page 39.) Built in the late 1890s, the schoolhouse is not box-and-strip; instead the framing is covered with shiplap siding. It was originally constructed as a part of the JA Ranch for the education of the children of cowboys and ranchers. Children were often told as they left with their lunch pails in the morning, "Watch for the snakes and mind the teacher." The sixteen- by sixteen-foot building received its light from two windows on each side and from the door when it was left open. Heat was supplied by a cast-iron potbellied stove in the center of the room. A shelf in one corner was stacked with books, and another shelf was reserved for the water bucket, not only a source for quenching thirst but a safeguard against fire.

Not all pupils were fortunate enough to enjoy the luxury of box-and-strip accommodations, even if the cracks were sometimes wide enough to let a cat crawl through. The first school in Mitchell County opened with fifteen students in a dugout. After a few weeks, the class moved to a tent where the only heat was supplied by a cooking stove. Merchandise boxes provided the first desks for pupils and teachers.

When a school was needed in Lynn County near Salt Wells, cowboys were sent by the owner of the Slaughter Ranch to help with the building. They may have been top-string cowhands, but they were less than perfect carpenters: "many were the times that the pupils in that little school amused themselves . . . trying to imagine that the hammer marks on the walls and ceilings were all sorts of animals, faces, and even whole scenes."

Called upon to accommodate many diverse purposes, Little Arizona School, built in 1895 for the Dumont Community in King County, was used during the summer for storing hay. Returning from the summer to discover bales of hay piled in the corners of the classroom, the teacher decided that since necessity was the mother of invention, she would use the bales as seats for the children. Desks had been ordered from the Sears-Roebuck Catalog but had not arrived.

C HURCH MEMBERS often shared the same conditions as teachers and students. In many communities schools were used for Sunday meetings. But before there were schools or courthouses to welcome the worshipers, one pioneer woman, living near Quanah, told about going to church under a hackberry tree. She also remembered "attending Sunday School in a rock dugout where the women wore black satin skirts and bow ties and 'high powered' perfume."

Saloons played a role, too. The Presbyterians were the first to hold religious gatherings in Mitchell County. The first sermon was delivered on 9 January 1881: "since no hall large enough . . . was available, a bar in a saloon was covered with a wagon sheet, and the saloon was utilized for the services."

In another hour of need, cowboys saved the Sabbath in Quanah. An itinerant preacher had promised a visit. The back room of the judge's quarters was to act as church for the day, but there was no organ. Learning of the dilemma, cowhands from a neighboring ranch volunteered to borrow one.

Next morning, sure enough the rooms had been readied, chairs and table for the speaker were in place and the miracle has happened—there was the organ! Two cowboys, freshly scrubbed and with hair slicked down, stood at the door requiring the other men [to] remove their spurs and six guns as they entered. Miss Zoe at a very prim and very precise sweet sixteen arrived and played the instrument that had been provided. How everyone sang! The visiting preacher spoke as only the rugged frontier servant of the Lord could preach. It was a memorable day. Only after the close of the service did the very proper Miss Harper learn that the cowboys borrowed the organ 'To the glory of God' from the neighboring saloon.

When the first churches appeared along the dirt streets of the new towns, they were often constructed in the familiar box-and-strip manner. Lubbock's first Episcopal church was built in the second decade of the twentieth century. At present it is a derelict, half hidden by unkempt lilacs and elm trees on one of Lubbock's busiest streets. The Episcopal congregation was spear-

(Opposite) Presbyterian church (now Lutheran) (1915), Post

Church of the Sacred Heart (1899), Menard

headed by Mrs. Sallie Coleman, whose religious convictions were well known. Her son wrote of his mother, "Many times I have seen her drive a wild cowboy or wild horse catcher from our camp. After he had removed his gun, put his pants legs outside of his boots and combed his hair he could return, partake of a generous meal and listen to a devotional."

Sad to say, Sallie Coleman died three years before work on St. Paul's on the Plains was begun in October of 1913. The church is a conventionally framed wooden structure with horizontal shiplap siding. It has a steeply pitched gabled roof. There is no tower. Perhaps to acknowledge a Gothic heritage, false buttresses of wood were added at the corners (see page 45) and two buttresses were spaced along the exterior north wall. In the same spirit, the windows and doorway were defined by pointed arches.

Although the building was not quite finished, the first service was held in the church on 11 January 1914, another indication of the speed with which a wood-framed structure could be raised. It was noted that a member of the church, Mr. Towle, contributed the paper for the walls; it was also reported that he pasted bits of colored tissue on the clear glass of the double-hung windows to produce the effect of stained glass. The heat was supplied by a stove burning coal and wood. Mary Elizabeth Randal, the daughter of the rector who served St. Paul's from 1926 to 1930, wrote in a letter, "The men in the congregation took turns stoking the fire during the service. The members who sat away from the stove froze in the wintertime and those closest to the stove fainted. At Easter it was not considered a successful service unless at some time someone would faint from the heat and had to be carried out. Those were the days."

In Post, a small wood-framed Presbyterian Church (now Lutheran) (see page 46) gives a clear picture of how St. Paul's on the Plains must once have looked. The Post church is dated 1915, a year after St. Paul's was completed. The two churches share so many features, it suggests that the same builder or contractor may have been employed for both. The churches are rectangular. The steeply angled gables create strong triangular compositions, possibly a reference to the Trinity. When lack of funds prohibited symbolic decoration, the church itself became the symbol. Of particular interest, the churches have the unusual feature of almost identi-

cal false buttresses. The harmonious proportions and pristine condition of the church at Post suggest the original charm of St. Paul's on the Plains.

The Menard Catholic Church of the Sacred Heart (see page 47) possesses the same simplicity and unaffected warmth as the white frame church at Post and a similar Episcopal church at Quanah. There is, however, a difference. The Church of the Sacred Heart, built in 1899, is constructed of carefully worked rusticated stone. The stone is coursed in diminishing sizes from the ground to the gable. The windows and door are framed by Gothic arches. There is a curious little diamond-shaped window midway between the pointed arch of the door and the cross at the apex of the gable.

St. John the Baptist Episcopal Church in Clarendon (see page 49) was consecrated in 1893, twenty years earlier than St. Paul's on the Plains in Lubbock. This is a reminder of the late settlement of pioneer communities on the Llano Estacado. Stylistically the churches should be reversed with the more sophisticated St. John Episcopal occupying the later date. The entry of the Clarendon church is located at the base of the bell tower at right angles to the facade which has as a central feature a large stained glass window contained by a pointed Gothic arch.

The Methodist church at Channing was built in 1898. (See page 50.) It has a tower that stands out from the rectangular building block. The spire is rather heavy. It is broken into three stages. The lower part is hipped and furnishes the base for a louvered square, presumably to allow light and air in the area where the bell is located. From this, the spire rises above overhanging and flared eaves. Joe Pickle reminds a younger generation that it was the church bell "whose vibrant, carrying peals called the faithful together [and that] when [it was] rung rapidly and incessantly, [it] warned the community of a fire or some other catastrophic event."

An almost forgotten Methodist church to which a few people still return stands in a field near the abandoned town of Sanco. (See page 50.) Four-square and resolute, the wooden structure seems to defy time. Totally devoid of decoration, the entry projects at the center. In the late afternoon sunlight, the church makes a powerful statement, drawing the mind back to those first New England meeting houses in the wilderness and to the religious roots from which this country came.

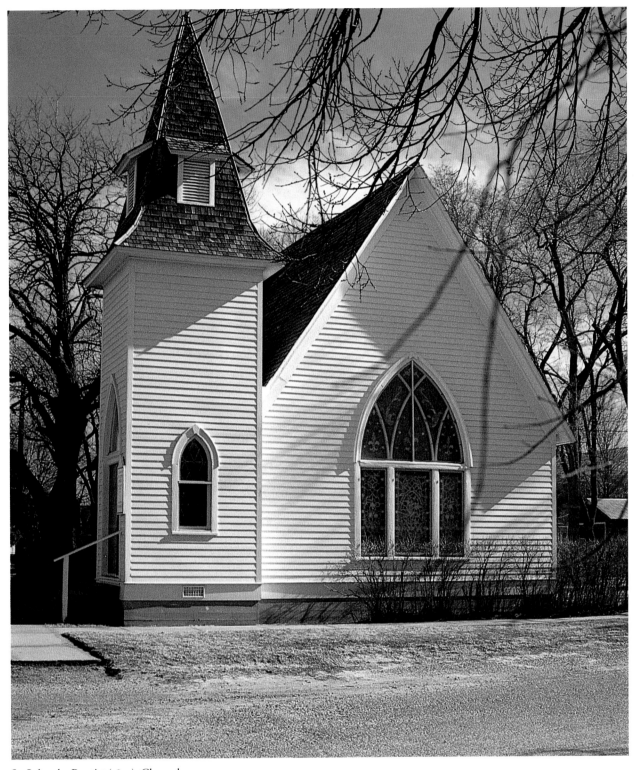

St. John the Baptist (1893), Clarendon

A short distance from the church, there is a wooden structure where camp meetings are still held during the summer. (See page 50.)

The revivals, which brought people together, are one of the special traditions of growing up in West Texas. At first the gatherings took place under brush arbors. The arbor had many of the same characteristics as the New Mexican *ramadas,* built in the pueblos and Spanish villages as shaded places for livestock or for women to carry on their weaving outdoors. The arbors for camp meetings in Howard County made use of tree trunks or spaced posts over the tops of these branches, lumber, and coarse wire were placed. This furnished the base for a matting of freshly cut brush. In hot arid climates, the arbor was a workable way of securing shade with a minimum of material and maximum air circulation. In the evenings, "lanterns were hung from posts, and in a few instances torches provided feeble illumination.

Methodist church (early 1900s), Sanco

First Methodist Church (1898), Channing

Church built at Porterville (1910) moved to Mentone
(1930), Mentone

Summer camp meeting site (c. 1915–1920), Sanco

Later there were kerosene and gas lights." Of the meetings that took place in such settings, Joe Pickle says,

> If there was a podium, it was a crude wooden affair to give the minister a bit of elevation. Makeshift benches, often made with lumber still bleeding resin or abounding with splinters, furnished seating along with primitive chairs, boxes, kegs, benches or whatever was handy. A pallet of quilts was spread to accommodate the babies. Dust (and rarely rain) beset the worshippers along with flies, mosquitoes and other insects. On hot still days, fans—ranging from fancy, folding lace-trimmed ones carried by milady in her purse, to plain pasteboard stapled to a stick—provided hand-powered air conditioning. The tempo of fanning often increased in direct proportion to the vividness with which the preacher called down visions of hell.

He continued, "Music centered around the universal instrument—the human voice. Most singing was a capella. An untutored layman started and was joined by others . . . perhaps he hummed or sounded a pitch pipe, and then he and the congregation took off."

Henrietta Nichols called the summer gatherings spent away from the daily chores at home "a real treat." She explained, "Cooks were hired [and] . . . the women and children stayed [in the church house]. The men took the older boys at night and used cowboy bedrolls to bed down in the bushes." Meetings were held under a brush arbor, which was covered with fresh shinnery limbs each year. The same method of cover protected the long narrow arbor where a plank table for food was set up. *Shinnery* is a well-known term to Texans from certain regions of the state, but a puzzle to others. According to David Caffey, the shinnery begins about halfway across the twenty-five miles from Abilene to Anson: "It was, in its essence, a dense thicket of native oak, shrubbery, and briars." The land, once the stumps and shrubs were grubbed out, was suitable for farming, but some shinnery was always left standing as a pasture for livestock and a supply of wood for the stove. Where brush was needed for arbor construction, the shinnery was a prime source; it also provided firewood for heating the "big wash pots [that] held food for three meals a day," the dutch ovens filled with biscuits, and the pot with coffee strong enough to walk away on its own steam.

A. C. Greene who writes about West Texas with a sensitivity and eloquence that fills those who love the country with something akin to reverence and not a little envy says of the religiosity that permeated this raw country from the beginning and brought folks together for camp meetings in country fields or under canvas tents:

> West Texas is like the Biblical lands, a hot, dry desert country. . . . Perhaps it is this kinship with the land of the Bible which caused it . . . to cling to dry, feverish beliefs which demand more [of people than they] are capable of offering even God.. . . The loneliness of the high sky makes men see God. But he is seen in the fiery sunlight. . . .
>
> Mostly [God] is represented by churches. Cities vanish but the lonely, little white frame churches, left over from the turn of the century are still sitting where there used to be towns.

In the last decade of the nineteenth century in West Texas, a white wooden church in which to worship (See page 54.) and a move from the dark dugout to a box-and-strip house in the sunlight caused feelings of pride and joy. But as families increased in size, as money became more plentiful, and as the rough, unpopulated prairie was gradually civilized, the box-and-strip houses—small, lacking insulation, devoid of comforts, monotonous in appearance—were no longer considered adequate. Trains brought in magazines and newspapers with pictures of more comfortable and fashionable architecture. Trips to visit relatives back east increased the longing for fashions. The houses that served as models for dreaming were often frame, but they were more spacious, and ornamented with a confection of gingerbread, turned with the lathe or cut with the jigsaw. Gingerbread had been on the residential menu in other parts of the country since the 1830s. Its proliferation in West Texas was the last gasp of the style that has, in recent years, been crowned with the title Queen Anne. How Queen Anne was received in West Texas is the next part of the story.

4
Box-and-Strip Meets Queen Anne

It was a big, squarish frame house that had once been white, decorated with cupolas and spires and scrolled balconies in the heavily lightsome style of the seventies, set on what had once been our most select street. But garages and cotton gins had encroached and obliterated even the august names of the neighborhood; only Miss Emily's house was left, lifting its stubborn and coquettish decay above the cotton wagons and the gasoline pumps.

William Faulkner, "A Rose for Emily"

THE VOGUE for the Gothic Revival was popularized in mid–nineteenth-century America by Andrew Jackson Downing and his best seller, *Cottage Residences,* first published in 1842. When it was printed, the Indians hunting buffalo over the grasslands of West Texas were hardly a receptive audience for a guide to refined domestic architecture. Four decades later, however, if the cattlemen and farmers had not been preoccupied with more important matters they might have appreciated Downing's opening comment that the first and basic principle to consider for a dwelling was "fitness or usefulness." Unfortunately, the author's next remarks would have drawn the same amused guffaws as a tenderfoot on a bucking bronco. To West Texans living in tents or dugouts while waiting to move into a box-and-strip home, the advice that a "bathing room" could "be easily constructed in any cottage" and that "no dwelling [could be considered complete without] a water-closet under its roof" would have seemed as farfetched as a Japanese inglenook with a parasol suspended from the ceiling. The jigsaw patterns and pointed arches of Gothic cottages were not choices offered settlers whose lumber had to be hauled by oxen or mules from distant railheads.

By the 1890s, however, the pioneer days on the High Plains were ending, just in time to welcome a successor to the Gothic Revival, the style named after Queen Anne. Two decades earlier in the settled parts of the United States, "Carpenter's Gothic," as it was called, had become old-fashioned and a bore. To break the tedium, Queen Anne entered and was pronounced honest, sincere, practical, and just a touch quaint. What is the Queen Anne style? Perversely, the answer begins with the facts that Queen Anne occupied the English throne briefly (1702-1714) and contributed little to the architectural scene except for a few pieces of graceful furniture. The reign of Anne was quickly eclipsed by the Georgian Age. Even in the nineteenth century, Queen Anne was only one more courtier in Victoria's largesse of architectural possibilities, which included the Italianate style, Richardsonian Romanesque, Second Empire, and a category known as Folk Victorian, to mention a few odds and ends.

Russell Lynes, in *The Tastemakers,* with tongue in cheek, refers to the Queen Anne mode as "a tossed salad of Elizabethan, Jacobean, and the style of Francis I with

Joseph Potton House (1901), Big Spring

J. D. Berry House (1869), Stephenville

the structural underpinnings of none of them. . . . it was picturesque at the same time that it was 'honest,' and 'artistic' at the same time it was 'practical.'" Its roofs were sharply peaked, and it had "second- and third-floor balconies, spindled verandas, occasional stained glass windows, and corner towers. . . . What was still more important, it was an architecture equally suitable to the wealthy and to the poor, and it demanded no skills in building of which every American carpenter was not the master."

When West Texans became aware of the Queen Anne manner with its indulgence in applied bric-a-brac, it had an immediate appeal. It offered a way to gussy up a plain box-and-strip home with a bit of fancy ornament. The result was a legacy, as John Maass phrased it, of some of the most "complex habitations ever designed for commoners." These complexities, led to a rejection of the traditional concept of unity in design. External appearances were distinguished by deliberate toying with irrational contrasts in texture, irregularities in ground plan, and unexpected positioning of parts. Every facade displayed a different elevation. The roof gave birth to families of dormers overlooked by bristling towers and crested ridges. Not only was traditional white paint abandoned in many parts of the country in exchange for rich, dark colors, but every conceivable trim was exploited

with an exuberance that would have left the Puritans predicting eternal fire and brimstone for carpenters and clients alike. There were wide porches extending along the front or wrapping around the sides, gables, balconies, bay windows, hoods and overhangs, stained glass, lathe turned posts, elaborate brackets, and friezes fashioned from delicate spindlework. Maass, reassessing what the critics of the mid-twentieth century rejected as chaos, wrote, "Paradoxically, this busy allover pattern created a unity of its own, very much like a patchwork quilt that makes a strong design out of many different fabrics."

It is understandable to react with surprise at the large serving of "gingerbread" offered by Queen Anne, since intricate jigsaw work was an earmark of the Gothic Revival. The differences in the characteristics of Carpenter's Gothic, as it was called colloquially, compared with the Queen Anne style are strongly marked and can be illustrated in the contrast of Stephenville's Gothic Revival Berry House with the wood-framed Queen Anne home of D. N. Arnett (dated 1899) in Colorado City (see page 55). The stone house in Stephenville is symmetrical with a prominent front gable. At the second story level, a balcony runs the entire length of the front porch. Access to the balcony is through a narrow door with a transom placed on the central axis. Above the door, a simple wooden circle with a cutwork design suggests stylized flower petals. The same motif is repeated beneath the chimneys at either end of the steeply pitched roof. (See page 56.) The verge boards have white arrow-shaped details. The front entrance is a plain double door with shuttered windows on either side. Although the windows are not defined by pointed arches, they are tall and narrow in the fashion typical of the Gothic Revival.

Built thirty years later in the Queen Anne mode, the Arnett house has cross gables and two stories. Below the front gable, there is a cutaway bay with corner bracketing. Over the central window of the bay and the windows at the side of the house, wooden sunshades are attached. (See page 57.) The ample porch has a spindle-work frieze between lathe-turned posts. (The vocabulary used to describe Queen Anne architecture is often as involved as the designs, but terminology is nothing more than an attempt to put into words what can be better understood by looking at a building. There is humor in the discovery that a snaggled brick pattern is called *mouse tooth*.) Another indication of the presence of Queen Anne at the Arnett home is the orchestration of intricate designs. The simplicity, symmetrical balance, and restrained use of gingerbread at the Berry House were no longer stylish. The effect required in the 1890s was a reflection of the embroidery on the fine muslin and lawn dresses of fashionable ladies, the fastidious curls of Spencerian script, or the uncoiling tendrils of ferns in a handpainted pot.

The recipe for the gingerbread offered by Queen Anne required new ingredients to suit changing conditions. But first a few words should be said about the puzzling term *gingerbread* as it is used in nineteenth-century architecture. John Maass's The *Gingerbread Age* traces an origin for the term to the medieval French *gingimbrat,* meaning "preserved ginger." When translated into English, the last syllable was mistakenly identified as "bread." English gingerbread, a relished sweet, was cut into fanciful shapes. A similarity was apparent between the gingerbread, artfully iced, and the carved decorations used by shipbuilders or applied by carpenters to English cottages. There was also a relation to the wood trim on Swiss chalets. The method of producing ornamental woodwork in the United States was quite different, however, from the Alpine tech-

D. N. Arnett House (1899), Colorado City

nique. In Switzerland, fretwork was handcarved with a knife, but on this side of the Atlantic gingerbread was cut from flat boards with a scroll saw worked by a foot treadle. The ornamental openwork that had been produced with a jigsaw (see page 58) was largely abandoned toward the end of the nineteenth century for lathe-turned porch posts and slender spindles often threaded with knoblike beads, identifying marks of the Queen Anne style. An example of a porch framed with intricate spindlework can be seen at 340 Patrick Street in Dublin. (See page 60.) Hoods over corner windows are filled with weblike spindles at a home on West Walnut Street in Coleman.

By the last decades of the nineteenth century, the foot treadle was replaced by steam-powered machinery. The outpouring of labor-saving devices invented to further American industry was a source of amazement to Europeans. At the Philadelphia Centennial Exhibition in 1876, one enterprising Ohio manufacturer displayed a line of patented "wood-workers" to be used for "jointing, squaring, smoothing, beveling, cornering, chamfering, tapering, mitering, rabbeting, tenoning, halfing, panel-raising, tonguing, grooving, hand-matching, rolling-joints, gaining, plowing, serpentine and waved moulding, fluting, beading, ripping, splitting, cross-cut sawing, straight, circular, oval, and elliptical moulding, dove-tailing, etc." No wonder there was an excessiveness associated with Queen Anne architecture. The style answered the challenge proffered by the can-do mentality, joined with the machine's ability to perform tasks better and to accomplish them faster and more expediently than anyone dreamed possible.

Not only was the mass-production of parts proven practical in building, but prefabrication of whole houses and storefronts became a flourishing industry. Prefabrication is usually thought of as a modern process, but structures prefabricated of both wood and iron were available and welcomed by an eager market in the late nineteenth century. Parts for refurbishing older structures could also be selected and ordered from catalogs. One ad announced, "A front of iron can be prepared and fitted at the manufactory and thence transported to the place of erection and put together with a wonderful rapidity and at all seasons of the year." An interesting example of cast-iron columns used for domestic architecture is found in the porch of a two-story Queen Anne house in Clarendon. (See page 60.)

Once the railroad came to the hinterlands of West Texas, ordering architectural parts by catalog eased the dilemma of having few professional architects to consult. A list of the pattern books and trade catalogs available would take up pages. A few examples include *Architectural Designs Issued by the T. W. Harvey Lumber Co.* (Chicago: T. W. Harvey Lumber Co., 1889); Daniel D. Badger, *Illustrations of Iron Architecture, 1865* (1865; rpt. New York: Dover, 1981); Louis H. Gibson, *Convenient*

Detail, J. D. Berry House (1869), Stephenville

Houses with Fifty Plans for the Housekeeper (New York: Thomas Y. Crowell, 1889); Henry Hudson Holly, *Modern Dwellings in Town and Country* (New York: Harper and Brothers, 1878); *Late Victorian Architectural Details, Combined Book of Sash, Door, Blinds, Mouldings, Etc., 1898* (1898; rpt. Watkins Glen, N.Y.: American Life Foundation and Study Institute, 1978); *Low-Cost Houses with Constructive Details,* Carpentry and Building Series, no. 2 (New York: David Williams Co., 1907); *Millwork Catalogue No. 121* (Fond du Lac, Wis.: Moore and Galloway Lumber Co., 1900); Robert W. Shopell, *How to Build, Furnish, and Decorate* (New York: Cooperative Building Plan Association, 1883); *Wooden and Brick Buildings with Details* (New York: A. J. Bucknell and Co., 1875). It was from such do-it-yourself handbooks that designs for scrolls and brackets and roof cresting and finials could be chosen and simplified to fit the work at hand.

Clever carpenters invented variations in keeping with their own inclinations and the tastes of their clients. Queen Anne architecture at its most extravagant reveled in orgies of foliate designs coiling from brackets and festooned in delicate beads and spindles, casting a net of shadows. The most flamboyant examples were associated with East Texas and the architectural fantasies of Galveston and the coast; nonetheless, West Texas had an unexpected wealth of "embroidered" houses. Some have survived almost untouched in smaller towns.

IN UVALDE, the John Nance Garner House was built in 1895 by Garner for his bride. The porch curving around at either side of the house is defined by the typical lathe-turned posts connected by a spindle work frieze. A gable is filled with a half circle of cutwork and beads that fan out from a small wooden circle. (See page 59.) Below the raised detail, there is a cladding of shingles in a diamond pattern.

Shingles used decoratively frequently appeared in gables or in bands accenting the surfaces of a building. The buildings were not always residential. At Fort Stockton, St. Stephen's Episcopal Church (see page 59), built in 1896, has bands of "fish scale," or scalloped shingles on its steeple. (See page 59.) The louvers of the lower windows are also particularly pleasing. This small and felicitous structure was not always in its present lo-

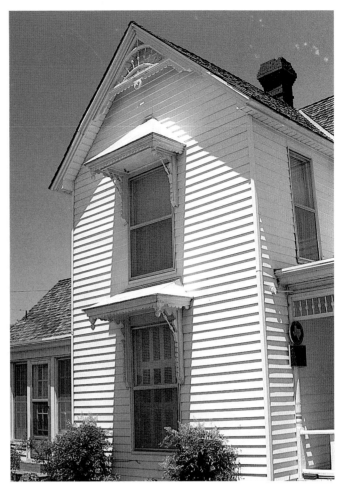

Detail, D. N. Arnett House (1899), Colorado City

cation. Once named for St. Mark, the small frame church was moved from Pecos to Ft. Stockton in 1958. There it was rededicated to St. Stephen.

The fish-scale shingle pattern found at St. Stephen's was only one of a wide variety of designs from which the builders could choose or combine in a bewildering profusion. The upper story and tower of the Tom Lovell House in Brownwood, dating from about 1889, was surfaced with "staggered" shingles, while a diamond pattern was introduced in the gables and repeated in a band at the level of the porch roof. (See page 59.) Tom Lovell, a native of Scotland and a contractor by profession, built a number of public buildings, including the Arizona State Capitol, several central Texas courthouses, and St. John's Episcopal Church in Brownwood.

In 1887, two years earlier than Brownwood's Lovell House, the White-Pool home at Odessa was more modestly designed for a Quaker family who migrated to West Texas from Indiana. Charles and Lucy White with their two sons loaded their possessions on a railroad car and made the long journey west attracted by the railroad land company's promise of good property available in Ector County. Within a year of the family's arrival on the South Plains, their two-story red brick house was completed. Brick, not often used in the 1880s

Tom Lovell House (c. 1889), Brownwood

(Top left) John Nance Garner House (1895), Uvalde

(Top right) Detail, St. Stephen's Episcopal Church
(formerly St. Mark's at Pecos) (1896), Fort Stockton

(Left) St. Stephen's Episcopal Church, Fort Stockton

(Opposite) Detail, house at 510 Denver (late 1880s),
Dalhart

House at 340 Patrick (1890s), Dublin

House at 314 South Jefferson (early 1900s), Clarendon

for West Texas homes, was delivered by rail to a point about two blocks from the small knoll on which the house stands. This oldest surviving structure of substance in Odessa reflects the sturdy simplicity of the Quaker life-style as well as memories of farmhouses familiar to anyone brought up in the Midwest. Relieving the substantial, no-nonsense brickwork, is a touch of gingerbread, which trims the front porch like an edging of white lace at the neck of a plain dress. (See page 61.)

Greater elaboration appears on a well-preserved house at 401 West Third Street in Hereford. Rows of octagonal and diamond-shaped shingles are combined in a gable pierced by a diamond-shaped window. (See page 61.) In another variation of textures, the gable surface of a Queen Anne house located at 305 Bowie in Menard is covered with alternating octagonal shingles and small squares. (See page 61.)

The projecting eaves and verge boards, or bargeboards as they are also known, begged for gingerbread.

At the Tubbs House in Lubbock, the decorated trim overhangs a cladding of octagonal shingles. (See page 61.)

The application of shingles as wall cladding became what amounted to a substyle. In some instances, the shingles were used only at the second-story level. In Dublin at 718 Patrick Street, the shingle treatment covered the support arches of an extensive porch. (See page 62.)

As the Queen Anne style developed in West Texas towns, there was a growing tendency toward delicacy in design. This is apparent if the cutwork in the gables, brackets, and porch balustrades of a house at 510 Denver Street in Dalhart (see page 61) is compared with a two-story house in Dublin. The porch of the Dublin home is defined by lathe-turned porch posts with a balustrade and frieze of light spindles. Above the porch roof there is a square tower, giving an asymmetrical balance to the composition. (See page 64.)

The growing popularity of towers dominated both small and large houses. Towers spark the imagination

(Top left) Detail, house at 401 West Third (c. 1900), Hereford

(Top right) Detail, house at 305 Bowie, Menard

(Middle left) Tubbs House (1908), Lubbock

(Middle right) House at 510 Denver (late 1880s), Dalhart

White-Pool House, (1887), Odessa

of children and cartoonists. Who can forget the cheery Christmas scene in a 1946 *New Yorker* of Charles Adams's monsters pouring boiling oil from the tower of a Queen Anne mansion (or is it Victorian Italianate?) on carolers expecting a different sort of wassail?

Towers came in many sizes and shapes—round in the case of the L. T. Lester House (see page 64) built at Canyon in 1904. Placed at a corner of the facade, a polygonal, two-story tower attracts attention to an unusual house in Brownwood. (See page 67.) The tower is covered by a tent type roof, a term designating a six-sided construction with the sides meeting in a point. (See page 66.) At the second level of the tower, the spaces between the windows are decorated with delicate swags reminiscent of the Adam Brothers' late eighteenth-century English ornament. At the lower stage, the sash windows have leaded glass in the top panels. The porch columns are classical, forsaking lathe-turned posts. In about a third of Queen Anne buildings, classical supports are present rather than posts with spindlework details. The Brownwood home, as a representative of Queen Anne, is even more lavish than usual in the selection of oddly assorted parts and noteworthy for the naïveté that assembled so many beguiling eccentricities.

After 1900, Queen Anne architecture gradually became simpler and often grander in scale. At Uvalde, a nineteen-room home was built in 1907 for Ford Moore and his wife. (See page 69.) A curving two-story porch with Tuscan columns extends three-quarters of the way around the house. A niece of the Fords remembered the good times such a big house provided for teenagers. The porch was an ideal place to put down mattresses for slumber parties with girlfriends. The 1907 footed bathtub—"almost big enough to swim in"—must have added novelty to such overnight visits.

Life had changed with remarkable rapidity for many families who a decade or two earlier had been living in tents or dugouts. The new generation of stately homes witnessed a shift in social life that in little more than a decade progressed from spelling bees and choral singing in one-room school houses and dances and town Christmas celebrations in the county courthouse to eggnog parties on Christmas morning in homes with twenty or more rooms and Christmas dinners served at long dining tables groaning beneath the hostess' "tradi-

House at 718 Patrick (c. 1910), Dublin

tional turkey and dressing" finished with "Lula's well known pies and Sadie's macaroon pudding."

In Uvalde close to the Ford home at the Kincaid-Ware family residence (see page 65), teenage dances were held on the third floor to the three-quarter time of waltzes played by local musicians. The attic story was also occupied by Mr. Kincaid's billiard table. Perhaps to unnerve his opponents, he arranged a life-size portrait of himself on an easel overlooking the green felt.

As a sign of the times, in 1909 the Kincaid carriage house was renovated to make room for an automobile. One account relates that "neighbors [remembered] seeing Frank Kincaid's Stutts-Bearcat car parked in the driveway and the girls coming home from Europe, wearing floppy hats and stylish dresses from their travel wardrobes."

Bridge parties, garden club meetings, even old-fashioned dominoes gave way to weddings. When a Uvalde belle married her childhood sweetheart on 11 November 1914, the ceremony, held in the bride's home, was described in detail by the *Leader-News:*

Reception rooms, hall and living room were filled with friends of the young couple. The double doors between the two reception rooms were thrown open, revealing tasteful arrangements of pot plants and cut flowers.

In the large front room the color scheme of green and white was artistically carried out in banks of fluffy white chrysanthemums and Boston ferns. In the adjoining room were exquisite masses of pink and white LaFrance roses and sword ferns.

As the hour of four-thirty approached . . . the bride and groom marched slowly through the long rooms and took their places at the altar. . . . At the conclusion of the ceremony, guests betook themselves to the dining room to inspect the gifts and to the living room where fruit punch was served.

The new generation of homes built at the turn of the century by successful ranchers, businessmen, bankers, doctors, lawyers, real estate entrepreneurs, and others signaled that the West, written off as uninhabitable a half century earlier, was well on the way toward assimilation into mainstream America.

The Queen Anne style, well suited to city life, also adapted to life in the country. Unfortunately, many of the older rural homes have been replaced by the comforts of modern ranch style architecture. A noteworthy survivor of country Queen Anne is the Barton House, built in 1909 by James Joseph Barton. Constructed from Tennessee architect George Barber's designs, which were published in a popular late nineteenth-century pattern book, it was originally located in Hale County at Bartonsite. False optimism had led Barton to the conclusion that the railroad would pass through the town to which he had given his family's name. The information seemed reliable enough to result in the building of a church, a school, a mercantile store, and the ever-present hotel. A lumberyard was ready and waiting for cut timber to be unloaded from the expected trains. As in so many other cases, the rail line was shifted east to Abernathy, and Bartonsite was left behind. The town's wooden buildings were transplanted closer to the tracks, only James Barton's home remained. For a time, it served as headquarters for a fifty-section ranch. Then in 1975, the house was moved intact, except for the front porch, along a forty-mile route to the Ranching Heritage Center in Lubbock. At its present location it represents the elegant house dreamed of by the families of farmers and ranchers who struggled against overwhelming odds to make a success of life in a dry and difficult land.

The Barton House presents the Queen Anne style favored toward the end of the period when gingerbread was becoming less palatable. (See page 65.) The frame house is asymmetrical with a hipped roof topped by a captain's walk surrounded by a balustrade that encloses two chimneys. Like many chimneys built at the time, these have corbeled chimney caps; that is, the brickwork was laid in three steps moving from a small top to a wide collar and, once again, a narrow stack. Such a seemingly minor detail added character and liveliness to the profile of a chimney as it stood out against the sky. On the porch, round columns make a timid move toward classicism. The porch roof flares out slightly and repeats the fish-scale shingling that covers the gables. On the porch pediment in low relief there are garlands flanking a wreath with a cross at the center. In the restoration, details of the trim have been painted a dark green; the gables are a lighter green. This brings up the problem of color, which is never far removed from Queen Anne architecture.

The questions are: What was the role of color in the initial building? What colors? What may the restorer legitimately do when faced with a choice of white or of hues that are in keeping with the style? White had been the preference of builders celebrating the new democracy on this side of the Atlantic. The home of the president of the United States is the White House. In the early nineteenth century, white paint covering brick conveyed the appearance of marble and established a symbolic association with the temples of ancient Greece, thus proclaiming an ancestral heritage linking the new nation with the democracy of the Greek city-states. Alexis de Tocqueville, a Frenchman traveling in the young United States in the 1830s, observed: "When I arrived for the first time at New York . . . I was surprised to perceive along the shore at some distance from the city, a considerable number of little palaces of white marble, several of which were built after models of ancient architecture. When I went the next day to inspect more closely the building which had particularly attracted my notice, I found that its walls were of whitewashed brick, and its columns of painted wood."

When Classicism was confronted with the Gothic Revival, the white and shining temples began to fall from grace. Andrew Jackson Downing held strong opinions on the subject of color. He wrote in his *Cottage Residences:*

The *color* of buildings may very properly be made to increase their expression of truthfulness. Thus a barn or stable, being regarded entirely in a useful point of view, may have a quiet, unobtrusive

House at 340 Patrick (1890s), Dublin

L. T. Lester House (1904), Canyon

tone of color, while a cottage or villa should be of a cheerful, mellow hue harmonizing with the verdure of the country. A mansion may very properly have a graver color than a cottage, to be in unison with its greater dignity and extent. There is one color, however, frequently employed by house-painters which we feel bound to protest against most heartily, as entirely unsuitable and in bad taste. This is *white,* which is so universally applied to our wooden houses of every size and description. . . . No painter of landscapes that has possessed a name was ever guilty of displaying in his pictures a glaring white house, but, on the contrary, the buildings introduced by the great masters have uniformly a mellow softened shade of color, in exquisite keeping with the surrounding objects. . . . To render the effect still worse, our modern builders paint their Venetian window-shutters a bright green! A cool dark green would be in better taste.

The architect Calvert Vaux rallied his support for color applied to architecture. He asserted that a white Classical Revival building lacked sympathy with its environment. He favored the picturesque union of house and landscape, but added the warning that any "attempt to force individual buildings into prominent notice is an evidence of a vulgar desire for notoriety at any sacrifice, or of an ill-educated eye and taste."

Joining the protest against white architecture, paint companies voiced their support. After all, the machinery was developed in 1870 to grind colored pigments in white lead mixed with oil. These ready-mixed colors could be packaged for safe shipping and only awaited the expanding railroads for increased business. As early as 1861, John Riddell had published the first pattern book for American architecture with full-color plates of domestic and residential buildings. By the 1880s, Wadsworth, Martinez, & Longman Company could point out that "extensive distribution of Color Cards,

Barton House (1909), Ranching Heritage Center, the Museum of Texas Tech University, Lubbock

Kincaid-Ware House (1903–1906), Uvalde

House at 1004 Beauregard (c. 1910), San Angelo

(Above) First Ware House (1890s), Amarillo

(Left) House at 402 West Third, (c. 1900), Hereford

Detail and above, house at 611 Coggin Avenue (c. 1900), Brownwood

Lithographs of Buildings in color, and many other methods placed before the public, to aid in making suitable selection of proper shades of color for painting" had provided the impetus for "change from simple white with green blinds to the many pleasing shades of color now presented upon almost every residence."

Once more the railroad entered the picture. It has been observed that if a family lived in a part of the country not reached until late in the nineteenth century by the spreading network of rails, the chances were strong that white was spread over the exteriors of the stylish Queen Anne homes. This seems to have been the case in West Texas. White paint was not controversial; it did not risk the unkind remarks of cantankerous neighbors complaining about gaudy colors. A comment on the Fretwell's home in Erath County seems to have offered the seal of approval for the family who "lived in a white frame house with all white accessories—cotton, chickens, turkeys, and a Spitz dog!"

Today when a colorful Queen Anne house is encountered in West Texas, like the brightly painted first Ware House in Amarillo (see page 65), now the office of Burger King, or the home in San Angelo at Washington and Beauregard (see page 65), it is likely that it is the work of a preservationist or architect who has made a study of the colors associated with the homes of the late 1800s.

It is difficult to imagine the fine Queen Anne home at 402 West Third at Hereford (see page 65) or its neighbor, the E. B. Black House (1909) (see page 68) dressed in anything but white. The Black home with its handsome veranda and refined craftsmanship, though retaining the asymmetrical composition, crested roof, and leaded windows of the Queen Anne style, as well as a spindlework gazebo in the backyard (see page 68), suggests by the absence of complex surfaces and the correctness of its Ionic columns that both Queens, Anne and Victoria, were beginning to fade into a period of Classical Revival

E. B. Black House (1909), Hereford

Gazebo behind the E. B. Black House, Hereford

and that America would once again be deluged with buckets of white house paint.

The resurgence of white was spurred by the enthusiasm resulting from the World's Columbian Exposition of 1893. Throughout the country, families traveled by train to Chicago and were dazzled by the classical imagery wafted on the lake breeze by fluttering banners and the gleaming white plaster temples of "The White City." Louis Sullivan, Chicago's prophet of the modern skyscraper, of new architecture for a new century, wrote with dismay, "The virus of the World's Fair, after a period of incubation . . . began to show unmistakable signs of the nature of the contagion. There came a violent outbreak of the Classic and the Renaissance in the East, which slowly spread westward, contaminating all that it touched. . . . The damage wrought by the World's Fair will last for half a century from its date, if not longer. It has penetrated deep into the constitution of the American mind."

There was a positive side of the exposition that is often forgotten in the cries of gloom. An out-of-door light spectacular amid the fountains and lagoons of the fair turned night into a fantasy from the *Arabian Nights*. Thomas Alva Edison was the wizard who had made this possible with his invention of the first practical incandescent light bulb. The fair illustrated the possibilities of turning night in cities into a wonderland, while lighting during the dark hours held out the promise of making life safer.

NEITHER THE INFLUENCE of the Columbian Exposition nor the Ecole des Beaux-Arts in Paris played a major role in West Texas during the first decade of the twentieth century. Experiments with grain production and cotton, accompanied by a necessary frugality, eliminated the most serious threats of building Rome on the Brazos or Athens in Yellowhouse Canyon.

The pioneering decades were too close to the population settling the High Plains to forsake practical considerations. One of the more improbable and interesting experiments was the building of concrete block houses with a small edge of gingerbread. In the Texas Panhandle for decades, ingenuity had been used to build shelters from the raw materials at hand—fieldstones, earth, sod, adobe, and—on the eastern fringe of the High Plains—logs. Now hand made stone houses

Ford Moore House (1907), Uvalde

emerged. One of the first concrete block structures was built in 1906 twelve miles northwest of Panhandle by Kate and Carroll Purvine. The building method was brought to the attention of West Texas and New Mexico by traveling drummers, who sold the molds from which the blocks were cast. The Purvines did not experiment on a small scale. Their home was planned with a large basement over which two stories would rise. The account of the work involved in the building operation began with the need to bring to the ranch site both water and sand for mixing the cement. Each block was poured by hand into a twelve- by eighteen-inch mold and allowed to dry. The blocks were hollow at the center, very much like concrete blocks today. The Purvines molded their blocks with beveled edges to give the impression of fine rock-faced ashlar. With very little help, husband and wife poured blocks day after day and set them in place until the ambitious project was completed. Today all that is left is one concrete block preserved in the historical museum in Panhandle, a few photographs, and

Detail and above, Joseph Potton House (1901), Big Spring

descriptions, among which the following paragraph was found:

> The ground floor, [contained a] living room with fireplace, dining room, kitchen, and pantry, two bedrooms and bath room. The rooms were plastered. The upstairs or top floor [was] one large room with dormer windows in the east, west, and south. . . . A large veranda or porch [extended] around the three sides of the house and this made a fine place for little girls to play. There was always a shady side on this deep, inviting veranda where cool breezes swept through in summer. . . . A large basement completed the house. It was a storehouse for the acetylene plant . . . that provided light. The basement was also a storehouse for meats and home canned vegetables—sparkling jars of yellow squash and pumpkin; green peas and beans, and ruby red beets set in neat rows on the shelves. . . . In the early days the basement also housed the coal supply for heating during the winter.

The shift from concrete blocks to real stone, in this case red Pecos sandstone cut with precision and fine craftsmanship, leads to Big Spring and the Potton House. This house was designed by the Fort Worth firm of S. B. Haggard and Son and built for Joseph Potton, master railroad mechanic for the 560-miles of rail that bound Cow town (Fort Worth) to the Mexican border. The date 1901 is recorded on the front gable. Above the date, there is a zinc medallion stamped with the lone star of Texas accompanied by foliage carved in wood relief. (The treatment of the carving resembles the pedimental detail at the Barton House.) Beneath the lone star and garland there is a pseudo-Palladian window surrounded by fish-scale shingles. Over the gabled entry to the porch, an oval window has a cruciform design made up of four spikes that resemble those used for fastening railroad ties. It would be an appropriate symbol for Potton's career with the railroad. The porch columns are made of painted cast iron. In the recent restoration, the gable surfaces were painted yellow with a dark green trim. The gables are flared, producing an oriental appearance. Overhanging eaves, with metal

Eddleman-McFarland House (1899), Fort Worth

gutters, are supported by carved brackets. The ridge on the top of the hipped roof, the highest point of the composition, has ornate cresting with elaborate finials at either end. (See page 52.)

In the manner of the Potton House, but quadrupling its grandeur, is the Eddleman-McFarland House built high above Fort Worth's present business district on what was nicknamed "Quality Hill." Designed by Howard Messer, it was finished in 1899, linking it closely in time with the sandstone Potton House in Big Spring.

With Fort Worth's rapid growth as a cattle market and railroad center, it is not surprising that many wealthy families wished to express their success and social position by building palatial Queen Anne mansions. The Eddleman-McFarland House (1899), and its neighbor the red brick Pollock-Capps home (1898) (see page 72) are among the few still standing. Initially, the Eddelman House was built for George Ball, a Weatherford banker, for thirty-six thousand dollars. In 1904, five years after it

had been completed, it was sold for twenty-five thousand dollars to W. H. Eddleman. Eddleman's daughter Carrie and her husband, Hays McFarland, were invited by her parents to join them in their new home. When the house was originally built, Edison's new invention, electric lighting, was installed. It is reported that a sign in the attic gave the following directions to the uninitiated, "Do not attempt to light with a match. Simply turn key on the wall by the door." The fact that social life in the Eddleman house was illumined not by gas jets but by electricity must have increased by many watts the brilliance of gatherings of Fort Worth society. The part played by electric lighting at evening parties was described by a resident of Palestine: "The great houses opened their doors, and that strange innovation, electricity, brightly lighted the parlours and fell upon lovely fabrics, dark woods, deep carpets, fine china and lovely objects d'art."

Pollock-Capps House (1898), Fort Worth

The description of a party in Palestine could as easily apply to the Eddleman-McFarland social whirl in Fort Worth. A 23 December 1898 soiree was reported in these words by the *Daily Visitor:*

The streets for two or three blocks about the elegant home . . . were thronged with carriages and gay equipages from 3 t o 6 o'clock yesterday evening. And through the wide halls and beautiful parlors were passed a continuous stream of elegantly dressed ladies. The guests were met at the front entrance . . . and ushered into Dr. Link's sanctum, at the right of the hall where they divested themselves of their heavy wraps. . . .

There was no special decorations, the handsome rooms needing none but there were lovely flowers, carnations, chrysanthemums, etc., disposed in bouquets . . . and filling the air with their sweet perfume.

Moore's Orchestra, from some invisible retreat, discoursed their heavenly music, but it was often drowned by the merry voices of the stately dames and fair damsels who filled the room to overflowing.

The food served at such an evening's entertainment deserves attention. A menu from an 1899 gala revealed:

The crowning feature of the evening was the lunch served in the dining room, twenty being seated at a time. A large table occupied the center of the room, and from the chandelier which was decorated with long sprays of asparagus fern above, hung a basket of exquisite flowers, from this pink and white ribbons were drawn to the four corners of the table. In the center of the table was an immense bouquet of pink and white roses. Full cut glass stands filled with luscious fruits were deposited about the table on elegant embroidered doilys and pink and white ice cream with every kind of cake and fruit made up the splendid lunch. . . . Very reluctantly the . . . guests said, "good bye."

If refreshments were a surfeit of ribbons, roses, cake, and pink and white brick ice cream (the term brick was probably added by society columnists to distinguish the product from common ice cream produced with great effort in hand-turned freezers), this was merely a reflection of the mélange offered in the name of architecture and

(Above and right) Eddleman-McFarland House (1899), Fort Worth

(Left and opposite)
Eddleman-McFarland
House (1899),
Fort Worth

Queen Anne by mansions like that of the Eddlemans. The spreading veranda and the house rested on rusticated stone masonry. The sculptured stone urns that introduced the stairs leading up to the porch and the column capitals were crisply carved in the Romanesque manner. (The terms *porch* and *veranda* are often used interchangeably, though in the strict sense there are differences. A *porch* associated with an entry is a strong part of the overall architectural composition; the *veranda* "is a special porch characterized by openness . . . and a continuous space surrounding the architecture on at least two sides of the building." A *veranda* reaches out toward the lawn linking it with the indoor space of the house. It parallels the concept that Frank Lloyd Wright called the "interpenetration" of inside and outside space.) The veranda of the Eddleman House flows into a circular pavilion which has the appearance of a small, solemn classical temple. Its roof, the architrave above the columns, the brackets upholding the eaves are all sheathed in copper, which has assumed a magnificent bluish green patina. (See page 73.) The upper stories and tall, narrow chimneys are of tan brick; the brick walls are finished at the corners with quoins of smoothly

cut brown sandstone (see quoins in the Glossary and the accompanying illustration). Usually quoins are made of a different material to contrast with the wall. Often the purpose of this change is to provide a strong accent to deliver the message, "The wall ends here." At the Eddelman mansion, there is an amusing and unexpected juxtaposition of parts, typical of Queen Anne nonchalance in the face of conventional treatment; above the classical pavilion, "chateauesque" chimneys rise over the flared roofs and gables. (See page 73.) For all of its quirkiness, the house was as urbane and polished, as unapologetic in its stance, as the portraits of gentlemen painted by John Singer Sargent. It was a suitable background for the bevy of ladies in formidable bustles and corsets that were intended to contrive S curves where nature failed. The Eddleman House is a totally secure work of architecture, unaware of changing styles, untouched by either slurs of the past decades or the growing enthusiasm of the present preservationists.

Before Queen Anne was excused from the scene, the style was joined by a host of borrowings from the past, many of which changed the appearance of Main Street, West Texas.

5
Main Street: From Hitching Post to Horseless Carriage

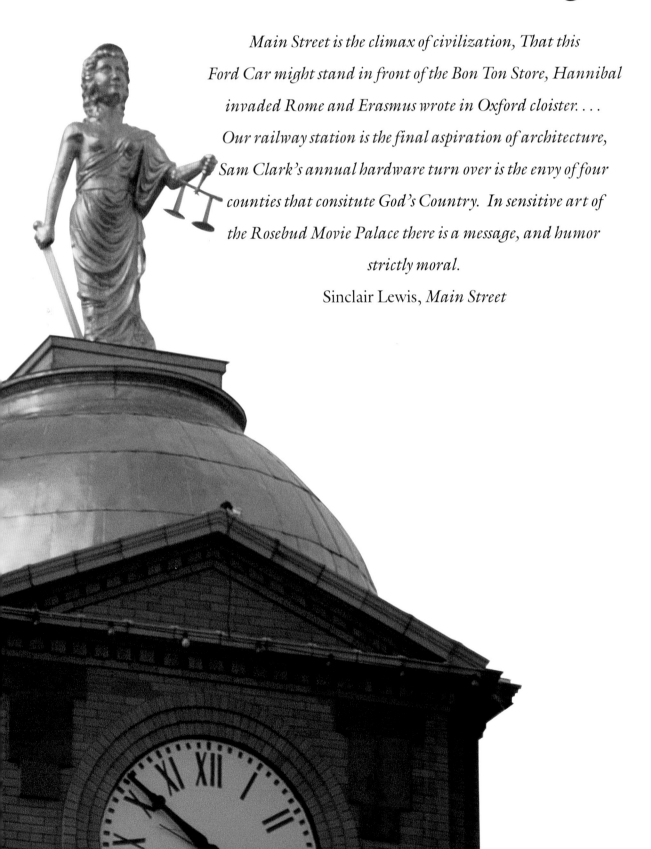

*Main Street is the climax of civilization, That this
Ford Car might stand in front of the Bon Ton Store, Hannibal
invaded Rome and Erasmus wrote in Oxford cloister. . . .
Our railway station is the final aspiration of architecture,
Sam Clark's annual hardware turn over is the envy of four
counties that consitute God's Country. In sensitive art of
the Rosebud Movie Palace there is a message, and humor
strictly moral.*

Sinclair Lewis, *Main Street*

S INCLAIR LEWIS might have added "courthouse" to "railway station." In the first decades of the twentieth century, both felt the pulse of the population. The station clocked men and women on the move; the courthouse filed the births and deaths and taxes of those who stayed. Railroad station and courthouse were the magnets drawing people and trade to towns. The old stagecoach routes, followed by the trail of iron tracks, promoted development of a settlement pattern like a spine with the vertebrae of business linked to the linear progress of rolling wheels. The impressions related by a young man leaving the train at Panhandle in 1919 present a verbal map of Main Street in West Texas. Having reached his destination, he wrote:

> I walked up town, on Main street, of course, because Main street at that time was the main street of the entire city. Most of the business part of town was located on Main, between First Street, which ran parallel with and a half block north of the Santa Fe tracks, and Second Street, better known as Broadway. The town's two banks . . . , three grocery stores, one general store, two dry goods stores, two drug stores, two barbershops, one hardware store, one furniture store, one small meat market, a doctor's office, one cafe, and post-office, as well as a jewelry shop in the back of one of the drug stores were all situated in the 100 block, that is, between First Street and Broadway. . . . Most of the homes were located east on Main and south on Ninth Street. . . . Main Street terminated at the grade and high school building.

In the last years of the twentieth century, Main streets like the one in the town of Panhandle still survive, though many of the schools were boarded up like the red brick building in Toyah (see page 78) and replaced decades ago by consolidated rural schools. Business blocks stand vacant. At Tolar there survives a line of old storefronts connected by covered porches. A wall of rough stone with brick quoins is visible now that an adjacent building has been torn down. The series of cornices facing the street are still fitted with pressed tin designs only slightly altered by time. Menard is another example of how Main Street looked in the last decade of the nineteenth century. In the 1890s, many mercantile establishments were constructed of rusticated stone, en-

Justice on dome of Jones County Courthouse, Anson

Detail, storefronts (c. 1910), Tolar

suring longevity. The names of owners were inserted in the location once occupied by advertising painted on box-and-strip buildings, for example, L. Simpson's (1893) at Quanah. (See page 79.)

But to turn to a second type of urban development affecting the layout of early West Texas towns, roads like arteries fed by the veins of smaller streets flowed to the town's heart—the courthouse square. The importance of the courthouse on the West Texas frontier did not differ greatly from that of courthouses built earlier in the South and midsection of the country. Nevertheless, there was an intensity of purpose in the new pioneering society and a sense of civic pride, which in the developed parts of the country had mellowed beneath the shadows of elms and maples that soften and blur the edges of the classical columns lining the porches of government. In the county seats of West Texas, where unpaved streets were flanked with flimsy box-and-strip constructions, a courthouse celebrated law and order and ushered in an optimistic future for the inhabitants, who were always looking slyly over the county line in the hope that their massive stone monument was not about to be outdone by ambitious neighbors. To achieve a suitable architectural symbolism, contractors or architects (often interchangeable in the 1880s) from Dallas and Fort Worth were often hired at a considerable cost to design and supervise the construction of an imposing building as a pedestal on which blind Justice could balance her sword and scales. (The architecture was usually more satisfactory than the sculpture.) There seems to have been little dissent over the price for importing stone and in some instances stonemasons. The variety of materials and textural counterpoint fulfilled all of the requirements of the Queen Anne style usually mixed with Romanesque and a helping of classical detail. A. Richard Williams might have had a West Texas courthouse in mind when he wrote, "Choices of elaborate and rich patterns rather than plain, even in the most vernacular

Abandoned high school (c. 1912), Toyah

settings, [reveal a desire] to communicate success and affluence, symbols of winning in a tough competitive world."

Many of the courthouses depended for their effect upon towers with spires punctuating the sky like exclamation points. The tower was a beacon during the day, announcing the proximity of a destination; at night, the four faces of an illuminated clock guided travelers or sent youngsters scampering home from a late party. When tall buildings began to take over the skyline in the 1930s, the courthouse was diminished. It was often pulled down to be replaced by a modern box without interesting foibles or eccentricities. There were exceptions, such as the courthouse at Eastland, where Old Rip, a revered horn toad, is entombed, and the grand courthouse for Cottle County. A few of the old guard survive presiding over the rooftops as reminders of the former glories of Main Street.

Among the survivors, the courthouse at Albany is one of the oldest public buildings in West Texas. (See page 80) Of it, A. C. Greene has written with affection born of a long acquaintance:

> You can come into Albany from six directions but the first thing you see, by any route, is the spire of the courthouse. . . . Albany's profile hasn't changed much since her picture-book courthouse was built in 1883.
>
> Albany sits in a bowl. . . . [From] the top of the courthouse tower you can see all around but not out. And the view has an exciting quality about it, for the viewer is denied the necessity of there being any other world except the world of his bowl. . . . Not many people have the luxury of that circuit of Albany because to get to the pinnacle of the tower you have to clamber out onto a rococo summerhouse of an affair, then take your mortal chances over a slick strip of sharply tilted copper roof, and, finally, share your summerhouse with the big bell that makes a clangerous outcry every half hour, scaring you out of your wits.

The Albany courthouse was built of rusticated limestone. The string courses between the three stories and the quoins at the corners are of a lighter and smoother stone. Designed by J. E. Flanders, a Dallas architect, the courthouse has towers that project at the four corners.

L. Simpson Building (1893), Quanah

Detail, L. Simpson Building, Quanah

Shackleford County Courthouse (1880s), Albany

It is saved from portly dignity by the graceful white tower and frivolous scallops around the clock faces.

On the courthouse lawn, there is a reconstructed bandstand awakening memories of concerts performed on warm summer evenings and ice cream socials. Upon the grander occasions of the glorious Fourth and Memorial Day the courthouse became the hub of the celebrations. Confederate Memorial Day was a perpetual reminder of the southern heritage and the war service of many of those who had moved to West Texas.

Confederate reunions were celebrations for both old and young. A reunion held in Dublin for four days every August was remembered by Wallace Reid. He wrote that people came from long distances in wagons and buggies. They camped on the outskirts of the fairgrounds. Among the concessions were "hot dog and hamburger stands, the lemonade stands, the cotton candy and the Hokey-Pokey ice cream—it was frozen in blocks and . . . wrapped in paper like . . . Eskimo pies." There was "a rifle range where [the crowds] could shoot at toy ducks." For each win, the prize was a kewpie doll. A merry-go-round and a Ferris wheel were among the most popular attractions. Mr. Reid's boyhood memories did not include details of the long-winded speeches made by the mayor and important political figures in honor of the aging veterans.

Among West Texas courthouses, the Donley County center of government at Clarendon is remarkable for its period. The usual Victorian *assemblage* of contrasting granite and sandstone, rusticated blocks, polychromy, cupolas and towers, mixed architectural metaphors is replaced by a smooth surface of rosy brick. It is an engaging building impossible to photograph to advantage because of the trees. Built between 1890 and 1891, it was designed by the Dallas firm of Bulger and Rapp. The characteristics of the Romanesque style are present in the rusticated stone watertable above which the smoother brick semisurface gives a pleasing contrast. The corner entry porch is introduced by round stone arches. Some of the semiattached columns that accentuate windows or are placed where two walls meet at right angles are assembled from circular drums and rest on rough stones inverted like upside-down mushroom caps. Unlike most buildings of the time, the interior arrangement is reflected in the external elements. The main stair on the southeast is indicated by windows in a

stair-step pattern with a large bull's-eye window at the lower level. There is a fan-shaped stained glass window, (see page 82) that provides a motif repeated in a carved detail on the stair post (see page 82). In the district courtroom on the second floor, the semicircular area for the judge's bench is suggested by the external curving wall. At the end opposite the bar, another semicircular space suggests the design of the Roman basilica.

No directives were given for the outside shells of the courthouses, but there were provisions for the division of interior spaces: "Each county was to provide one or more district courts for the trial of felony cases by twelve man juries and county courts for the trial of misdemeanors with six man juries. Courts of justices of the peace were required to deal with minor offenses." Jury rooms were another necessity. It was customary to locate the spaces for county business on the ground floor with areas designated for the use of the tax assessor–collector and the clerk in charge of county business. The district courtroom might gain added stature by combining the second and third floors into one large open area. This

Donley County Courthouse (1890–1891), Clarendon

(Above and below) Donley County Courthouse (1890–1891), Clarendon

expansive height with windows opening on opposite sides allowed cross ventilation and the circulation of air so welcome in the stifling summer heat.

Built nearly twenty years after the courthouse at Clarendon, the Jones County seat at Anson (1910–1911) belongs to the period when Queen Anne excesses were being tamed and restrained by the Classical Revival spurred by memories of the Chicago Fair. (See page 83.) Architect Elmer Withers accented smooth brick with a reddish sandstone trim. The materials and detailing have a sophistication foreign to the 1890's taste for rusticated surfaces. Standing at the summit of the dome, Justice is equipped with sword and scales as well as the physical attributes of Marilyn Monroe. (See page 76.)

The trend toward classical elements is even more apparent in the white marble of the Deaf Smith County Courthouse at Hereford. (See page 83.) The simple symmetry provides a startling contrast to the Victorian love of complication. The porch, a distant relative of the Roman portico, is mounted on a podium and approached by a double flight of steps. A lone star looks down from the center of a modest pediment. At first glance the columns, without fluting, seem to have had the capitals omitted. A careful search, however, identifies a wafer-thin slab placed between the column shaft and architrave.

The announcement of a new courthouse was an event of sufficient importance for the railroads to offer reduced fares on trains taking excursions to the site of a cornerstone leveling. This ritual was performed in the midst of barbecues, parades, band concerts, and endless speeches and orations. The following description is given by Willard Robinson in his book *The People's Architecture:*

The cornerstone was a symbol of strength and [revealed] pride in the accomplishments of the builders. Reflecting centuries-old traditions, cornerstones on public buildings ordinarily were laid by Masonic fraternities. Usually placed in the northeast corner, symbolic of light, the stone was cemented into place by Masons attired in formal ceremonial dress. It was consecrated by the master of the lodge in charge, who scattered corn and poured wine and oil on it, emblematic of plenty, health and peace.

The stone itself, usually a hollow block of fine stone with two rubbed or polished faces, communicated information about the building and reflected something of the values of society. Ordinarily, on the face was carved the name of county officials, the architect and contractor, and the date sometimes in both anno Domini and anno lucis (the Masonic date) computations. . . . Into the hollow cornerstone was placed a metal chest or casket containing a variety of interesting articles. . . . In the commemorative block of the Coryell County Courthouse were deposited both a bottle of whiskey and a list of Women's Christian Temperance Union officers.

In 1897, a time before the horned toad was declared an endangered species, horned toad Old Rip was buried alive, a parallel to the storyline of Aïda, in the cornerstone of Eastland County's courthouse. When the building was torn down in 1928 to be replaced by a new structure, it is reported that Rip was resurrected and ready for a go at the twentieth century. Information dims at this point, but the durable toad has finally found permanent repose within the present courthouse.

The Masonic implication of the cornerstone is appropriate because Masonic Orders played an important part as did other fraternal societies in the town life of West Texas. A life-size knight in armor looks down on Main Street from a niche in the Knights of Pythias Building in Fort Worth. (See page 85.) Built in 1881, the structure was rebuilt in 1893 and again in 1901. (See page

Jones County Courthouse (1910–1911), Anson

Deaf Smith County Courthouse (1910), Hereford

85.) It is red brick with a corner tower and a steeply pitched roof hidden behind a curvilinear gable end.

In Weatherford (see page 85), a brother knight in shining armor (a not-so-distant cousin of the Tin Woodman) stands "alert within a niche, looking brave but doubtful as he faces the world with a raised shield and half-lowered sword." He stares down on the courthouse square from the shelter of the old brick lodge complete with Gothic crenellation.

ACROSS FROM the Crockett County Courthouse (1902), the Ozona National Bank shared nothing with the medieval guise of the Knights of Pythias meeting place except space on the second floor for Masonic lodge members. It was part of the changes in the architectural style attracting attention in the years before World War I. The new mode centered around the revival of classicism stimulated by the Columbian Exposition with its orgy of white temples based on the Ecole des Beaux-Arts training of a generation of architects along the Eastern Seaboard. Refurbished Classicism was a favorite architectural choice throughout the country for large public buildings and stately homes, the demand for expensive materials notwithstanding. "Nowhere outside of the United States," Marcus Whiffen noted, "were the classical orders to be drawn up in so many parade formations. . . . Nowhere else were fine materials to be so lavishly employed; one would not be surprised to be told that more marble was used in buildings in the United States in the years 1900 -1917 than was used in the Roman Empire during its entire history."

West Texas contributed to the popularity of the classical style, if not to the abundant use of marble. For the banks that flourished on Main Street, like the handsome brick building in Memphis (see page 85), Classicism possessed the proper traditional mystique, the noble firmness of purpose associated with ancient democracies, that would assure investors that their money was in safe hands—no flimsily constructed facades, only unflappable stability conveying fiscal responsibility. On the streets around the courthouse square, banks had a tendency to occupy corner sites. An entry was located where two streets met; thus, the doorway was equally accessible to those approaching from either street.

Such a corner was selected by the State National Bank (1909) in Big Spring. (See page 87.) The bank was constructed of brick with a classical pediment and moldings of marble around the doorway. The simple, even austere, design furnishes an interesting contrast compared with Stephenville's First National Bank built ten years earlier. (See page 86.) The primary material employed at the Stephenville bank was stone laid in a random ashlar. Actually, this type of ashlar is not as random as the name implies. Stones of varied sizes are squared and put together in an intricate repeated pattern that is not immediately clear to the observer. It is another example of the pleasure in complexity associated with the Queen Anne style. Framing the arched doorway of the Stephenville bank are coupled columns of veined marble topped by capitals that interpret the Ionic order with more exuberance than knowledge. On the second story, an oriel window curves out to define a half tower covered with metal sheathing. The free-standing spire is sheathed in the same material. *Quaint* is the appropriate adjective.

Quaintness also dominates another corner building linked to an equally quaint opera house in Uvalde, dated 1891. The architect was B. F. Trester. The corner entrance and sidewalk are covered by a metal canopy supported on cast-iron columns. (See page 87.) Above the doorway, the tower bay has three sash windows. The upper sashes are bordered by the small squares of colored glass, an identifying mark of the Queen Anne style. The spire rises from a crown of small triangular openings that repeat the shape of the dormers set in the hipped roof. A wrought-iron dragon is wrapped around the rod at the top of the spire. Following the usual custom, the opera house stage and auditorium occupied the second story, which was approached by a broad flight of stairs. Attention is attracted by a decorative pediment, announcing in easy-to-read block letters, Grand Opera House. (See page 87.) Under the apex of the triangle is an urn of foliage in sculptured relief and beneath the squared letters of *Grand*, the head of a jester. Tradition suggests that this may be a portrait of Trester.

A block from the Uvalde opera house, there is a now empty store which is a small gem. (See page 89.) Built in the 1880s, it has escaped vandalism and other willful acts of destruction. It is jewellike in the late afternoon sun. The material used is brick with an overhang protecting

Knights of Pythias Building (1906), Fort Worth

Knight from Knights of Pythias Building (1889–1901), Fort Worth

Knight from Knights of Pythias Building (1890s), Weatherford

First National Bank (c. 1910), Memphis

First National Bank (c. 1899), Stephenville

State National Bank (1909), Big Spring

Opera house (1891), Uvalde

Detail, opera house, Uvalde

the sidewalk. The cornice is simple but decorative. Urns stand out against the sky on either side of a small central pediment. The squares of colored glass surrounding the upper window sashes identify Queen Anne as surely as a royal fingerprint.

In the company of the opera house, banking establishment, and courthouse, the hotel shared the honors as one of the most important gathering places near a town's center. Most of the first wave of hotels are gone, though the Algerita in Post has survived; nevertheless, memories linger and have become the stuff of legends. One of Colorado City's memorable events was the Stockman's Ball held in 1885. The St. James Hotel had just been completed. It was a three-story brick building with barbershop, a bar, and indoor plumbing. The local cowmen decided to throw a party for their ranching friends from across the state, in fact, as one story goes, "from any place where men rode horse back and branded cattle—their own or anyone else's." According to the recollections of Dick Pierson, who was there,

> A fifty piece orchestra was brought from St. Louis to play for the dancing. Cowmen's wives and daughters wore beautiful gowns and flashing jewels. The festivities extended from the hotel to the Frenkel Opera House a block below, and to prevent soiling the afore-mentioned gowns, a solid walk of red brussels carpet was laid between the two buildings. Beside the wives and daughters walked more than one young cowman whose boot heels were adorned with spurs inlaid with gold and silver whose rowels made of twenty-dollar gold pieces tinkled in perfect time to the silken swish of his companion's skirts.

Pierson claimed that "1,800 pints of champagne were iced and served gratis to guests attending the 'Ball.'" Add to these libations, "the necessary drinks; friendly drinks; throat clearing ones; those pledging undying friendship and those necessary to clear up various and sundry misunderstandings of brands, fence lines and water rights—all taken straight—and the affair must have been a howling success with far, very far reaching effects."

From hotel to church, physically at least, was often only a matter of a few steps. In the older and thriving towns of West Texas, by the dawn of the twentieth cen-

tury, churches were matching the standards set by the finest public architecture. St. John's Methodist Episcopal Church in Stamford was built in 1910 by James Edward Flanders, the architect for the Shackelford County Courthouse in Albany. (See page 90.) The contrast with Lubbock's small white frame St. Paul's on the Plains, not finished until 1914, is dramatic. St. John's does not belong to any one particular style but makes use of bits and pieces of Gothic, Romanesque, Classical, and a seasoning of late Queen Anne. It is warm orange brick, which turns golden in the late afternoon sun. The bricks are narrow rectangles, laid in a "running bond." The smooth surface produces a quality of refinement. The wide overhanging eaves of a small tower protect a frieze of terra cotta. (See page 90.) The pattern is similar, if not identical, to Louis Sullivan's ornament, or to the designs of El Paso's Henry Trost, who was influenced during his student days in Chicago by Sullivan. In a letter to the author, Jim Steely, director of the National Register programs for the Texas Historical Society, observed that the similarity to Sullivan's ornament happened "because Chicago terra cotta producers made such things available through mass production and catalogues," shipped by the railroads. The higher tower stretches a hundred feet in the air and once enjoyed the reputation of being the tallest church tower between Dallas and El Paso.

Memphis is the site of the sophisticated and satisfying First Presbyterian Church. (See page 89.) It was constructed in 1911 at the corner of Eighth and Robertson streets, and the contractor was J. S. Cobb. An enthusiastic Memphis resident described the church in these words: "Built to last forever of bricks burned in the Memphis kiln, the . . . church is an imposing edifice with a domed roof, like St. Peter's Cathedral in Rome but on a much smaller scale. There are beautiful European stained-glass windows throughout, some plain, and others with portrait designs. . . . [The] beautiful old pipe organ is listed in the American Organ Historical Society because of its beauty and quality of tone. The pipe organ was originally operated by water pressure and later electrified." The porches at the front and side are flanked by well proportioned Ionic columns. The church possesses a harmonious relationship of parts that pleases and gives the promise of a tranquil place of worship.

Storefront (c. 1890s), Uvalde

The Gothic Revival, inspired by English parish churches, was a source for St. John's Episcopal Church at Brownwood, dated 1892. Tom Lovell, a Scotsman, was the contractor/architect for the project. His familiarity with medieval architecture in Scotland and England doubtless accounts for the accuracy of Gothic details: the mullions dividing the windows, the small buttresses that seem to be useful as well as ornamental, the Celtic crosses at the points of the gables.

Also at Brownwood close to St. John's on Center Avenue are several early twentieth-century mansions with Classical Revival designs. The R. B. Rogers House, at 707 Center Street, was finished in 1904. The brick house has Ionic columns that extend for a full two stories. The entry porch forms a segment of a circle and is topped by a balustrade that continues along the roof line. (See page 91.) These are major characteristics of Neoclassicism in domestic architecture during the first decades of the twentieth century. The columns generally belong to the Ionic, Corinthian, or Composite orders. The builders of the earlier Greek Revival houses preferred the Doric order and employed Corinthian and Ionic columns less frequently. One reason for the change in favor of the sculptural details of Ionic and Corinthian column types may have resulted from mass-produced plaster capitals cast in molds. This eliminated

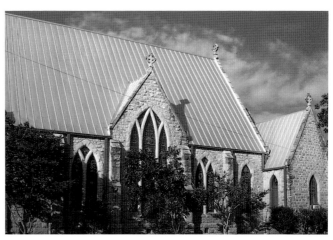

St. John's Episcopal Church (1892), Brownwood

First Presbyterian Church (1911), Memphis

(Above and detail below) St. John's Methodist Episcopal Church (1910), Stamford

(Opposite) R. B. Rogers House (1904), Brownwood

the need to rely on expensive and time-consuming work in wood or stone by master craftsmen.

Ready acceptance of mass production was a characteristic peculiar to Americans, including West Texans. For pioneers on the High Plains, the coming of the railroads meant trains crossing the Panhandle loaded with precut lumber and machine-made nails. These materials made it possible for houses to be built and towns to grow with incredible speed. Function over beauty dominated vernacular architecture, though in the end both often came together to produce a handsome whole. Frontier practicality and the democratic impulse approved methods of duplication that could make Corinthian capitals or necessities like "Aladdin" lamps and gasoline tractors available for the largest number of people. Why should time be spent making one–of–a–kind objects for the benefit of a few? Mass-produced column capitals, ordered from catalogs, only enhanced the desire for the fine homes that new fortunes were building in West Texas towns.

The Lee Bivins House, built in 1905 at 1000 Polk Street in Amarillo and now occupied by the Amarillo Chamber of Commerce, is a two and one-half-story brick home designed by the office of the Echols Brothers, architects/contractors. (See page 92.) Their client,

Lee Bivins, was the owner of one of West Texas's largest cattle ranches put together in part with property purchased from the LIT and LX holdings. Gas was discovered on the land in 1918, thus opening the biggest gas field in the world. The giant front porch is held on tapering unfluted columns which are doubled beneath the central pediment. The pediment, sheltered by a very pronounced raking cornice, has a fan light at its center. There is the familiar motif of a balcony and window lifted above the front door. The doorway is surrounded by a Richardsonian arch of rough cut limestone with a keystone on which Bivins's initials are carved.

Another of the notable Amarillo homes is the Landergin-Harrington House at 1600 Polk Street. (See page 93.) Its classical elements are associated with Georgian Revival, a style whose symmetry and substantial presence signaled the arrival of this grande dame of architecture. (See page 94.) Fulfilling the early twentieth century's taste for the past, the two–and–one-half–story brick residence was constructed for two brothers, John and Pat Landergin. The architects were Shepard, Farrer, & Wise. In 1940, the mansion was purchased by D. D. Harrington. During the 1980s, it was given to the Panhandle Plains Museum in Canyon. The Harrington House, as it is best known, is open to the public as a museum that preserves the fine furniture and decorative objects of a few decades ago.

Of equal distinction is the Krueger home in Lubbock at 2703 Nineteenth Street. It, like the Landergin-Harrington House, is an excellent example of Georgian Revival. It is a two-story brick design symmetrically arranged with a fine portico of Corinthian columns lifting the architrave and pediment to a strong focal point above the level of the gabled roof. Commissioned by Kreuger, a pioneer surgeon, the home dates from 1935 and was the work of Lubbock architect S. B. Haynes. (See page 94.)

Thistle Hill in Fort Worth is a monument to a cattle baron's success. It epitomizes the rapidity with which West Texas ranching headquarters and line camps could become the catalysts for a luxurious life-style enjoyed by the rancher's children. The house begun in 1903 was a wedding present from W. T. Waggoner to his daughter, "the fabulous Electra," a young woman who combined the disquieting virtues of Annie Oakley and Isadora Duncan. This "honeymoon cottage," as it has been called,

Lee Bivins House (1905), Amarillo

(Opposite) Landergin-Harrington House (1914), Amarillo

had eighteen rooms and six baths and was completed by the architectural firm of Sanguinet and Staats for thirty-eight thousand dollars. (See page 95.)

Electra and her husband, A. B. Wharton, Jr., a Philadelphian, entertained with appropriate panache. Newspaper reports sketch a vivid picture of the frolics of the rich and famous in the decade before the world was disrupted by war. There were luncheons for two hundred guests. Costume parties with a dizzying sequence of themes ranging from North Pole figures (the ladies wore ermine) to characters from the Orient. The decorations were expensively appropriate: "cherry blossoms and wisteria for Japanese parties, lilies and palms for New Year's, with the fireplace filled with ferns and the mantel covered with moss and leaves or, another year, long stemmed American beauty roses in vases and jardinieres. On one Fourth of July the house was draped in

Detail, Landergin-Harrington House (1914), Amarillo

Krueger House (1935), Lubbock

(Above and left) Thistle Hill (1903), Fort Worth

red, white, and blue bunting, with tiny flags on the porches and fences and thousands of dollars worth of fire works were set off. Nothing was done modestly or without flair."

The only other private owners of Thistle Hill were the Winfield Scotts. Scott was also a rancher, but he diversified his fortune by investing in downtown Fort Worth property. As soon as Thistle Hill was offered for sale, Scott bought it for ninety thousand dollars. Extensive remodeling began at once. When the mansion was first built the brick structure was decorated with wooden detailing. At the second floor level, a porch with a white wooden balustrade stretched across the entire front of the house. The roof was covered with wood shingles. The Scotts wished to give a Georgian appearance to their new home. To do this the wood was stripped and marble and stone were substituted. The house was reroofed with green glazed ceramic tiles.

One of the most elegant features of the entry is the Palladian treatment of the doorway with rectangular side lights and a graceful fan window over the door. Contemporary brides often use the house, now owned by the Fort Worth Historical Society, for their weddings.

(See page 95.) Ceremonies often take place at the stair landing in the hall before a stained glass window that echoes the Palladian design of the front door.

There is only one remaining subsidiary building on the property dating from the Waggoner period; this is the carriage house. Electra's husband added a gas pump and storage tank converting at least a portion of it into a garage. This would seem to have been a necessity since Wharton owned five cars.

With the arrival of automobiles driving up and down Main Street, life and transportation were reordered and new categories were added to the architectural bill of fare. Livery stables and carriage houses were on their way out, and family garages for protecting the four wheeled wonders were in. The era was dawning when a house without a garage would be unthinkable. Automobile salesrooms were a necessity. In Ozona, a block from the courthouse, a sculptured relief of an automobile wheel with the date 1917 formed the crest of a building that functioned as a combination auto salesroom and garage for repairs. The filling station was indispensable. Without a prototype, the design was often borrowed from domestic architecture.

The new-fangled means of transportation posed all sorts of hazards to life and limb. By 1906, Fort Worth had ninety automobiles. To preserve the city's sanity from this onslaught, a speed limit was imposed of seven miles per hour. In 1909, the city council in Memphis set a higher speed limit of eight miles per hour, but added the requirement that all motorists had to have attached to their cars "a bell or other appliance giving notice of approach, so that when the bell is rung it may be heard at a distance of 300 feet." When encountering a vehicle drawn by horses, drivers were required to ring the bell first and come to a full stop. Colorado City issued, in the same year, leather license plates, measuring fourteen inches by eighteen inches, with numbers painted in white. (The first licensing of a car in Texas took place in Austin in 1895, but the state had no registration law until 1917.)

By 1912, wagons and buggies were rapidly being replaced by motor cars. Model T Fords with acetylene lights were bumping along brick streets in town and skirting chuckholes in the country. There was one unexpected danger waiting for unwary motorists. A native,

Filling station (1920s), Clarendon

Fire Station No. 1 (1907), Fort Worth

living near Post, pointed out that "Model T curtains were no match for West Texas winds. Once while driving past a gin yard in Southland, a hot ember from burning burrs blew in through the curtains" and caught the driver's clothes on fire.

Fire was always a threat to those living in both city and country. On farms located beyond the help of volunteer firemen, if a fire fanned by high winds was observed rolling over the pastures, all the farmer could do was attempt to save his house by plowing furrows around it. Most of the ranches and farms were protected by these fire guards plowed well in advance of the dry seasons when fires were most apt to be swept ahead by strong winds.

A colorful account of fires in the Panhandle relates:

> If the numerous shootings didn't provide enough excitement, fires did. Winds blew from the north and then from the south. . . . On one occasion when a farmer burned his straw stack (in those days the straw from the wheat harvest was stacked in huge stacks and burned) at around 6 o'clock in the evening a high wind storm developed and the town was in danger of burning. All available farmers plowed around the town to keep the fire from spreading. On another occasion when citizens of the town were decorating floats for the Fourth of July parade, a fire broke out in a "honky tonk" and both sides of four city blocks were destroyed. Guns were fired to call out the bucket brigade, blankets were dipped in barrels of water and put on the roofs of buildings to keep them from catching fire.

As early as the 1880s, in East and Central Texas fire stations of considerable architectural presence often were designed with towers from which alarms were sounded. The tower, which was open rather than enclosed like the towers and cupolas of courthouses, according to Willard Robinson, "signified 'fire house.'" Volunteer teams gradually became professional fire fighters, accompanied on their mission by steam-powered pumps and hook and ladder wagons pulled by hand or deployed by teams of horses.

By 1907 when Fire Station No. 1 was built in Fort Worth several blocks from the Tarrant County Courthouse, the telephone had eliminated the need for a

Fountain on Tarrant County Courthouse lawn (1890s), Fort Worth

tower. (See page 96.) The tan brick building was an urbane addition to Neoclassicism treated simply and functionally with an abstract symmetry in the arrangement of the arched window over the door and a smaller window with an arch and lighter keystone on either side.

Before fire department and milk wagons and buggies were replaced forever by trucks and cars, in 1892, the Woman's Humane Association of Fort Worth placed a watering trough and fountain on the grounds of the Tarrant County Courthouse for all four-footed creatures. An inscription has nearly worn away, but some lines can still be deciphered:

> masters 'a weel earned due [to] humble beastie gie.
>
> [j]ustice an' mercy's blessings flow nae less for him than ye.

Carnegie Library (1909), Ballinger

Off of Main Street, but not far off, other necessary services were housed. A few ice houses (see page 100) still stand as relics of the past when a favorite pastime of children was to run along behind the ice wagon and beg for small pieces of ice that were chipped off when the iceman cut blocks to match the weight indicated on the cardboard signs placed in front windows.

The old-fashioned grocery store would seem as alien as the ice wagon to a youngster accustomed to supermarkets. A child would have been confronted by "large black scales with weights . . . the bins of flour, beans, sugar, and coffee (underground). There were barrels of pickles, crackers, sauerkraut, lard and huge round cheeses on the counter. All were scooped out of the bins and barrels and weighed, then sacked or wrapped in brown paper and tied with string." One customer, remembering the good old days, said the grocery bill for an entire year was usually about one hundred dollars.

The public library had early beginnings, but few towns were as fortunate or as proud as Ballinger, which in 1909 received funds for a Carnegie Library. Andrew Carnegie himself gave five thousand dollars to be used for expansion. The design for the two-story building is credited to a local Presbyterian minister, J. D. Leslie. The jaillike appearance of the rusticated stonework may be excused as a symbolic protection of knowledge, but the austerity is lightened by the Neoclassical portico with paired Ionic columns on either side of the entry, a pediment painted white, and white trim.

Other buildings located close to the town square or along the main highway were post offices, cafés, hospitals, and sanitariums, like the Proton Sanitarium at Post. Dating from 1913, this two-story structure with sandstone veneer is in the Neoclassic Revival style. The Doric

Proton Sanitarium (1910), Post

columns are, however, concrete. There is a second-story porch above the entry and a pediment with stickwork ornament. The masonry was laid by Scottish masons, using stone quarried from the Caprock Escarpment. The Sanitarium was one of the earliest hospitals in the region to introduce steam heat, fund an X-ray lab, use a sterilized operating room, and to have a training program for nurses. Charles Post, the city's founder, was responsible for the farsighted planning.

The story of the city of Post is remarkable. It begins with the agricultural potential of the Panhandle and South Plains. By the turn of the century, wheat, oats, millet, corn, and kaffir corn were among the crops grown by West Texas farmers with considerable success. As the railroad pushed west, grain could be delivered to the railheads for freighting. Storage, often over considerable time, was needed. This led to the tall grain elevators that stand above the flat landscape like medieval guardians.

The men and women settlers who migrated west, often from the southern States and East Texas, were determined to farm, yet they seem to have given little thought to raising cotton. As time passed, it became apparent that the semiarid climate was not promising for the successful cultivation of grain year after year. It was also evident that beef cattle could not be raised profitably on small plots of land. In Hall County in the spring of 1892, some farmers met and decided to try their luck with cotton. Cotton was produced but there was no gin close at hand. The county's first cotton gin was financed by a group of Memphis men. Power was furnished by the horse driven machinery of a thresher. In those days, the "seed cotton was carried from the wagons to the gin-stands in baskets, then the lint cotton was conveyed in the same manner to the press. Small boys 'tromped' it down until a full bale could be packed in the press box. . . . It was compressed more firmly by the old fashioned screw type machinery and tied. A part of the machinery was located in the street and if all went well three bales could be ginned in a day." In a number of West Texas towns, more gins were built between 1894 and 1908. At first cotton seed was thrown away, but then it was discovered that the manufacture of cottonseed cakes and cottonseed oil turned a profit at the oil mills. Cotton gins and cotton compresses took their places as a part of the new industrial structures.

Grain elevator, Shamrock

When Charles Post, a Texanized Yankee, arrived on the Caprock he was convinced that agriculture, not ranching, was the key to the success of the region. Like Robert Owen and other Utopians, he dreamed of a model city and industry to support the products grown by the farmers. To this end Post City was born on 19 May 1907. A new town needed buildings: supplies for this purpose were brought by twenty-four new and shiny wagons drawn by seventy-two Missouri mules all the way from Big Spring, the nearest railhead at the time. Limestone came from a Caprock quarry site. A machine shop, hotel, and other essential businesses together with fifty houses were completed in the first year.

Water was supplied by a concrete reservoir on the rim of the Caprock situated three hundred feet above the town. The water source was a field of wells on the plain overlooking the reservoir. A dependable supply of water for farming was a preoccupation of Post's. He was one of the initiators of irrigation on the High Plains. He had six-inch wells bored on his experimental farmlands. Gasoline engines were installed to pump water into irrigation ditches at the rate of two thousand gallons per minute.

Given irrigation, cotton was judged by Post to be a financially stable crop, so he established a gin in 1911. The next year he announced the construction of Postex Cotton Mills. The mills were planned to contain ten thousand spindles and 480 broadlooms. This was the first plant in the United States designed to use the supply of cotton brought directly from the fields and to turn that cotton into finished sheets and pillow slips.

Jack Maguire, who assessed Post's triumphs in "The Cereal that Won the West," determined that Post had only one failure of judgment. This was in his misguided evangelical efforts to protect his ranch hands' health. Having invented Postum, the drink which he was convinced would cure the evils of coffee consumption just as it had improved his own fragile health, Post ordered the cook to serve nothing but the healthful substitute for ten days. Cut off from the daily overdose of caffeine, the cowboys rebelled. In spite of high wages and excellent working conditions, they threatened to ride off into the sunset if coffee did not reappear in the customary battered pot. Post, until the end of his life, grumbled that "cowboys were a sickly lot . . . because of their addiction" to that dangerous beverage. It may have been in an effort to offer first aid that the sanitarium was built.

If WEST TEXANS were exposed to black coffee, burning burrs from the cotton gins, fires, and an occasional bank robbery, their imaginations could be diverted by a new entertainment: the cinema. The humble beginnings of the great film emporiums were cellars and tents. A sample of adolescent ingenuity took place in Chillicothe in 1908. Thirteen year old William Webb decided to make a magic lantern. According to the account, "He got his machine together and set it up in the cellar. He asked his mother for a piece of white cloth for a screen. She was busy and told him to get one out of a certain box of scraps. A short time later he came to her and insisted that she go with him to the cellar to see

Ice house (1920s), Albany

the picture on the screen. She went with him [and] saw picture—projected onto the big scrap of white linen she had been saving."

Mrs. Webb forgot the "picture," but she did not forget the shock of seeing her good linen hanging on the dirty cellar wall. The story had a happy ending. Dr. Webb, pleased by his son's interest in motion pictures bought an Edison projector and they opened the first moving picture theatre in Chillicothe. "The theatre was open week-day nights and on Saturday afternoon. [There was usually] a serial for Saturday afternoon . . . and the same picture that night. The admission price was five cents for children six to twelve years of age and ten cents for adults."

Often traveling entertainers would come through the West Texas towns and rent the opera house for magic lantern shows or entertainment provided by hand-operated motion picture projectors. Guthrie was host to a traveling showman who set up his production with bleachers and a small screen surrounded by canvas side walls. One young spectator remembered the excitement when the film reached a climactic shooting scene. He said, "I got scared and set up a yell. I don't remember for sure, but I believe the projectionist fired a pistol to give the show sound effects." Another moviegoer in those primitive days summed it up by saying, "Those who never saw a pioneer silent film can not imagine how crude the performances were. There was [sic] no screen explanations. An employee stood near the rear and read the script as the plot developed. The film broke often and there was constant trouble keeping the two carbon electrodes separated properly to produce satisfactory light. No strong light bulb had come into use."

The first "picture show" in Clarendon was built by Homer Mulkey. It was located along the railroad track, and the building was corrugated iron. This was "sometime before 'the flickers' came into being but there were pictures. And the 'piped in' music was a cylinder record player with a morning glory horn operated by a small boy winding the machine and changing the records."

In Fort Worth, with an ordinary bedsheet for the screen, the first motion picture was shown about 1903. One of the films attracting customers was *The Great Train Robbery;* it was viewed in Rosen Park at the Odeon, which was built in 1910. Admission to a one-reel movie cost five cents.

If picture shows became a bore, there were other diversions not far from Main Street, though usually "across the tracks." In Colorado City, as

new brick buildings, residences, churches, and public buildings were erected and the town grew in size, so grew the *red light district* along the east bank of the river. . . . Principal attractions . . . were four or five prominent dance halls, which had combined with them saloons and theaters of approved frontier type. Among these was the Gayety, the People's, and one or two others whose names have been forgotten. . . . Theatrical performances consisted of buxom chorines, weepy soubrettes, vaudeville acts and a piano pounding "professor."

There were more uplifting forms of entertainments for those with a yearning for culture. Chautuaqua, underwritten by the businessmen of a town, was one of these. Presented generally under a large tent, the programs sponsored by the cultural group, originating in Chautauqua, New York, brought to small town America an opportunity to see and hear lecturers on subjects ranging from Hawaiian volcanoes to great literature, impersonations of Abraham Lincoln, musicians, humorists, slide shows, plays, magicians, and mornings devoted to entertainment and instruction for the children in the community. For three days or sometimes a week, a town closed down to allow ticket holders to attend matinees and evening programs. After dark, small

farm roads in all directions were an unbroken chain of cars with lights flickering like fireflies as families drove slowly home from an evening performance.

To restate what has already been written, the role of the tent in West Texas is a remarkable chapter in the story of urban development. The covered wagon was a tent in motion; tent towns were set up while waiting for lumber to be hauled in or delivered by the promised trains and rail lines. Tents were pitched above dugouts burrowed in the ground. "Long tents were the only rooming houses" in the first days of Quanah's development. In the beginning, newspapers might be published under canvas. Itinerant photographers operated from tents. Schoolchildren and church congregations met in tents before permanent structures could be built. Revival meetings took place in large tents. Chautauqua and silent films attracted an audience to pitched tents before the cast and crews moved on to the next town. The tent was a partner in building West Texas. It functioned because of the climate—months of mild or hot weather, sun, and little rain. Tents were made for the desert and arid lands, and West Texans proved the tent's efficiency.

Naturally, the grandest tent of all was the big top that accompanied the circus to West Texas, and Main Street was the scene of the circus parade. Molly Bailey's circus traveled by horse-drawn wagons. One who saw the parades recalled, "The tents and equipment, the animals and performers made a [procession] across country, showing wherever night overtook the caravan. . . . Molly Bailey . . . always rode in the lead wagon, a gaily painted circus van drawn by six little mules, two lead, two swing, and two wheel mules. . . . But by far the most fascinating of all of the circus wagons was the one carrying the birds, a hack pulled by one mule, filled with cages and perches . . . holding birds of all kinds. Macaws, cockatoos, myna birds, and canaries kept up a raucous chatter as the circus moved to a location and set up for the show."

Another circus paying visits to West Texas was the Adam Forepaugh & Sell's Brothers Circus. In 1906, the largest crowd ever gathered in Quanah came to see the show. The one and only hotel was filled, so many of the eight thousand ticket holders had to content themselves with sleeping on the streets. By this time the circus traveled by rail. There were forty-four cars required to transport the performers, tents, cages, and animals. The most famous of the performing animals was a white elephant, the rival of Barnum's much advertised beast. Barnum's "sacred" elephant was light gray, like all authentic white elephants, and had cost a fortune. Forepaugh did not bother to send to Burmah or Siam to acquire a pachyderm with the Good Housekeeping seal of authenticity. He prepared his white elephant "by the sacred use of sufficient paint, and with careful applications every other day."

If this seems to have strayed too far from architecture, the reader has only to remember the famous White Elephant Saloon in Fredericksburg, which still stands on Main Street. It was one of several Texas saloons given this title. Main Street in Fort Worth had a famous, or infamous, White Elephant Saloon owned by none other than Winfield Scott of Thistle Hill. It was the site of the notorious shooting of Jim Courtright. James J. Corbett and John L. Sullivan, along with "Iron Jaw" McGraw and Father Malone, pastor at All Saints, are said to have been among those who bent their elbows at the bar. The reason for the name and the symbol of a silvery little elephant in the recess above the door in Fredericksburg is not clear, though it probably is associated with the crest of eating and drinking establishments in Europe.

A West Texas encounter with an elephant in Donley County is sufficiently strange. It goes like this: "One of the most heated arguments ever to occur in Giles concerned a man and his elephant. No one knew from whence they came or where they were going. They just appeared on the east bank of the Buck Creek bridge, one fine day. The town fathers were afraid the weight of the beast would cause the bridge to collapse. So, after much discussion, the wayfarer was compelled to cross the creek bed with his elephant in tow."

It calls to mind the Chinese philosopher Lao Tze, (whose name in translation means "good old boy") and his water buffalo. After lingering briefly at the farthest outpost of the Great Wall to write out his philosophical beliefs, man and buffalo went off into Tibet and were never heard from again. It is an apt parable for all of those who left Main Street behind to go farther west or south to the border.

(Opposite) White Elephant Saloon (1890s), Fredericksburg

6

South to the Rio Grande

About twenty miles southeast of Alamosa the first sign of Spanish adobe

culture appeared in a little village . . . with houses built of earth, under

grand cottonwoods, on a gentle slope above the river encircled by

fine hills. This scene made of slow water, bounteous trees, earthen

brick and irrigated fields, is like a symbolic image of much that

is to follow as the river goes south . . . In many places along its

course you can see preserved illustrations of different ways

and times of its human society, as though the river cut through

the laminations of history as it does through

those of the earth's crust.

Paul Horgan, *The Heroic Triad*

To that composite American identity

of the future, Spanish character

will supply some of the most needed parts.

Walt Whitman

TRAVELING SOUTH from far West Texas after the spring ploughing, one finds the landscape cut by brown furrows stretching for mile after mile beneath the vacant sky. Here and there the horizon is broken by grain elevators or an occasional windmill. A mirage glimmers fitfully in the early summer heat, and dust devils, trying to escape the monotony, spiral up like twisted ropes.

After Midland, the fields are dotted with oil pumps moving up and down like the heads of prehistoric birds who are pecking at the earth for nourishment. Cattle roam through clumps of rough grass and, for a few weeks a year, wildflowers cover the ground with a quilt of colors. Gradually the spaces become lonelier and less inhabited by man or beast. The land is a tawny blanket stitched with cacti and those bushes with melodious Spanish names—tornillo, popotillo, and the waving wands of ocotillo burning with poker red tips. Ocotillo is indelibly printed in the memory by Paul Horgan's description. He observed, "A bush of ocotillo looks like a hank of rattlesnakes clutched together by their tails and made to strive upward in all directions against air and sunlight."

When the Rio Grande emerges from between the mountains that hem it in, it is often no more than a sluggish band of muddy water edged with salt cedar, but its siesta is sometimes disturbed by sudden downpours spawned by summer storms. Then the awakened river turns violent. It is at Presidio that new life flows into the Rio Grande when it is joined by the Rio Concho and its major tributary the Rio San Pedro. Close to Del Rio, the dry desert heat turns stagnant and damp and the river begins its journey toward the flood plains. Here, too, the rim of mountains melts in the baking sun; craggy cliffs turn into small mounds fringing the horizon.

The changes in the valley as the river flows toward the Gulf are no more diverse than the cultures that have met at the river's banks—first Indians and Spaniards, and then Anglos, Germans, Poles, and many others. The blend of languages, customs, life-styles, religions, and the arts have a counterpart in the architecture that developed as a result of available materials, needs, and memories of distant places.

An account of early South Texas family shelters survives, written by J. O. Langford, a homesteader who moved south to the Rio Grande valley in 1909 in the

Picket and sotol house (1904), Ranching Heritage Center, the Museum of Texas Tech University, Lubbock

Picket and sotol house (1904), Ranching Heritage Center, the Museum of Texas Tech University, Lubbock

hope of finding improved health. His efforts stand as an example of the utilization of available resources and the development of vernacular architecture that evolved from the most primitive protection to a comfortable home. The family's story begins like that of so many pioneers moving into West Texas. In Langford's words, "Near our chosen campsite was an old abandoned dugout, with its rock walls in an excellent state of repair. Over this I stretched one of our tents, then erected the other just out in front. This gave us a two-room dwelling, one for sleeping quarters and storing our furniture, the other for setting up our dining table."

The first real house was to have been built of pine planks but Langford reconsidered when he discovered the price of lumber and the expense of having it hauled to a remote location. Sensibly, he looked around and saw that the adobe houses of his Spanish neighbors were made of materials found right on their own land—"native stone, adobe bricks, and cottonwood poles for rafters." A squatter renting a piece of land from Langford was enlisted to help make the adobes. For ten dollars, Cleofas agreed to make one thousand adobe bricks measuring twelve inches by four inches by eighteen inches. The adobe was made in the traditional way from an admixture of mud, grass, and goat manure. As the ingredients were combined and put in a hole dug for the purpose, Cleofas's brood of children tramped the paste to make sure it was thoroughly mixed. Once the right consistency was reached, the mud was packed and shaped in wooden molds, then taken from the molds and put in the sun to dry. To dry evenly the bricks were turned and finally put on end until they were properly cured. If the usual procedure was followed, the bricks were laid in a mud mortar very much like that used in making the adobes.

The assembling of the house, which measured twelve feet by fourteen feet with a height of nine feet, was detailed by Langford. Combined with the thick adobe walls, door sills were laid with long flat stones dragged from the surrounding hills. He continued:

Such stones were also used for headers above the doors and windows and to frame the fireplace. We wrecked an abandoned hut a mile up the valley and dragged off such timber as we could use. One

long straight log we used as a center pole. There were some smaller poles, too, which we used as rafters. We cut cane from along the river with which to roof the rafters, tying the cane down hard with strings of split yucca blades. Then over the cane we heaped a six-inch layer of damp clay, which dried and hardened to make a good waterproof roof and later did much to keep our house cool in the summer.

Nails, hinges, and a small amount of lumber were ordered from Marathon, in addition to one small window. The cost was about ten dollars Langford recalled. This was the total outlay in cash, since the labor on the adobes was credited to Cleofas's rent.

When two additional rooms were added to the adobe house, the material chosen was rock. Langford had learned something about working stone from a German who had been apprenticed to a stone mason in Germany. Rocks were selected from the loose stones that had fallen from nearby cliffs. Watching Herman Jacobs at work on a project, Langford summed up his methods. Fellow workers collected the rocks, washing and scrubbing them with a steel brush, while others mixed the mortar. Langford explained: "all of us together couldn't keep Herman in mud and rock as fast as he called for them. He could take one glance at the pile say of a hundred rocks and say: 'Bring me that one.' And nine times out of ten that rock fit exactly the place he had in mind for it. If not, one or two quick strokes with his stone hammer made it fit."

The new rooms added to the Langford house were framed with willow poles and cane and then covered with corrugated metal roofing, which satisfactorily shut out heat and rain. As in the earlier room, stone was used to frame the floor and windows, but concrete flooring was poured "for smoother walking."

Common building materials used in construction by pioneering families in southwest Texas were cedar pickets and sotol. A picket and sotol house, dating from 1904 and originally located thirty-five miles southwest of Ozona, was moved to the Ranching Heritage Center in Lubbock, where it was carefully restored. (See page 104.) The ingenious ways of using meager resources—cedar brush from which pickets could be made, crumbly rock, and sotol, a yuccalike plant—represented a triumph over the hardships of survival in an arid region.

Sotol has received its share of admiration. The Indians and Hispanic settlers baked its roots in hot coals and considered the results a culinary delicacy. Mr. Langford was another admirer. For him, the sotol plant was worthy of notice "with its huge stump of glistening light green . . . blades, thrusting out in all directions from the base, with its tall bloom stem in the center holding aloft huge clusters of creamy blossoms." He added, "try to imagine an area eight miles through, where almost nothing grew except the flowering sotol. Thousands upon thousands of big white flower clusters, with here and there the sight of deer feeding on the sotol buds."

Admiring the white flowers was the bonus, the nitty-gritty of building a picket and sotol house first required finding cedar posts, spacing them about four feet apart, and setting them vertically in the ground. Sotol stalks were then nailed horizontally, inside and out, to the pickets. Earth and rubble were packed between the stalks for filler and insulation. (See page 106.) The roof was framed with cedar timbers to which sotol stalks

were fastened. The next step was thatching the roof. Thatch was made of coarse grass called *sacahuiste;* this was bound in bundles and tied to the roof framing in overlapping swatches. (See page 110.) When the picket and sotol house was reconstructed in Lubbock, José Maria Martinez of San Antonio and Juan Enriqué Martinez and Felix Vela of Laredo all donated their labor and expertise in thatching the roof using the age-old methods handed down in their families. The two rooms of picket and sotol were extended by the addition of a third space constructed of cedar pickets and roofed with shingles. A stone chimney on the end wall was laid with mud mortar. A small window fitted in a cut lumber frame would have been transported at considerable expense and effort from the nearest town. A vernacular shelter such as this was commonly found in the sheep and goat country along the Texas-Mexican border.

Picket houses, however, were not limited to the Rio Grande region. In Carson County in 1880, Clara Sully Carhart lived in a house built of pickets "made by standing poles upright and daubing the cracks with mud. The poles were cedar from Palo Duro Canyon, and the

Ledbetter picket house (1870s), Albany

shingles for the roof were made from cottonwood trees from McClellan Creek. In dry, hot weather the shingles curled out of shape, but when wet with rain, they flattened out and turned water nicely."

When Mary Hampton moved from East Texas to land near Abilene in the 1880s she remarked that she saw "rooms built of pickets and covered with poles upon which sod had been heaped to keep out the rain. . . . The rooms were about six in number and were about 8 feet square and floored with flat stones a bountiful supply of which could be found near the door. The series of rooms were built on economical plans. The inner wall serving for the wall of two rooms through-out an entire row."

Buildings made of vertical pickets daubed with mud or sod were referred to as jacal. (See page 108.) Langford, upon arriving at Boquillas at the foot of the Chisos Mountains, wrote that the village "comprised a store, a school building, and some ten adobe cabins. There were several *jacales,* or huts, made of sotol and maguey bloom stalks, with ocotillo roofs on which clay was laid about six inches thick."

It was adobe, however, that served as the primary material used in Southwest Texas. When the Spaniards came to New Mexico, they found Indians practicing agriculture and living in sun-dried adobe pueblos that rose in multi-storied terraces. Ladders connected the platformed stages and made it possible to move from level to level or to enter a room through the roof. Pre-Columbian pueblo walls were usually constructed of puddled adobe. The Spaniards taught the Indians to use wooden molds (a technique they had learned from the Moors) to shape bricks of uniform size. The adobes were put in the sun to dry. Thick adobe walls were roofed with *vigas,* sturdy poles made of tree trunks or large branches, spaced several feet apart that connected one side wall with the wall opposite it. The length of the *viga* determined the width of the interior space; this was usually no more than fifteen or twenty feet. Smaller tree branches, called *savinos* or *latias,* were laid across the *vigas* at right angles, or they were arranged in a herringbone pattern. (See page 110.) The rooftop was packed with brush and earth and plastered with as much as five or six inches of clay paste for waterproofing. The Spanish newcomers adopted this same method for roofing their adobe homes and mission churches. The *vigas* usually projected externally ensuring a striking shadow

pattern on the plain adobe walls. Heavy wooden gutters, or *canales,* were introduced by the Spanish settlers; these issued from the walls like miniature cannons (see page 111) to carry off rain that collected on the flat roofs. By the late nineteenth century, the roofs of adobe houses were frequently gabled instead of flat and were protected by sheet tin shipped by rail.

Adobe houses are a familiar presence in Alpine. Many are in excellent repair and have been added to over the years. Others return tranquilly to the earth from which they were made. (See page 111.) Original dates are difficult to determine after decades of rebuilding; but continued use suggests the comfort provided by the massive walls that insulate against chill in winter and that warm slowly in summer, maintaining a cool retreat. In climates where heat and aridity are ever present, only small windows pierce the adobe walls, ensuring the walls' integrity and keeping the interior a shadowy refuge from the glare of the out-of-door light.

Unlike the Pueblo Indians whose apartment units rose in several stories above an open plaza, the Spanish strung their rooms together along the ground. A porch, or *portal,* its roof supported by posts, extended the length of the living space. This provided shade and invited breezes to penetrate on three sides. It served as a corridor for communicating between rooms, though there were usually interior doors as well. The linear arramgement made it easy to extend the plan when the need arose.

The outside walls were finished with several coats of adobe plaster. Each spring, after the rainy season, the women added a coating of fresh mud plaster. Floors of packed earth were sprinkled several times a day to keep dust at a minimum. The interior walls, coated with whitewash, posed a problem. The dilemma was not unlike that faced by pioneers living in dugouts, where dust and dirt drifted from the ceiling. Susan Magoffin's diary explained the problem of plastered adobe walls and revealed a solution. She wrote the following report about a space that served as both parlor and dining room: "[this] is a long room with dirt floor [as they all have], plank ceiling, and nicely white-washed sides. Around one half to the height of six feet is tacked what may be called a schreen [*sic*] for it protects ones back from white wash, if he should chance to lean against it: it is made of calico, bound at each edge and looks quite fixy;

Vigas and *latias*, Nuestra Senora de la Concepción del Pueblo Socorro (1683–c. 1840), Socorro

the seats which are mostly cushioned benches, are placed against it."

The nuisance of flaking whitewash in adobe homes cured by calico was the result of feminine ingenuity; but the dugout housewife did not hold any delusions of a "fixy" solution offered by her canvas hangings. Susan Magoffin continued, "the floor too at the same end of the room [where calico is used on the wall] is covered with a kind of Mexican carpeting made of wool and coloured black and white only. In short we may consider this great hall as two rooms, for one half of it is carpeted and furnished for the parlour, while the other half has a naked floor, the dining table and all things attached to that establishment occupy it." This seems to imply the expectation of scraps thrown to the dogs and wine spilled in the midst of heated political arguments.

In addition to rooms extending single file, many houses along the Rio Grande and in New Mexico followed the Spanish custom of rooms arranged around a *placita,* or courtyard, with a bland facade facing the street. An example in which the linear design and the placita were combined is the Magoffin House in El Paso, now known as the Magoffin Home State Historic Site. (See page 112.) In 1850, James Wiley Magoffin, a relative of Susan Magoffin's husband, settled in the valley where El Paso now stands. He developed a small community called Magoffinville and built an adobe hacienda a few blocks from the present Magoffin home. The adobe house was swept away in the flood of 1867. In 1875, a new house was begun by James's son Joseph, acclaimed as one of El Paso's most esteemed elder statesmen. He appears to have wished his new house to have a design closely related to the home that had been destroyed almost a decade earlier. Instead of selecting the Gothic Revival style popular at the time, he chose the traditional Spanish manner, making use of adobe brick for the walls that enclosed the one-story sequence of rooms that developed in a U shape around a large courtyard. The south and east wings were aligned one room deep with entries from the exterior as well as in the walls shared by adjoining rooms. The north wing broke with traditionalism and formed a block of four rooms, two rooms deep, on either side of a central hall. The hall stretched from the street entry to a doorway (see page 113) on the opposite axis leading to the *placita.* The entrance hints at a relation to the Spanish Colonial

(Top) *Canales*   (Above) Adobe house, 607 West Avenue G, Alpine

(Above and opposite) Joseph Magoffin House (1875),
1120 Magoffin Street, El Paso

zaguan, or roofed corridor, which connected the front of the house to the stables and other buildings at the rear. In appearance, the north block, instead of maintaining the earlier Spanish adobe facade with a *portal,* is related to the New Mexican Territorial style. Greek Revival details were grafted onto the adobe construction. Small pedimental forms appear above the shuttered windows. (See page 112.) The walls were covered with lime plaster and then scored to give the appearance of blocks of coursed masonry. Today, the scoring has been redone in the cement plaster that has been applied to preserve the building fabric. It is amusing to contrast the geometric and unyielding lines of the "false" masonry with the *canales* that look slightly embarrassed as they project over such regularity and perfection of alignment.

ALONG THE RIVER and east of El Paso are three venerable adobe churches. Two trace their origins to the seventeenth-century mission program, and one served at least briefly as a chapel for the military. Their origins are a couple of centuries earlier than the guidelines set by this book, but there is a loophole: all three have been rebuilt several times, in some cases as late as the second half of the nineteenth century or the

earlier decades of the twentieth. Fine examples of the Spanish pueblo style, they are often by-passed in the rush to focus attention on the missions at San Antonio.

Moving east from El Paso, the first encounter is with what may be the oldest Spanish Colonial building in Texas: the present Community Center at the Tigua Indian pueblo of Isleta del Sur. (See page 115.) The pueblo traces its beginnings to a home established by the Franciscan Fathers for the displaced Tiwa people who chose to leave New Mexico during the 1680 Pueblo Indian Revolt. The construction of an adobe refuge was begun sometime between 1682 and 1690. The thick mud brick walls were coated with several inches of adobe plaster made of river clay mixed with straw. Cottonwood and pine logs, a foot in diameter, were selected for the *vigas* to support the roof. The smaller *latias* were cut from willow branches, covered with tule (leaves of river cane), and then plastered with mud. A restoration project initiated by the state building commission was carried out in the late 1960s. The work was done by Tigua Indians living nearby.

The present church corresponds to Corpus Christi de la Ysleta del Sur, built in 1744. A flood in 1849 damaged the structure and left it and the Indian pueblo on the U.S. side of the Rio Grande. Rebuilding took place, but disaster struck again in 1907 when a fire destroyed everything, including the five-foot-thick adobe walls, leaving only the ruins of the altar area. The church was once more rebuilt, and a three-story beehive dome on wood scaffolding was raised over the tower. The mission church, originally known as Corpus Christi, is also called the Church of Our Lady of Mount Carmel. To add to the confusion it is dedicated to Saint Anthony of Padua. The death of Saint Anthony in 1231 on the thirteenth of June corresponded to the early summer performance of the traditional Green Corn Dance of the Tigua. Today the dance takes place on St. Anthony's Day. The celebration of the two events is a subject with which Lenore Hughes is familiar. Her account begins:

> The dance is led by the Tribe's Cacique (patriarch). The procession goes toward the church in the midst of gunblasts of the pistaleros who are the processional guards. . . . The dancers sing and wave stalks of corn.

Joseph Magoffin House (1875), 1120 Magoffin Street, El Paso

After two ceremonial circlings on the porch of the mission, while still singing songs, they form a line in front of the porch and [move] back and forth rhythmically. . . .

Bells are rung vigorously, loud and fast. Guns are exploded. They go into the church followed by the waiting crowd. The shrine of St. Anthony is situated near the altar and a choir sings to the accompaniment of a guitarist, a tambourine player, and a saxophonist. When mass is ended, the shrine is carried out of the church and in a procession around the mission. Then the tribal members dance until noon.

Going east from Ysleta, the Mission de la Purisima Concepción del Socorro shared a series of misfortunes similar to those afflicting the church at Ysleta. The church now standing is the third church. (See page 116.) Reconstructed in the nineteenth century, it was carefully stabilized in 1984. It ranks with New Mexican missions for its elegant and gently contoured adobe walls. The facade belongs to a category referred to as a *campanario,* that is, instead of flanking towers or a single tower, it has a pierced wall for the placement of bells. Here, the wall rises above the central doorway in a graceful parapet based on a Pueblo stepped motif. The roof and the choir gallery over the entry are supported by *vigas* of cottonwood and cypress. The timbers rest on carved corbels, each one different in design. Some of the corbels may date from the second church, since it is said that materials saved from the destructive flood were reused in the new church. An early guidebook, which indicates points of interest in the Lone Star State, relates an amusing story about the statue of Saint Michael (see page 117), which is placed in a niche near the sanctuary: "Legend says that this statue was intended for a New Mexico mission, but that while it was being freighted overland the cart stuck in Socorro and three yoke of oxen were unable to move it, so the people of Socorro bought it and made the saint their secondary patron."

The villagers were so deeply convinced that their church was St. Michael's special domain that when the statue needed repair, they refused to allow the figure to be taken away even temporarily. Persuaded that the saint could only be refurbished at the mission near Is-

Corpus Christi de la Ysleta (1682, 1744, 1849, 1907), Ysleta

Nuestra Señora de la Concepción del Pueblo Socorro (1683–c. 1840), Socorro

leta, the statue finally made the journey accompanied by a shotgun patrol, who never left it until it was safely returned to its own place at Socorro.

There are other interesting customs associated with Socorro. In her book *Holy Adobe* Lenore Hughes writes:

> There is an unusual graveyard in the rear of the rectory. Here the Indian neophytes buried their dead in layers, one above the other, only one grave being allowed to a family. In the mission churchyard, east of the mission, is another unique burial ground. Four *decansas,* or resting places, are located at the four cardinal points of the compass to each of which the deceased is carried by mourners before the burial. (See page 118.) The Spaniards believe that when a person dies, his soul will never get lost if it goes to the corners of the cemetery and will always know its resting place. There are two large cornerstones remaining in the cemetery and they are known as *Portales.*

The reference to the markers at the four corners of the cemetery is especially interesting because it suggests a relation to the four *posas,* or small chapels, Mexicans usually built at the four corners of mission courtyards after the Conquest. The purpose of the *posas* remains a matter of speculation.

The third in the group of adobe churches is about five miles east of Socorro near Clint. The Capilla de San Elizario stands on the south side of a sleepy plaza. (See page 118.) It is flanked by one of the older houses in the valley, whose long *portal,* looks out into the dusty square where a bandstand has been decorated with spray-painted graffiti. The town of San Elizario was founded as a *presidio,* that is, a military establishment, after the New Mexican Indian Revolt of 1680. A *presidio* always had a chapel to minister to the spiritual needs of the soldiers. San Elizario as it appears today was under construction between 1877 and 1887. Like the church at Socorro, San Elizario has a bell wall with several bells above the entry, but here the resemblance ends. There are four buttresses in front, two on either side of the entry, and buttresses along the sides of the structure. These seem to serve a decorative, rather than a functional, purpose. The plan, which is nearly square, does not resemble New Mexican missions or those in the Rio Grande Valley. The number three, a symbol of the Trin-

San Miguel at Nuestra Señora de la Concepción (mid–nineteenth century), Socorro

ity, intentionally or unintentionally plays an important role. There are three aisles divided by three columns on each side, three apses, and three windows along each side wall. Three doors give entry into the sanctuary: a double door opens at the front of the church; and a door on each side of the church is accented by a fan light. One of the most pleasing features of the design is the consciousness of the intense West Texas sunlight. The buttresses produce strong shadow patterns and

Capilla de San Elizario (1877–1887), San Elizario

Decansa, burial ground of Nuestra Señora de la Concepción, Socorro

contrasts of light and dark, creating a powerful and dramatic effect.

In other small towns in southwest Texas there are less venerable but no less pleasing adobe churches and public buildings. In Sierra Blanca, there is an abandoned adobe chapel with an entry dominated by a tower built in two stages and covered by a small dome. It stands out starkly in the bright sun. (See page 119.) Sierra Blanca is famous for its adobe courthouse, dating from 1917. (See page 119.) It is said to be the largest adobe structure in Texas.

WHILE DISCUSSING adobe architecture and the strong vernacular statements made by the sculptured earthen walls patterned with shadow streaks from the projecting vigas, the position of Queen Anne along the Rio Grande is difficult to determine. The "Queen of Gingerbread" in the late nineteenth century did not hesitate to apply a touch of spindlework or even elaborate brackets to sunbaked brick. Unfortunately, inasmuch as adobe perishes when neglected and loses its original character after it has been refurbished in a contemporary idiom, houses with spindlework have rarely survived. One of the survivors

(Above) Abandoned church (late nineteenth century), Sierra Blanca

(Right) Hudspeth County Courthouse (1919), Sierra Blanco

Detail, Annie Riggs Hotel (1902), Fort Stockton

is the Annie Riggs Hotel on South Main Street at Fort Stockton. Opened in 1902, it was presided over for nearly two decades by the woman for whom it was named. It is now the Annie Riggs Memorial Museum. The walls are thick adobe bricks that act as insulation against the year-round sun. A veranda with spindlework offers visitors shade and protection from the heat. At the rear, an open courtyard is flanked by many of the guest rooms. Ornamental shingles and a touch of gingerbread continue to decorate the gables.

If Queen Anne with jigsaw trimming lavished on adobe is not easily found in West Texas, there are examples of "icing" on stone and brick along the Rio Grande. The Glenn-Dowe House in Del Rio is a storybook cottage. (See page 122.) It was begun in 1900 by builder David Glenn and sold to Mrs. Dowe in 1906. It belongs to the gabled-ell cottage type. The porch with spindlework trim is tucked into the wing. Above a projecting wall with a single window, a hood curves up almost to

Courtyard at rear, Annie Riggs Hotel, Fort Stockton

(Opposite) Orfila House (c. 1880), 1701 Matamoras, Laredo

the top of the gable. The impression is reminiscent of a Chinese pavilion.

Laredo has an especially flamboyant Victorian residence known as the Orfila House. White as a wedding cake, it is believed to have been built about 1880. Accounts say that it was a boarding house, but rumors persist that it may have been the place of business for shady ladies. Tradition relates that it was designed in the French manner of New Orleans architecture. Built of brick, it is one story lifted on a raised basement. The porch is connected to the ground with a curving stair. A balustrade at porch level connects handsome Corinthian columns. The roof, hipped and covered with sheet metal, rests on a decorative cornice and brackets.

The Orfila House flaunts an exuberance characterized by an abundance of ornament that rarely appears in such lush profusion farther north in West Texas. In Mexico, the pre-Columbian Indian sculpture—friezes and roof combs and stelae—at temple sites coalesced with the decoration and fantasy of Spanish Baroque and the more refined detail associated with the Churrigueresque style. This taste for extravagant design and rich textural effects is reflected in several El Paso buildings. One of these is a three-story, red brick structure at 312 East Overland Avenue. (See page 123.) The cornice is centered by a plasterwork head of an Indian with a feathered headdress. (See page 123.) The date 1904 appears in a ribbon motif below the cornice. (The Indian may have been suggested by the Indian head penny or the profile on the reverse side of the buffalo nickel.) The facade is divided into three bays. Rusticated pilaster strips with Ionic plaster capitals separate the central bays from the vertical band of single windows on either side. The windows are topped with elaborate pediments resting on ornate consoles. At the third story, the pediments are decorated with pleasantly demonic creatures: one seems to have hands, and the other looks like a placid mastiff. At the second level, the triangular pediments have snarling toothy creatures about to leap down on unsuspecting pedestrians. The windows looking out on the street have been modernized, and a trace of the original doorway remains.

Almost as complex in its detail, El Paso's Merrick Building, at 301 El Paso Street, was built in 1887. (See page 124.) It faces El Paso Street (301 El Paso). An elongated side extends along Overland. Designed by John J.

Glenn-Dowe House (1900–1901), Del Rio

Orfila House (c. 1880), 1701 Matamoras, Laredo

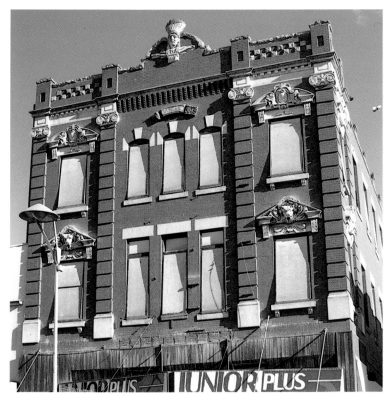

Business building (1904), 312 East Overland, El Paso

(Below) Detail, business building, El Paso

Stewart and William J. Carpenter, local architects, it was built for Charles Merrick by contractors Richard Caples and Lewis Hammer. First known as the St. Charles Hotel, today the street front neon delivers the information "Hollywood Cafe." The second and third floors are politely called "a residential hotel." Basically sound, it is in dire need of tender loving restoration. It is a remarkable example of the Queen Anne style applied to a commercial building. Above the ground floor, there seems to have been little change. It illustrates the Queen Anne dislike for plain walls and the effort exerted for multiple textures. Brick and terra cotta insets join the projecting bay windows in order to eliminate bare flat surfaces. Tin facing and patterned tin shingles frame the bays and add further embellishment to the cornice. (See page 124.)

Emphasizing the patterned walls and the use of materials developed in the multicultural environment close to the border, the Merrick Building contrasts strongly with the National Security Bank in Quanah. (See page 125.) Both buildings are brick and share approximately the same date. The corner bank is a substantial two-story structure with a rusticated foundation and rusticated stone arches framing the doorway and windows

(Above and below)Merrick Building (1887), 301 El Paso Street, El Paso

along the street. The arches over the windows at the second story are brick accentuated by a narrow eyebrow of rusticated stone and stone keystones at the center of the brick half circles. The cornice is handsomely detailed (see page 125), but it is restrained and almost Puritanical in contrast to the multiple textures of the Merrick Building.

MANY OF El Paso's most gracious buildings during the first three decades of the twentieth century were the work of an Ohioan, Henry Charles Trost, born in Toledo on the fifth of March in 1860. Because Trost's work in the Southwest, his adopted land, represented virtually every trend present in the period before he died in 1933, his training and architectural contributions are of particular importance. Until Lloyd and June-Marie Englebrecht's biography *Henry C. Trost: Architect of the Southwest* was published in 1981, the architect and his buildings had attracted little attention, despite the fact that for three decades, beginning in 1900, he was one of the most significant architects practicing in Southwest Texas, New Mexico, and Arizona.

Trost's parents migrated from Germany to northwestern Ohio. The elder Trost kept a grocery store, but he was better known as a skilled carpenter and a builder/contractor. It is likely that young Henry absorbed a

Security National Bank (1890s), Quanah

working knowledge of construction from his father to which was added an appreciation of finely detailed carpentry and the crafts. After attending classes at the Toledo Art School, where he developed his talent for drawing, Trost was employed as a draftsman in Toledo architectural offices—this was the way in which many young men who wished to become architects received their professional education.

At the age of twenty, Trost seems to have fallen under the spell of the Wild West. He boarded a train, "that nineteenth-century symbol of freedom, space, and mobility," and arrived in Denver in 1880. He moved to Pueblo, but like a great many adventurous Midwesterners, he became restless and left for Dallas. The architect referred to Big D as "a little country town" and went to Fort Worth. By 1884 Trost was in New Orleans helping to design the World's Industrial and Cotton Centennial Exposition. The trail next led from New Orleans to Dodge City. Toward the end of the 1880s, Trost caught a northbound train. This time his ticket read Chicago, the most active architectural center in the country.

The eight years that Trost spent in the Windy City prepared him for his permanent destination in the Southwest. The 1890s were the years of Louis Sullivan's great successes. In 1893 Frank Lloyd Wright, who had

Detail, Security National Bank, Quanah

Quanah, Acme & Pacific Railroad Depot (1909), Quanah

been employed to do drafting in the office of Adler and Sullivan, began his own independent practice. There is some evidence that Trost may also have worked in Sullivan's office during his Chicago sojourn. Marcus Whiffen accepts this as a fact. Another source of information is an article on the firm of Trost and Trost, published in 1954, in the El Paso newspaper. At this time Henry's brothers and associates were still living. The account observed that Henry Trost has been employed by Adler and Sullivan and that he had "worked beside a bright young man, Frank Lloyd Wright, and under the direction of the father of modern architecture, Louis Sullivan."

This was the period in which Sullivan's personal style of ornament, freed from Ecole des Beaux-Arts' influence, was developing, based upon observation of nature and the organic growth of plants. Sullivan insisted that both building and ornament must be planned simultaneously: ornament should never be applied as an afterthought; it should develop with the total design concept. During the years when ornament was being liberated from the classical and Gothic traditions, it is significant that Trost became a designer of ornamental metal. In 1888, he was accepted into the prestigious Chicago Architectural Sketch Club. One of his sketches, published in *The Building Budget,* was given an award

by what must have been one of the most distinguished panels of jurors ever assembled: Louis Sullivan, John Wellborn Root, and William Le Baron Jenney. The sketch was for a "wrot iron gate," it was submitted anonymously under the appropriate pseudonym *Smithy.*

When Trost left Chicago for Tucson in 1899, his admiration for Sullivan's ornament would soon be enhanced by the discovery of the Hispanic Baroque designs that surround the portal of the Church of San Xavier with richly polychromed swags and symbols. The eighteenth-century church, as well as the mingling of Spanish and pueblo adobe buildings, must have heightened Trost's interest in the role of climate, function, and aesthetics in the world of desert heat and long stretches of rainlessness. He wrote in a brochure:

Back of this Spanish mission style is more than mere imitation. . . . The atmosphere of the southwest is wonderfully clear. The mountain masses are rugged and their shadows and contrasts are sharply defined. The sunset tints are primary colors, illuminated with wonderful gold and purple. The horizons are infinite—long, distant, level lines, broken only by the far-off mountains or the scrubby desert vegetation against the sky. The dominant characteristics of the arid southwest are:

plenty of elbow room, sharply defined contrasts, long unbroken lines, low firm masses, and vivid colors. With accurate instinct, the old Spanish builders adapted their structure to the requirements of environment.

But they went still further. The climate of the arid southwest, as well as the physical aspect, is marked by sharp contrasts. The difference between night and day temperature is 30 to 40 degrees, or double that if the day temperature be read in the sun. The sun's rays strike the earth directly, for the atmosphere is dry, and there is no blanket of water vapor in the air to absorb and retain the heat, for the same reason, it is always cool in the shade, and the breeze blows constantly. Natural vegetation is scant and neutral in tone. The object, therefore, is to build so as to cut off the intense heat of the sun in the summer, to retain the artificial warmth of the house in the winter, and to create a green, flowery oasis for man's pleasure and comfort. This threefold end was attained by the Spaniards with their thick walls, patios, deep porches, and large, high-ceiled rooms.

Trost learned the lessons of the desert early and well. They remained a part of whatever style he chose for his work. After a brief and productive stay in Tucson, in 1903 Trost moved to El Paso. It could be said that Trost was made for El Paso and that El Paso was made for Trost. The city on the border enjoyed a cultural heritage that united Hispanic and Anglo customs accommodating Anglo practicality and concern for new inventions and industrial materials with the architectural richness, color, and respect for craftsmanship inherited from Spain and Mexico. El Paso also provided Trost with the sun and aridity that he found so congenial.

Among the first residences designed by Trost in El Paso were the Wingo House and the Williams House. Both are examples of the Mission style popularized in California in the 1890s. The Columbian Exposition that had stirred the overwhelming enthusiasm for a revival of classicism was also responsible for directing the public's attention to California's Mission architecture. This was brought about by A. Page Brown's California Building for the fair. Brown refused to bow to the "politically correct" classicism handed down by the eastern

establishment. He drew his inspiration from the eighteenth-century Spanish missions built along the California coastline. The railroads moving West to California were quick to grasp the significance of stations in the mission idiom. These would pique the curiosity of travelers and direct their attention to sunny California. The station/hotel in Quanah, Texas, with its white stucco walls and red-tiled towers, projected that aura of romance—the promise of adventure and the carefree life of a Spanish *caballero*. (See page 126.)

The Williams and Wingo houses in El Paso followed the characteristic pattern associated with California Mission design. The elements usually included were arches covering arcaded walkways and defining ample porches, low-pitched tile roofs and facades with parapets centered by a circular or quatrefoil opening. The smoothly plastered walls were left undecorated thus separating Mission style from the Spanish Colonial Re-

Wingo House (1907), 4115 Trowbridge, El Paso

Williams House (1915), 323 West Rio, El Paso

vival that followed in the 1920s. After World War I the free-wheeling approach to design based on the Spanish culture in the Southwest ended. Spanish Colonial Revival emphasized an architecture that was historically accurate. The publication of books illustrated by handsome photographs, as well as degrees in architecture that included required courses in architectural history, provided incentives for a new generation of architects. Graduates of the rapidly multiplying schools of architecture traveled throughout the Spanish colonies in the Americas and then visited Spain for further inspiration.

Although Trost did not make pilgrimages to Mexico or Spain, in the 1920s he became quite as comfortable with the Spanish Colonial Revival mannerisms as he had been earlier with the Mission style. One example is El Paso's now endangered Westminster Presbyterian Church, finished in 1911. It was purchased by the St. George Orthodox Church in 1951 as a place of worship

St. George Orthodox Church, formerly Westminster Presbyterian Church (1910–1911), East Rio Grande Avenue and North Florence Street, El Paso

Gray House (1904), 1205 El Paso Street, El Paso

for the Greek Orthodox congregation. A new church is in the planning stages, and neither interest nor plans for saving Trost's structure with its fine tower are in evidence.

Like a chameleon, Trost could change his historical coat with an ease that satisfied his clients' tastes. One of the most curious and original of the El Paso residences is the Gray House. Built in 1904, it is now unfortunately in a state of deterioration. (See page 128.) The two columns flanking the deep porch offer an eclectic buffet. They have been whimsically referred to as Egyptian-Doric. The fluting on the column shafts and the general shape of the capitals are borrowed from Greece, but the echinus moldings swell with alternating lotus buds and lotus flowers, a concept that would have spread horror through Phidias's veins. To add to the tongue-in-cheek atrocities, Trost bordered the porch with a frieze in low relief that could be mistaken for the work of Louis Sullivan.

If liberties were taken with the Gray house, the William Ward Turney House, now the El Paso Museum of Art, wears an imperturbably Neoclassical facade accented by two-story wooden Corinthian columns. Turney was born in Marshall, close to the Louisiana border. This may have caused him to want a home wrapped in the glow of Southern tradition. Turney's mansion was ready for occupancy in 1909, the same year that Trost's own home was completed. (And the year Frank Lloyd Wright built the Robie House in Chicago.) If architecture is capable of presenting portraits of its owners or designers, the proof might rest in the contrast between the nostalgia for the Old South chosen by Turney and Trost's own choice, a design recalling memories of the years spent in Chicago (see page 131) at a time when Prairie houses were flowing from Frank Lloyd Wright's pencil and taking physical form in Oak Park and the towns of northern Illinois.

The Prairie style was the result of new needs in the field of domestic architecture—fewer live-in servants, smaller families, new methods of heating and lighting, garages replacing the stables at the back of lots, the interrelation of indoor-outdoor space, the economic need to rely on mass production instead of handcraftmanship, and the elimination of ornament and influences

Turney House, now El Paso Museum of Art (1908–1909), 1205 Montana Street, El Paso

borrowed from Europe's past. The Prairie house was usually two stories with one-story wings moving out from the central block and ending in porches or a car-port. The low roofs were frequently hipped with ample overhangs appropriated by Wright from the Japanese, as were many other elements selected by the architect to suit his own purposes.

Wright's first contact with Japanese architecture may have been a Japanese Pavilion at the 1893 Fair. The Japa-nese Shoin style suggested interior space that elimi-nated the walls boxing in rooms. Japanese architecture reinforced Wright's asymmetrical compositions, his use of dark wood strips in contrast to light plaster walls, and the garden visible through ample windows. The Prairie houses also placed an emphasis on earth-hugging hori-zontal lines of brick walls accented by light stone or cement coping and the ever-present pedestals with flat-tened urns for vines or flowers.

Trost's home at the corner of West Yandell Drive and Hawthorn Street suggests the way in which the Prairie house, intended for the Midwest, was successfully grafted to the stony soil and arid climate of El Paso. The wide, overhanging eaves protected the walls and win-dows from direct sunlight. Trost designed a double roof with a layer of air separating the upper and lower seg-ments, thus, achieving ideal insulation from the heat. Before the city was built up, as it is today, the site took full advantage of a landscape extending to the Rio Grande below and the mountains to the south. Tawny bricks and cream tones were in harmony with the beige and brown of the landscape. Wright's open plans when introduced into the hot climate of El Paso allowed a welcome circulation of air, instead of confining life to a series of small poorly ventilated rooms. The Engel-brechts were enthusiastic in their description of an inte-rior wall design that captured the spirit of the region. They wrote: "The interior wall frieze is an authentic link with the Southwest. In leather tones of tan, brown, and burnt orange, relieved by soft greens and yellows . . . a continuous, repetitive motif derived from the thistle, the palm and cactus was stenciled in place on huge sheets of seamless paper which had been applied to por-tions of the walls."

(Above and top right) Trost House, now Malcolm McGregor home (1909), 1013 West Yandell Drive, El Paso

Detail, Alhambra Theatre (1914), 209 El Paso Street, El Paso

Alhambra Theatre (1914), 209 El Paso Street, El Paso

This painting presents a clue to the exterior frieze of deeply sculptured cream-colored all-weather plaster beneath the protective overhang of the roof. Carefully examined, the motifs resemble the southwestern plants stenciled inside the house. There are abstractions of thorny thistles, vines and bulbous cacti.

The story is told that when Frank Lloyd Wright visited El Paso in 1957, he was taken to see the Trost house. His first remark was, "How did that get out here?"

In the period before the First World War, Trost's remarkable versatility was exercised in ways other than domestic architecture. His multistory office buildings changed the character of downtown El Paso. The architect might have revised Caesar Augustus's famous remark, "I found Rome a city of brick and left it a city of marble." Trost could have said correctly, "I found the business center of El Paso a district of brick; I left it a district of concrete." Concrete was used sparingly except for foundations in the 1800s, but with the dawn of the twentieth century, its use increased rapidly. In 1900,

Trost pointed out, there was not a single reinforced concrete building in El Paso; then seven were built in rapid succession. To make this possible, the city's first cement plant became operational in 1910. The Richard Caples Building, designed by Trost, was El Paso's first large building to use poured concrete; the concrete was not left exposed, but was faced with brick. The interest of the public in concrete construction was highlighted by the *El Paso Herald,* which gave the following explanation: "When the concrete is mixed sufficiently it is sluiced off in a big trough . . . and hoisted to the floor above, where the boxes [forms] have been prepared for its reception, [and] where, with the assistance of a a crew of Mexican laborers, it is dumped into the molds the same as molten metal. . . . Floor after floor is laid in the same way, the concrete being poured into the boxes containing the steel reinforcing."

Trost, while designing tall office buildings, continued to rampage through usual and unusual sources for eclectic borrowings. One of his most satisfying designs was for the Alhambra Theatre at 209 South El Paso Street. Later referred to as the Palace Theatre, it opened in August 1914 at the outbreak of the world war in Europe. The theatre was intended to serve as a stage for live drama and as a movie house. With silent films in mind, a large organ was installed for the background music accompanying action unfolding on the silver screen. The plaster lacework veiling the facade resembles the walls of the Palace of the Alhambra in Granada for which the theatre was first named. (See page 131.) The Moorish detailing used by Trost preceded by a decade the vogue for the opulence of Moorish Spain that dominated the architecture of so many theatres in the 1920s.

One of Trost's most exotic and unlikely sources was foisted on him by a painter and *National Geographic.* The main classroom building of El Paso's School of Mines, now The University of Texas at El Paso (UTEP), burned in 1916. In the April 1914 issue of the *Geographic* an article had appeared on the architecture of Bhutan that apparently captured the imagination of El Paso artist, Helen Worrell. After the fire, she conceived the idea of a new building based upon Bhutanese Buddhist monasteries. This might have remained an unfulfilled fantasy had Helen Worrell's husband, George Howard Worrell, not been a dean of the School of Mines. Trost & Trost was invited to participate in the project in 1917.

Henry Trost's earliest drawings did not please either Dean Worrell or the faculty. Worse still, Worrell insisted that his faculty should make drawings and plans to help Trost out. This would be enough to send wall-to-wall vibrations through any architect's office. Trost proved himself as expert at diplomacy as he was at architectural design. His next submission to the dean met with grudging acceptance and the comment from Worrell that Trost & Trost "succeeded in working out a plan for the main building which will, I think, be very beautiful, decidedly more so than the plan they had before." But insisting on the last word, the dean added that this happened because the architects had made good use of "the faculty plan." Eccentric as the design source was, the building proved not only in harmony with the rugged environment and barren rocks of El Paso's steep hillsides, but also dramatic, making an impact unusual for a college campus structure. The Engelbrechts have commented on the characteristics derived from architecture of the Himalayan Kingdom of Bhutan. These include, "the low hipped roof; the ornamental frieze of brick and tile below the roof line, broken by the windows of the top story; the three corbels under the central window; battered outside walls which increase in thickness toward the bottom by seven inches per ten feet." The greater thickness resulted in deep-set windows on the lower stories, a device especially appropriate for eliminating the direct rays of the hot sun. El Paso American Institute of Architects chapter member and researcher Patrick Rand has called attention to the band of red brick at the upper level of Old Main, which in Bhutan and Tibet identified a building as a religious institution or a monastery, while the circular *mandalas* decorating the building are derived from the Buddhist Wheel of Life.

It was not only the variety of architectural design and the quantity of work undertaken by Trost, but also the high standards of excellence he maintained, that seem in retrospect incomprehensible. Trost studied and developed each assignment with more than just competence. He possessed a certain élan combined with unflagging energy and enthusiasm. Equally remarkable was Trost's ability to predict, several decades before

Old Main (1921), The University of Texas at El Paso Campus, El Paso

they were generally accepted, the array of styles that would besiege the early twentieth century. His work before and during World War I offered a preview of the eclectic fancies and fashions that dominated the 1920s and 1930s: the so-called Prairie architecture that helped to popularize the bungalow; the Spanish Colonial Revival that succeeded the Mission style; Hispanic blends of Moorish decoration; continued Neoclassicism; and the clean lines of reinforced concrete office buildings. If this were not enough, in 1929 it was Trost who designed the O. T. Bassett Tower in El Paso, a fine example of *L'Art Deco*, the most original style of the postWorld War I period. In the midst of such varied fare, Trost never lost sight of the special characteristics of the Southwest—the effects of an arid climate, sunlight, and an austere landscape on the buildings for which he was responsible.

7

The 1920s: Bungalows and Eclectic Borrowings

[The automobile] changed the face of America. Villages
that had once prospered because they were "on the railroad"
languished with economic anaemia; villages on Route 61
bloomed with garages, filling stations, hot-dog stands, chicken-
dinner restaurants, tearooms, tourists' rests, camping sites,
and affluence.... At the beginning of the decade [the 1920s]
a single traffic officer at the junction of Main Street
and Central Street had been sufficient for the control of traffic.
By the end of the decade, what a difference! —red and green
lights, blinkers, one-way streets, boulevard stops, stringent and
yet more stringent parking ordinances—and still a shining
flow of traffic that backed up for blocks along Main Street
every Saturday and Sunday afternoon.
[Made accessible by the auto,] attractive suburbs grew with
amazing speed, blossoming out with brand-new Colonial
farmhouses (with attached garage), Tudor cottages (with
age-old sagging roofs constructed by inserting wedge-shaped
blocks at the ends of the roof- trees), and Spanish stucco
haciendas (with built-in radios).
Frederick Lewis Allen, from *Only Yesterday*

Hotel El Paisano (1930), Marfa

Santa Rita #2 (1924), Permian Basin Petroleum Museum, Midland

IT WAS OIL that supplied the gas that fueled the cars that encouraged the suburbs that housed the refugees from the growing cities. If cotton had brought a new cash crop to West Texas in the first two decades of the twentieth century, oil wells gushed-in the post–World War I era. A Fort Worth hostess is said to have interrupted a dinner party to load her bemused guests into a caravan of cars waiting to drive them to her ranch to witness an oil well "come in." It did, right on schedule, spewing out a geyser of oil blacker than the night sky.

Just as cattle and grain and cotton produced their own vernacular buildings—windmills and bunkhouses, grain elevators and gins—so the oil fields produced their rigs, which Mrs. John Berry remembered as "just like bristles in a hairbrush in Burkburnett in 1918." She added, "You looked out the door and it was just like a cactus."

Close to Midland, the Permian Basin Petroleum Museum preserves in an out-of-door setting some early skeletons of the oil industry. One of the exhibits is Santa Rita #2. Located seventy miles southeast of Midland, a part of the Texon Oil and Land Company area owned by Frank T. Pickrell, the Santa Rita field was destined to be touched by the miraculous, or just plain luck. The unlikely story is that shares in the proposed field were sold by Pickrell to some good Catholic women from New York City. Pickrell seems to have been one of those promoters who could have sold bikinis to Eskimos. After an extended period with no word of their investments, the ladies grew restive and turned to the parish priest for guidance. Not well versed in oil wells and a doubting Thomas into the bargain, the priest recommended the only action that seemed appropriate: he suggested that the ladies invoke the aid of of Santa Rita, patron saint of the impossible. This was done and a sealed envelope with a message was carried back to Texas by one of the developers and to the site where drilling was taking place. When the envelope was opened, it contained a letter and a red rose. The letter requested that the rose petals be scattered over the rig and that the oil field should be christened Santa Rita. One report says that it was Frank Pickrell himself who scrambled to the top of the rig and sent the petals cascading, blown by West Texas winds. The field was duly christened as requested. The patroness of impossible events must have been amused at the sight of a West

Texan oilman tossing rose petals after "black gold" and flattered to have an oil field as a namesake. Twenty-one months later, the first Santa Rita well began production. As Judge Orland L. Sims put it, "Old Santa Rita No. 1 can still produce a few barrels of oil and stands as a landmark for the gents who are not afraid to attempt the impossible."

With the opening of the oil fields in the 1920s, a new generation came to West Texas looking for a chance to better their lives. This time they came to the boomtowns, not in covered wagons, but in Model T's and trucks packed with boxes and tents and children. These new "pioneers" were not cowboys who rode the range or nesters who lived in dugouts while they filed for land and built simple box-and-strip homes. They were oil field workers who picked up and moved whenever there was word of a new site being opened. They were a hard-working lot, and like the cowboys who roared into town after a cattle drive, they liked to play hard: "oil boom towns appealed to restless young men looking for a good time." As was so often the case, it was the women for whom life was most difficult. They gathered up a few household necessities and remained at their husbands' sides, living under the most adverse conditions during the two years it took to drill a well. "Bing" Moddox, who was there, described Borger, a typical boomtown. "It was," he said, "made up of corrugated sheet-iron buildings, tents, one-by-twelve lumber shacks, people living in their automobiles and trailers . . . two wheel and four-wheel open wagon bed trailers."

Like the earlier settlers (both cowboys and nesters), many oil field workers came from the farms. They were accustomed to "rugged outdoor work done with lots of muscle," and "they could get by without indoor plumbing, central heating, and a grocery store around the corner." Their values were West Texan. They helped their neighbors when the need arose, because for those who were on the move, there were rarely friends or kin close by. They respected self-reliance and endurance, and they were suspicious of anything limiting their personal independence. Gradually the transient life-style changed, and the change was brought about by paved roads. When paving replaced the dirt roads, axle deep with mud if the rains came, it was possible for a family to live in town. Civilization was only a few hours' drive from the place where drilling was taking place. Children

were able to go to school on a regular basis, and isolation was replaced by the chance to participate in the activities of a community. From jerry-built shacks, a family could move into a bungalow with the help of a loan from the bank. The bungalow became a link between box-and-strip houses of the late nineteenth century and the ranch style homes of the post–World War II period.

Finding a generally acceptable definition for the Bungalow style is the equivalent of updating the medieval squabble over how many angels could stand on the head of a pin to how many flappers could Charleston on a Victrola needle. The origin of the *bungalow*, a title causing such terrible puns as *bungalowner* and, worse, *bungaloner*, it is generally agreed, can be traced to India during the British Colonial Period. In seventeenth-century India, a bungalow, given varied spellings including *bangla*, was a Bengali peasant hut. The floor was raised a foot or two above the ground to counter the periodic rains. The framing of the hut was bamboo plastered with mud, and the roof was thatched with grass. By the early 1800s the bungalow of an Englishman living in India was situated in a large compound, which served as an extension of the house, that is, an out-of-door room. It was built from local materials by native laborers who used traditional methods of construction. It was lifted on a platform a foot or two in height. The framing for the one-story structure might be of wooden posts and the walls of burnt brick. The rooms were surrounded by a wide veranda.

With its background of English colonialism, it is not surprising that the bungalow migrated to the British Isles before being introduced in the United States. The title *bungalow* was first given to a holiday house built in 1869 on the north coast of Kent. Increasingly fast and convenient travel by rail made an informal vacation home a desirable way of escaping urban pressures. It was not long, however, before the bungalow invaded the suburbs. Anthony King referred to the bungalow in these words, "A cottage is a little house in the country but a bungalow is a little country house." It was more than this neat turn of phrase. It was a product of the Industrial Revolution and an answer to new needs. The growing middle class placed value on owning property, even a pocket handkerchief of land. A bungalow with its one-story plan (but not all bungalows were limited to a single story) lessened housework and reflected the availability of fewer and fewer servants. Invalids in wheelchairs had access to all of the rooms. With no stairs to cause falls, the hazard of injuries was reduced, and loss of life by fire was less threatening because the family could crawl out windows close to the ground. The morbid thought was expressed that the problem in two-story houses of carrying a coffin down narrow stairs could be eliminated. Most bungalows were vernacular structures built without expensive architects; therefore, building a bungalow saved money. Plans and variations were widely published in the last years of the nineteenth century by builders' magazines and ladies' journals. Patented building materials were available as well as prefabricated units.

Of course, it was not long before the bungalow moved across the Atlantic and took root in the United States, or, one might say, was reinvented in California. An early bungalow was built in 1895 near San Francisco by A. Page Brown, who had introduced the Mission style at the Columbian Exposition. It was the well-known California architects, the brothers Charles and Henry Greene, who were major contributors to the popularity of what was called the "California bungalow." In spite of an association with the Greenes, the bungalow usually had little to do with important architectural offices. Frederick Hodgon wrote in 1906, "The little bungalows . . . are rarely designed by architects. . . . They are . . . the sort of thing that the ordinary California country carpenter knows how to build [as a] result of a popular tradition." Fanning out from California throughout the United States, the bungalow gradually replaced regional architectural styles and became the first nationwide suburban vernacular. (See page 139.) Pattern books and sets of working drawings could be purchased for as little as five dollars. The availability of precut lumber and detailing made it possible for bungalows to be assembled quickly by local carpenters and builders. One result was that identical bungalows could be found hundreds of miles apart. Rapid transportation by rail of uniform parts, standard heating systems, and air-conditioning, insulating materials, and electric lighting later reduced the importance of climate and locally available materials in determining design.

The bungalow reached its maximum growth in the years between 1900 and 1930. Marcus Whiffen has said that if compelled to choose a single bungalow type, the example would have two broad gables facing the street: "the gable of the porch-veranda in front echoed by the body of the house behind and to one side." Although bungalows are rarely spoken of as relatives of Frank Lloyd Wright's Prairie style houses, they, nevertheless, shared many of the same features. They were built to spread out horizontally, not to accent vertical lines. Emphasis was placed on practical everyday living and on the recognition that the servant class that had once performed the household tasks was vanishing. For greater convenience built-in furniture was designed. The quality of materials was important, but at the same time the need to make use of machine-produced materials was acknowledged. The garage was included in the plans as a necessity of a new age. The admission of light and a view of the garden, accompanied by an ample porch, were characteristics of both the Prairie style house and the bungalow.

In the years before the Second World War, the romantic appeal of a cottage in the country in the midst of the disappearing wilderness and the mournful howl of coyotes offered less attraction to West Texans than the desire to move into town. As children grew up and left the ranches and farms for other states and countries, a smaller house in a pleasant community was an ideal solution for older couples. The bungalow was modest in appearance, stressed convenience, and was built on property owned by the individual. It was close to other families, dispelling the loneliness that existed when there were miles between one farm and the next. One of the most curious characteristics of West Texas towns to newcomers from the East or Midwest is the way in which lots are crowded close to one another and backyards are enclosed by high fences. In many parts of the country where there is less vacant land on which to spread out, suburban homes are built on large lawns separated from neighbors not by fences but by shrubbery. Children play from yard to yard, unless instructed by parents that certain lawns are off limits. If a fence is built between backyards, it is customarily handled with the tact associated with upper echelon diplomacy and the assurance that a gate will give easy access. The price of real estate is sometimes offered as a reason for small lots that force houses to rub elbows. In the 1920s and 1930s, when tumbleweeds blew into town and piled up

Bungalow on Huff Avenue (1920s), Wichita Falls

House at 406 Bevans (1890s), Menard

like desicated snowmen and lawns used up the supply of water, small yards may have made sense. But it seems more likely that in some obscure part of the pioneer memory, there was a need to be close to people after enduring the isolation of land unrelieved by close contact with other humans.

By the 1920s in some parts of the country, the bungalow and the escape to the suburbs had taken on a sentimentality expressed in song. Bix Beiderbecke in an RKO Recording from about 1928 spun out a ditty that crooned:

> Far from the city
> Somehow it seems
> We're sitting pretty in
> Our bungalow
> Of dreams.

The bungalow was often dominated and distinguished by its porch. One of the variables in design was the treatment given the supports for the porch roof with its ample overhang. These supports might be short square columns resting on massive piers, or pedestals, which began at the foundation. In other instances, they rose from the porch balustrade and had "battered" sides, that is, the shape tapered toward the top from a wider base. Some porches had a projecting portico. In the case of a Fort Worth bungalow, the entry was flanked by coupled columns that supported a vault fitting neatly beneath the clipped gable of the roof. There was no particular material favored by bungalow owners. Bungalows were built from brick, concrete, concrete block, wood, stucco, or stone; false half-timbering was frequently applied as decoration.

The use of decorative timber was an offshoot of the Stick style, associated with both Queen Anne and Tudor revivals. Neither revival displayed a high regard for historical accuracy. A Queen Anne house in Menard illustrates the use of stick work for bracketing under the eaves. Applied to mansion and bungalow, stick decoration had its origins in the half-timbering of the Middle Ages. But in the nineteenth- and twentieth-century application, the original functionality had been lost, and the timber was nothing more than applied design with little or no structural integrity. The most elaborate examples of the style had a tendency to occur where wood was abundant, particularly in the Northwest and on the

Bungalow at 1816 Hurley (1920s), Fort Worth

Business block (1920s), northeast corner of Broadway and University, Lubbock

Pacific Coast. In West Texas, patterns were restrained. A Fort Worth bungalow on Hurley Street limited the design to the pediment above the porch. The stick details, painted white, are joined by a gray stucco fill.

The Tudor style was not limited to domestic architecture. It was applied to tearooms and filling stations, dentists' offices and pharmacies. In Lubbock, across from the Texas Tech University campus, a block of shops with half-timbered Tudor gables and elaborate (and nonfunctioning) chimneys has sheltered generations of students.

The old rhyme "sticks and stones may break my bones" might be revised to read "sticks and stones may *house* my bones." The popularity of the stick vogue was matched by richly textured stone walls. To West Texans, stone houses were known by the colloquialism *rock*. Found throughout the region, the rock house was a vernacular expression applied with particular zest during the 1920s and 1930s to bungalow construction.

The individuality of rock houses, which at first glance seems to blur into monotonous sameness, depends upon the selection of the stones, the way in which they are put together, and the textures and colors. A rock house at Junction (see page 141) is constructed of rough

Rock house (1930s), Junction

Rock house at 217 South Washington (1930s), San Angelo

cobblestones, projecting irregularly from the mortar. At 217 South Washington in San Angelo, a porch with a clipped gabled roof conveys the impression of an entry into a grotto. The walls on either side are designed to give the appearance of having been effected by time and weather. Some stones project above the surface which is set randomly in what is called "puzzle" or "cobweb" rubble. (See page 142.) The question seems to be, Wouldn't it be fun to collect a house?—that is, the stones from which to build it, stones with extraordinary shapes, like pudding stones and stone wasp nests. A Lubbock house on Fifteenth Street displays a smoothly cut lone star inserted in the rough wall surface.

Like half-timbered designs, rock structures were adaptable. Storefronts and tourist courts were built with a flare for the unusual. There is a rock motel in Sierra Blanca and a ruin of what appears to have been a motel in Early. (See page 142.) Little is left standing in Early but the indestructible arches, which look as if they might have been put together by a disciple of Antonio Gaudi.

WHILE THE owners of rock houses displayed their geological finds cemented into the walls of their homes, other families, after the end of the First World War, were anxious to build spacious mansions inspired by a wide selection of styles from various historical periods. The eclectic smorgasbord offered a menu gathered from the Nile River to the Seine, including the Italian and Spanish Renaissance and Spanish Colonial styles—everything but the kitchen sink.

In Laredo, there is an unusual example of Renaissance Revival occupying a corner lot at 1512 Matamoras.

(See page 143.) It was built about 1924 for Rosa de Benavides, inspired by the design of the home of Dr. F. R. Canseco and his wife Margarita Zambrano Berardi. The Canseco home had been finished a year or two earlier. Before moving to Laredo, the Cansecos had lived in France, where Dr. Canseco lectured at the Sorbonne. It is said that the doctor had been charmed by a detail at the Palace of Versailles, though it seems more likely that it may have been the Grand Trianon with its pink marble. He wished to build his new home in a similar manner. Whatever the case, Dr. Canseco purchased some stone-cutting machinery in France and had it shipped to Laredo to ensure that the stonemasons could cut the stone as he wished it for his new residence on Chihuahua Street. Captivated by the appearance of the Canseco home, Rosa de Benavides asked if she might have a house constructed in the same manner. The kind doctor appears to have offered no obstacles and also loaned her the stone-cutting equipment. Surrounded by the wrought-iron fence, the house with its pink rusticated stone trim is handsome and not precisely what might be expected in West Texas.

Trost also turned his attention to the use of Spanish Renaissance details. Early in the settlement pattern of West Texas, businessmen and entrepreneurs had understood the value of the hotel in attracting settlers and profitable business to the region. The need for luxury hotels did not diminish, and at El Paso, the gateway between the north and Mexico, the firm of Trost & Trost led the way in creating designs for such projects. The Hotel Paso del Norte was opened to receive guests in 1912. (See page 144.) The fashionable hotels of the period were usually rectangular in plan and built with a light well, often beginning at the third floor to allow expansive

Detail, puzzle rubble (1930s),
Lubbock

Motel (1930s), Early

space for a two-story lobby. This was the manner in which the El Paso del Norte was planned. The arched windows above the sidewalk on the San Antonio Avenue side of the building are elegantly detailed with modillions acting as keystones and wreathed motifs in the Renaissance fashion. The building is brick with white marble at the lower stories and repeated as a decorative trim for a tenth floor added to contain the ballroom. An interesting feature of the lobby is a stained glass dome that may be a product of the Tiffany studios, though there is no documentary evidence. The lobby also has the only known sculpture signed by Henry Trost. This is a round plaque over the registration desk depicting an Indian and a Spanish friar. In retrospect the hotel seems to have been a harbinger of the Spanish Colonial style, which was the successor of Mission design.

The Spanish Colonial style, or Spanish Eclectic as it was also called, was popular from about 1915 until the 1940s. Although it spread to other parts of the country, it was always at home in the Southwest. Its origin is credited to Bertram Grosvenor Goodhue, a California architect who had studied Spanish Colonial buildings extensively. Goodhue was chief architect of the Panama-California Exposition held in San Diego in 1915. The thousands of visitors who poured into the exposition grounds to celebrate the opening of the Panama Canal were introduced to the seductions of the most elaborately conceived influences of Mexican Baroque architecture, which reached a feverish peak in Goodhue's California Building. Spanish Colonial Revival harvested design motifs and fragments from the entire history of Spanish architectural design: architecture that took root in the centuries of Moorish domination in Spain; architecture from the Renaissance with its richness of patterns that contributed the term *plateresque* (borrowed from the work of silversmiths); architecture from the baroque period, associated with the Churrigueresque style and committed to emotional dramas in sculpture for flamboyant ecclesiastical monuments; and *tequitqui*, architectural improvisations on Spanish Colonial design by native workmen inserting Indian motifs. The Spanish Colonial style was far more faithful to historic examples than the Mission style had been. After World War I, travel to Europe became the way to spend a vacation. The itinerary often included Spain and then led back across the Atlantic to Mexico and South America,

Rosa de Benavides House at 1512 Matamoras (1924), Laredo

Hotel Paso del Norte (1912), corner of North El Paso and West San Antonio, El Paso

Paramount Theatre (1932), Abilene

La Rita Theater (1929), Dalhart

where firsthand information could be absorbed about Spanish post-Columbian architecture.

By 1925, Spanish Colonial or Spanish Eclectic had become a craze. Its popularity was enhanced by Hollywood where Latin stars were matinee idols—Delores del Río, Ramon Navarro, and the exotic Rudolf Valentino who had introduced the tango in *The Four Horsemen of the Apocalypse*. Movie "palaces" chose appropriate imagery for south-of-the-border romance.

A movie theater in West Texas that adopted a Hispanic format was Abilene's Paramount. Designed in 1932 by George Castle, an Abilene architect, the tan brick exterior is ornamented with large panels of brightly colored terra cotta placed along the parapet. Designs alternate coats of arms with medallions containing helmets, swords and other paraphernalia associated with the Spanish conquerers. At either end of the frieze, there is a false balcony with a curving wrought-iron balustrade. A theater of less grand scale but with picturesque Hispanic influence is at Dalhart. La Rita (1929) has a rosy brick facade with a white trim. At the upper level, a diaper pattern of slightly raised brick forms a

background for three windows separated by twisted semiattached columns.

The Spanish Colonial Revival was both popular and versatile in its adaptability to many building types. With an earlier interest in the Mission style, it is not surprising to discover that Henry Trost directed his design skills to the new vogue and that he succeeded brilliantly. In 1918 just before the end of the war, Trost drew up plans for Hotel El Paisano in Marfa. Work was not begun, however, for ten years. When it was completed in 1930, the sculptural design framing the main entrance possessed a boldness that suggested a transformation from the more refined plateresque idiom that Trost used earlier to a fully realized baroque grandeur. (See page 135.) During the years while El Paisano waited in the wings, Trost was at work on the eleven-story Hotel Cortez in El Paso. (See page 147.) The hotel was known, when it first opened in 1926, as the Orndorff; then as the Hussmann, and finally, in keeping with the impact of Spanish Colonial design, as the Cortez. The plain beige brick walls provide a foil for the intertwining relief patterns at the street level. In sculptured bands above the ground floor there are rondels with the heads of conquistadors projecting from the circles. (See page 147.) The possible sources for the portrait heads are interesting to explore.

An early Renaissance use of the motif was incorporated by Ghiberti in the design of the baptistery doors at Florence. But there are also Spanish Renaissance examples: encircled heads standing out in sculptured relief decorate the entry portal at the Casa de las Muertes at the University of Salamanca; similar heads with religious identities are present at Salamanca's Convent of San Esteban. Far from Renaissance Spain, in 1891 Chicago, there was an alignment of terra cotta heads of German culture heroes pushing from the circles decorating Adler and Sullivan's Schiller Building. Brendan Gill has suggested that the heads were "probably designed by Frank Lloyd Wright." Trost was listed in the Chicago city directory as early as 1889, and the Englebrechts, in their study of Trost's architecture, state that the young man would most likely have been in the Adler & Sullivan office sometime between 1891 and 1892. How amusing if the idea for the heads at the Cortez were less Spanish Colonial than a remembrance of Sullivan, Wright, and the Chicago days.

There is a building in downtown Stamford that is so much like the decorative work applied by Trost to the Cortez that it begs for an investigation of the architect's identity. At present it serves as the office for West Texas Utilities and is located at 120 South Swenson. (See page 148.) There are three entries separated by piers, each with a central panel of cast-relief in a design of urns and scrolls. The architrave has shield designs that alternate with heads in low relief confined by circles.

Heads staring down from round frames are also a feature of the administration building at Texas Tech University. From the building's north wall, portraits of historical figures survey the changing campus. (See page 148.) This first building of the new college and the conquest of the the windswept South Plains by the Spanish Renaissance were simultaneously initiated in 1924. By 1926, the administration building (see page 148) stood finished but as isolated as El Escorial, while students walked along unpaved paths, picking up an occasional arrowhead. William Ward Watkin, founder and dean of the School of Architecture at Rice Institute, had been placed in charge of the master plan and the design of Texas Technological College. In the 1920s, he was

one of those who had been drawn to Spain where he discovered a strong kinship with the architecture of the sixteenth century. When the opportunity to design a new campus on the flat South Plains arose, he was struck by the relation between the landscape of central Spain, with its seasonal aridity, its starkness, its burning sun and clarity of light and the dry land and overwhelming sky of West Texas. His choice of the Spanish Renaissance style for the new college was not a whim. In the *Campus Bulletin,* at the request of Tech's first president, Dr. Paul Whitfield Horn, Watkin explained his choice of a historic prototype. He wrote:

> In its architecture, "Texas Tech" is carrying on the traditions of the early architectural history of the State. That tradition is recorded in the old Spanish missions. This style of Spain which was the background of the missions in Texas, was one of the most impressive and inspiring of Europe. The architecture of Spain in the middle of the 16th century, as one sees it in such examples as Leon, Alcala de Henares, Salamanca, and Toledo, carr[ies] the simple splendor of the wall more for robust and at the same time for artful work than is characteristic of the other countries of western Europe in their periods of Renaissance. . . . The great table lands of west Texas upon which the buildings of the new college are being built have a likeness in color and character to the table lands of central Spain, and this group of college buildings . . . can carry the early traditions, fittingly tying-in the bond of tradition, the old history and the new, the past, the present and the hope for the future.

The concept for the administration building was in a general way influenced by the sixteenth-century city hall in Spain and more particularly the University of Alcala de Henares. The materials chosen for the building, as well as for the campus, were tawny brick with tones ranging from light brown to darker shades. These were not laid in a rigid pattern but were blended together in a random arrangement. Mission, or Spanish (barrel), tile with its warm colors was used as the roof covering. The stone for the trim came from Leuders in Jones County. It was relatively soft and not difficult to work. Where stone was subjected to unusual wear and abrasion, Bedford limestone was shipped from Indiana.

(Above and below right) Hotel Cortez (1926), northeast corner of North Mesa Street and Mills Avenue, El Paso

Detail, Hotel Cortez, El Paso

West Texas Utilities (1920s), Stamford

(Detail above and below) Administration Building (1926), Texas Tech University, Lubbock

Following the Spanish example introduced by the Moors into Spain, smooth wall surfaces were used, strengthening the contrast provided by the intricacy of the plateresque decoration that dramatized doorways and windows.

Symbolic sculpture was an important requirement that appealed to Tech's first president. Dr. Horn was committed to underscoring his goals for Texas Tech with likenesses of great men of the past and memorable quotations. A phrase of Mirabeau B. Lamar's, chiseled in stone, reads, "Cultivated mind is the guardian genius of democracy. It is the only dictator that freemen acknowledge, the only security freemen desire." In keeping with this dictum, carvings of ten important historical figures were placed between the double arched windows at the second level of the north facade. These heroes ranged from Columbus to Davy Crockett, Washington to Lee, and, of course, a bow to James Hogg and Sam Houston. No women were included. After all, they had only had the vote for a few years. The encircled heads were done at about the same time that Trost was placing Spanish explorers on the outer walls of the Cortez.

The south facade of the administration building looked out on a courtyard. Here carved panels were decorated with urns and torches intertwined with references to Janus and pairs of grotesque beasts in a pattern of scrolls, vines and foliage. (See page 150.) It is also claimed that there is a cartoon head of Ward Watkin (see page 151.) by Ruth Young McConigle, the first woman graduate in architecture from Rice Institute and an employee in Watkin's Houston office. Her pencil was responsible for much of the detailing, which gave interest and graceful accents to the first building program of Texas Tech's architecture.

Across the long grassy axis from the administration building, the textile engineering building anchors the north end of the plan. The entrance is one of the finest examples of plateresque detail and Spanish Colonial Revival design on the campus. (See page 151.) Instead of the deadening effect of the north light, which falls over the facade of the administration building, the southern sunlight creates a complex relief intensified by dark shadows. The entry arch is bordered by a half circle of small cusped arches. The carving on the semiattached columns is made up of swags and crisp acanthus leaves. On either side of a second-story window above the

arched entry there are two niches, usually a retreat for saints who look down benignly. Here the university substituted two stylized bales of cotton, symbols of the cotton growers and textile workers. The legendary Rose Window at the Mission of San José in San Antonio may have suggested the design for the opening above the second-story window. At the top of the parapet, a stone urn and carved knobs stand out against the sky.

On the west side of the lawn between the administration and textile engineering buildings, the West engineering building took its place in the 1920s building program. The design element emphasized was an arcaded *portal* stretching along the entire facade. This could have been borrowed from a cloister court or from the shaded promenade around a part of the Plaza Mayor in Salamanca. The central arch pushes out slightly from the shadowy walkway and leads into the passage between the two wings of the building. At the upper level above the arched entrance there is a balcony crested with stone cupids holding shields whose heraldic designs represented the disciplines taught: civil, mechanical, and electrical engineering and architecture, a department chaired by Florian Kleinschmidt, an ardent champion of the Beaux-Arts' system of education. (See page 152.)

For anyone in the 1920s seeing the campus for the first time, nothing could have seemed more lacking in logic than a "technological" college in the Bible Belt where students—children of hardy, self-sufficient pioneers—walked to class in cowboy boots and Levis beneath the arched portals and towers of sixteenth-century Spain, a country at the very heart of Catholicism, the Inquisition, and monarchy. But flip the coin to the opposite side. In an atmosphere of bone-bare brick walls, would the teaching of the arts and sciences, engineering, and agriculture have been as balanced without this reminder of history and the South Plains' heritage from Spain and Mexico? Did the Renaissance and baroque spirit plant subconsciously a graciousness of mind as students were blown to class in a whirl of dust? Did this incongruous setting in a cotton patch carry the imagination to distant lands where someday bodies would follow? Does an architectural setting help to determine or modify lives?

For better or worse and for several decades, the Spanish Colonial Revival, sparked by the university, and the

Detail, Administration Building (1926), Texas Tech University, Lubbock

Textile Engineering Building
(1926–1927), Texas Tech
University, Lubbock

Detail, Administration Building
(1926), Texas Tech
University, Lubbock

West Engineering Building (1926–1927), Texas Tech
University, Lubbock

Lubbock High School (1930), Nineteenth Street, Lubbock

tan brick used ad infinitum, rubbed off on many Lubbock buildings. Lubbock High School, one of the most
handsome, was designed in 1930 by by W. L. Bradshaw.

The Spanish Colonial Revival spread throughout the
South Plains as an appropriate style for municipal buildings. It possessed a monumentality that added dignity
to a city center, and it reflected the pride of a region that
was associated with the lore of Coronado's march
across the Llano Estacado and of the cowboys' debt to
the Mexican *vaqueros.* There must have been a wish,
too, to express the character of towns, not yet fifty years
old, in a way that would underscore the phenomenal
transition from unpaved streets lined with box-and-
strip stores to thriving cities with an appreciation of
world culture and the value of education. The choice of
Spanish Colonial architecture can never be considered
entirely apart from the factor of climate—the many days

of sunlight that bring out every nuance of plateresque scrolls and curves and the gleam of colored tile. In a rainy climate or one where fog is frequent, the subtle details of ornament would be blurred and lost.

Wherever municipalities craved elegance, Spanish Colonial Revival could be found. The Big Spring Municipal Building was built in 1932 by Peters, Strange, and Bradshaw. Beige bricks and a tile roof enclose an auditorium and city offices. The auditorium is the dominant feature, suggesting, just as the opera houses of an earlier period did, the concern of the townspeople with obtaining programs to enrich life away from large metropolitan centers. Of the municipal buildings adopting the Spanish Colonial style, one of the most successful is a similar arrangement of city hall combined with an auditorium in Wichita Falls. (See page 154.) Its date is 1927; it was built under the design and supervision of Lang, Witchell, Voelcker and Dixon. There is a splen-

didly designed octagon possessing a sophistication that reoccurs in the pleasing scale and detailing around the entrances to the auditorium.

Laredo is an excellent place to look for the link that relates the exuberance of the Spanish Renaissance with the new style of the 1920s known as *art moderne*. A building that serves this purpose is the Hamilton Hotel. Heroic measures are currently being taken to preserve this landmark. In brief, its beginnings go back to the mid-1880s, a time when Laredo was enjoying a railroad boom and many Mexican citizens were coming across the border to escape the revolution. The first hotel on the present site was a three-story Victorian structure that was partially preserved when a larger seven-story addition was constructed in 1923. Five additional stories were added in 1928. (See page 155.) The corner tower and tile roof are Spanish Colonial. A comparison, however, with Trost's Cortez Hotel in El Paso presents an en-

City hall and auditorium (1927), Wichita Falls

Detail, City hall and auditorium (1927), Wichita Falls

tirely different treatment given the outer walls. There is no plateresque sculpture encrusting doors and windows. Instead the wall surfaces are flatter and depend upon the patterns and color added by glazed tiles. The use of tile is typical of both Mexico and Spain, but here the design is not strictly traditional. Borders of black, olive, blue, peach, and beige frame mosaics at the second level and outline the arches above the street. Between the arches, tiles in pastel colors are glazed and joined together to represent large stylized figures of eagles. The eagle is a symbol for the countries both north and south of the Rio Grande.

The Texas eagle, a scrawny bird carved sometime before 1845, according to Elinor Horwitz, was inspired less by the Great Seal of the United States than by the Mexican legend that explains the Aztecs' choice of an island on Lake Texcoco as the site for their capital, Tenochtitán. The wanderers had been directed by the sun god to travel until they saw an eagle perched on a cactus plant with a snake held in its talons and a berry in its mouth. This symbol is now on the flag of Mexico. Aside from legends associated with eagles, the birds on the glazed tile at the Hamilton Hotel are harbingers of a change introducing a more stylized and colorful decor— Art Deco of the 1920s.

Hamilton Hotel (1923), Laredo

8

Art Deco in West Texas

*Birds have justly been the messengers between the skies above
and the earth. . . . Birds are associated with transformation.
Transgressing the limits of humans, they seem to be special
messengers of prayers. . . . One bird, probably the eagle,
was transformed by legend into the Great Thunderbird. . . .
"Great birds in the sky, wrapped in clouds," according to
Indian legends, bring rain with the thunderheads,
but also sow death, hurling thunderbolts . . .
The thunderbird is a powerful mythological presence.*

Carla Breeze, from *Pueblo Deco*

THE NEW STYLE, Art Deco, as it was later called, swept into West Texas on eagle wings, partly as a heritage from the popular thunderbird sign of the New Mexican Indians (see page 156) and partly as a patriotic symbol at the close of a war won for democracy. During the 1930s, the eagle would blaze on postage stamps as a reminder of the National Recovery Administration initiated in 1936 by Franklin D. Roosevelt and of new hope for an end to the years of the Depression.

The eagle had little to do, however, with the origins of the new *art moderne*. The style's beginnings, like so many other explosions, was partly the result of an international exposition. This time Paris was the fountain-head, and the event was L'Exposition Internationale des Arts Décoratifs et Industriels Modernes. The glittering display was held in 1925. Submissions, which included furniture, textiles, ceramics, glass, metal, and many other contemporary products, were to have no traces of historic influences. Modern ideas, functionality, new materials, and machine products were sought. In spite of this, there were still some older designers who rewarmed past motifs, leaning lightly on neoclassicism. The avant-garde sent tremors rippling through the viewers with their synthetic fabrics printed in brilliant colors with cubist designs. Experiments with molded glass, chrome tubing, and aluminum attracted attention. If historic copyism was taboo, designs inspired by the recent discoveries of Howard Carter in Tutankhamen's tomb, bold motifs from native art, or the sets and costumes of the Ballet Russe were acceptable. A major contribution of the exposition was the use of reinforced concrete in the exhibition buildings. Concrete was already a part of commercial building construction in Europe and America, but in Paris at the exposition simple masses, streamlined design and the values of machine produced materials were graphically illustrated in the exhibition pavilions.

The United States was not represented by an exhibit at Paris; but delegates were sent to observe the innovations and report to the American public. The following year, in 1926, a traveling show of pieces from the exposition was organized and circulated in a few American museums. Three years later, the Metropolitan Museum organized a show with the title "The Architect and the International Arts: An Exhibition of Contemporary American Design." For the Metropolitan show, eight

Cottle County Courthouse (1930), Paducah

American architects were asked to mount room settings with furniture and accessories indicating the progress of industrial products and machine production incorporated into architecture in the United States. The new manner, which originated in Paris and became the rage on this side of the Atlantic, was called art moderne (or modernistic, a word that quickly took on derogatory connotations, perhaps because of the popularity it enjoyed in shoddy Hollywood set design). It was not until the late 1960s that the term Art Deco was invented as a title for a book by British art historian Bevis Hillier. Art Deco captured the brassy, jazzy atmosphere of the twenties, gaining instant popularity and quickly erasing art moderne from the working vocabulary.

Today, the Art Deco image invokes bobbed hair, short skirts, cigarettes, and powder puffs; sleek greyhounds and less-than-sleek raccoon coats, cocktails, and speakeasies; saxophones and jazz; and world fairs and streamlined engines. It also invokes the "dressing" for two decades of skyscrapers and tall office buildings. It is true that some tall buildings preferred to lift touches of Gothic up to the clouds. But reinforced concrete, steel, and glass lent themselves to decorative zigzags and chevrons, abstract flowers and arcs. Deco was the ally of hard edges, high polish, and the products of industry. The zigzagging lines and points of skyscrapers rising in layered terraces above the streets hidden in dark canyons called for designs produced with a compass and straight edge in homage to industrial growth and "a century of progress."

It must be pointed out immediately that Art Deco of the 1920s and 1930s did not exert an influence on the structural development of architecture. The setbacks associated with tall buildings were not deliberately created on the drawing board but were the result of zoning ordinances (passed in New York City as early as 1916) requiring high rise structures to move back in stages toward a pyramidal top thus allowing some penetration of light and air for humans on the streets far below. Art Deco was responsibile for a distinctive style of ornament that introduced a different and *moderne* look. It made use of glazed terra cotta, aluminum, stainless steel, chromium plating, etched or frosted glass, glass brick, and bronze. Stripped of the decorative details, an Art Deco building would have looked like any other commercial building of the period.

Machine-made products were used in unexpected combinations and textures. Colors, as well as logos of offices and shops, were influenced by flashy billboards and neon advertising. The glittering effect was dramatized by gold and burnished metals and by slabs of polished stones. From the eagerness with which the opulence of Art Deco was grasped, it is apparent that the United States was not ready for the asceticism of Walter Gropius and Le Corbusier.

Art Deco was spread throughout the forty-eight states by its association with business. Large corporations opened branches in smaller towns and specified the designs for the building programs from a central office located in a metropolitan center. The day of regional architecture was passing rapidly. The same name brands appeared on grocery shelves whether in Kansas City or Amarillo. Similar labels were found on clothing, and familiar ads assured the public. "Once camels carried wisemen, now wise men carry Camels." The Burma Shave signs strung along highways from Maine to California made driving less tedious with teeth-grinding jingles. For example:

> Henry the Eighth
> Prince of Friskers
> Lost five wives
> But kept his whiskers
> Burma-Shave.

Art Deco migrated to the hinterlands from New York and Chicago and Los Angeles by way of Kress stores, oil companies, utilities, railroad stations, hotels, and movie theater chains. It came to West Texas like the breath of spring with a chain of logos featuring a nymph with torch and caduceus in either hand balanced on a globe labeled the "Spirit of Progress." (See page 159.) Having read too many ads for Coty or Roger and Gallet powder, the poor girl's complexion is pure white—glazed enamel—as she cavorts over a green-glazed background. Throughout the Panhandle, these chaste maidens performed their aerobics on the parapets of stores whose facades were covered with a veneer of ivory tile.

It is impossible to discuss Art Deco without pausing to look more closely at terra cotta, which became the material of choice for a building's exterior, a primary material for ornamental details, and a covering for interior walls and even floors. Its advantages were legion. It was fireproof; maintenance was simple; broken pieces could

Terra cotta Art Deco design, "Spirit of Progress" (1930s), Brownwood

be replaced. The glazed and fired clay, when compared with carved marble and granite, was more than cost-efficient, and the price per design unit was reduced in proportion to the number of pieces to be duplicated. Clay was malleable and could provide crisp edges or subtle detail. Most of all, at a time when bright colors had entered the architectural vocabulary, the available range of hues seemed unlimited. The colors did not fade, and the need to repaint every year or two was eliminated. A colorful and unexpected terra cotta facade for a restaurant, theater, store, or other commercial enterprise was worth its weight in advertising. Hundreds of patterns to mix or match could be ordered from the catalogs published by terra cotta manufacturers. If architects wished to design their own ornament, their designs could be cast in the numbers required.

One of the architects whose Art Deco work continues to draw attention and praise is Edward F. Sibbert, the architect/designer for Samuel H. Kress Company. Between 1929 and 1954, the years Sibbert worked for

Kress, he designed more than two hundred stores. Carla Breeze writes in *Pueblo Deco* that of these, more than thirty are either on the National Register of Historic Places or in designated historic districts. One of the most grandiose designs is the S. H. Kress Building at Oregon and Mills streets in El Paso. (See page 161.) It is dated 1937. This building (as well as several others included in *Dugout to Deco*) falls outside this text's time frame, but it is worth relaxing the rules to observe the development and versatility of Art Deco at its best. Like Trost, Sibbert was a master at adapting motifs from other cultures—in this instance, Spain and Mexico—and making them his own. In the Kress Building, Sibbert used a Spanish rope motif around windows, wrought-iron balconies, and insets of decorated tile closely related to Hispanic designs and colors. Finials spaced along the parapets are drawn from Moorish patterns embellished with baroque fancies. Attention is unerringly carried to the boxlike tower that rises above the roof. (See page 160.) It seems to relate to the *mirador,*

(Opposite and detail above) Kress Building (1937), Oregon and Mills streets, El Paso

an observatory or porch located on the roofs of colonial houses in New Spain. The walls of the cube are covered with colorful repeated patterns of tile, but this is no protected spot for dark eyes to look down at the street below. Instead it conceals the mechanical equipment. The flamboyance of the Deco style was admirably suited to the layered cultures of the border city.

A few years earlier, in 1934, Sibbert had designed a Kress store for Lubbock that was totally unlike the El Paso building. The three-story brick facade is faced with a pale butter yellow terra cotta. The parapet has a handsomely scalloped detail at the center connected by

moldings with smaller baroque features at either end of the roofline. It has been compared, with more humor than accuracy, to a rephrasing of the parapet of the Alamo. The central crest displays the word KRESS which appears to be metallic gold terra cotta, the result of a technique "involving the melting of metals onto the tiles in a second high temperature firing." One of the more amusing flights of imagination is the resemblance between the molded brackets holding the tie-rods (bracing for the canopy that extends over the sidewalk) and heads of Hereford cattle. (See page 162.)

Theaters were at the center of the Art Deco style, from the signs glowing with light bulbs or neon above a small-town movie house in Spur (see page 162) to an example of Deco's glory days in El Paso. El Paso's Colon is one of Texas' best 1930s movie theater designs. It has remained virtually unknown. (See page 162.) Another cinema worthy of preservation is the former Wichita Falls opera house, which was funded by public subscription in 1908. The first play presented was *His Honor, the Mayor*. Its boards supported the oratory of William Jennings Bryan, the ballet slippers of Pavlova, and the portly figure of Madam Schumann-Heink. It was remodeled for silent pictures and a player piano in the 1920s. Unlike the sumptuous motion picture palaces flooded with streamers of neon, this is the Zen of the Deco style. (See page 163.) Circles and half circles in red and black decorate the marquee and are repeated in the paving as well as on the ticket window. The design is closer to Malevich than to Radio City.

As early as 1900 in New York City, electricity was flowing "into nearly 1,500 incandescent lamps arrayed on the narrow front of the Flatiron Building to form America's first electrically lighted outdoor advertising sign." Movie marquees illuminated the night after the war, and added color to Main Street America. Electric lightbulbs were soon joined by neon. Like Art Deco, neon was introduced to the United States by the French, more specifically, in 1923 by the firm of Georges Claude. Surprisingly, despite the attention directed to industrial techniques at the L'Exposition des Arts Decoratifs, there is no mention of neon. This suggests that handicrafts, though no longer quite respectable, were still exerting their weight in the realm of design philosophy. Until very recently, neon was considered too brash and too commercial—a vernacular manifestation. Rudi Stern's *Let There Be*

(Top left) Kress Building
(detail) (1934), Lubbock

(Top right) Palace Theatre
(1930s), Spur

Colon Theatre (1930s),
El Paso Street, El Paso

Old opera house (now a movie theatre) (1930s), Tenth and Indiana, Wichita Falls

U Drop Inn Cafe (1930s), Routes 40 and 83, Shamrock

Neon led the way in a reevaluation of the role played by neon design. He noted, "Neon . . . became symbolic of American energy and inventiveness, its Continental roots giving rise to a spectacular flowering of American showmanship in the late 1920s and early 1930s."

Neon is associated with nightclubs and honky-tonk joints as well as with filling stations and cafés. These popular places for local entertainment were the scene of Folk Deco. Clocks and beer signs and nickelodeons radiated with neon tubes and "modernistic" chrome and leatherette. A filling station–café in Shamrock is Deco at its most amusing. The emphatic vertical textures of the station walls climax with a tower—Heaven forbid, a parody of the Choraigic Monument of Lysicrates in Athens—holding a green flower like a tripod at its apex. It is assumed that this is a symbolic shamrock. Adjoining the gas station and repeating the vertically striated design is the U Drop Inn Cafe. It, too, has a monument

like an athletic trophy rising from an octagon inscribed *CAFE*. The slender pole holds what might be mistaken for a basketball for leprechauns.

In West Texas, Art Deco was not always the exclusive possession of commercial enterprises. The style was considered suitable for public buildings and courthouses. One of the most interesting courthouses, designed by Voelker and Dixon, was built in 1930 for Cottle County in Paducah. Its brick-veneered walls, particularly the buttresses at the entries, suggest a Sumerian ziggurat whose upper terraces have eroded. The sculpture increases the atmosphere of the ancient Tigris-Euphrates valleys. The two figures framing the entrance have Babylonian facial characteristics and robes with wavelike patterns common in Babylonian sculpture (see page 165.). This symbolism is not necessarily misplaced when one remembers Hammurabi and his Code of Laws, written, of course, in an arid land. An

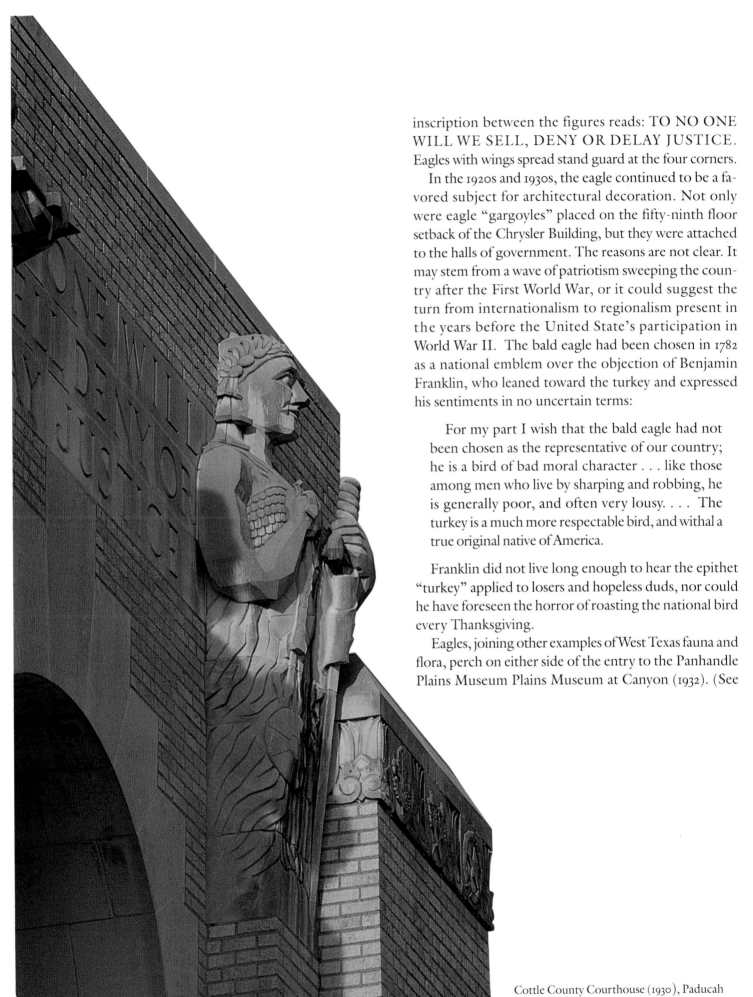

inscription between the figures reads: TO NO ONE WILL WE SELL, DENY OR DELAY JUSTICE. Eagles with wings spread stand guard at the four corners.

In the 1920s and 1930s, the eagle continued to be a favored subject for architectural decoration. Not only were eagle "gargoyles" placed on the fifty-ninth floor setback of the Chrysler Building, but they were attached to the halls of government. The reasons are not clear. It may stem from a wave of patriotism sweeping the country after the First World War, or it could suggest the turn from internationalism to regionalism present in the years before the United State's participation in World War II. The bald eagle had been chosen in 1782 as a national emblem over the objection of Benjamin Franklin, who leaned toward the turkey and expressed his sentiments in no uncertain terms:

> For my part I wish that the bald eagle had not been chosen as the representative of our country; he is a bird of bad moral character . . . like those among men who live by sharping and robbing, he is generally poor, and often very lousy. . . . The turkey is a much more respectable bird, and withal a true original native of America.

Franklin did not live long enough to hear the epithet "turkey" applied to losers and hopeless duds, nor could he have foreseen the horror of roasting the national bird every Thanksgiving.

Eagles, joining other examples of West Texas fauna and flora, perch on either side of the entry to the Panhandle Plains Museum Plains Museum at Canyon (1932). (See

Cottle County Courthouse (1930), Paducah

Panhandle Plains Museum (1932), Canyon

Entry, Panhandle Plains Museum

Detail, Panhandle Plains Museum

page 166.) The architect was E. F. Rittenberry. The carvings were the work of sculptors employed by Texas Quarries, Inc., of Austin. Once again heads project from circles; this time the heads are those of animals—a coyote, a jackrabbit, a buffalo, and a pronghorn. The cornice line is decorated by a swag of prickly pear. Between the scallops of the plants, cactus flowers are carved like decorative buttons. In sharply chiseled intaglio, an Indian and a cowboy face off on the piers flanking the entrance. A recessed door is surrounded by squares, each corraling a brand from a Panhandle ranch. Presiding over these symbols is the head of a Texas longhorn. (See page 166.)

The ornament at the Panhandle Plains Museum represents human, animal, and plant life on the Llano Estacado. In contrast, the Public Market in Fort Worth reveals little about the city or the market. It was built in 1930 by an Oklahoma developer who employed architect D. Gaylord Noftsger. This hybrid design, intermingling Churrigueresque with Art Deco, formerly housed a farmers market and retail shops. The spaces are now taken over by Cadillac Plastics and small businesses. Approaching the site, a tall corner tower of tan brick in the Spanish Colonial Revival style attracts attention. Beneath the pinnacle capped with a tile roof, a long narrow stained glass window is filled with an abstract pattern of squares and rectangular shapes in the Art Deco manner. The doorway is introduced by columns whose spiral shafts and capitals end in elaborate finials. Placed over the door, the background of the tympanum is laid with wine-colored tiles against which a polychrome relief of drinking horns filled with vines and grape clusters embrace a Greek vase decorated with bacchanalian dancers. (See page 168.) One amusing discovery may be made on a capital of an attached column close to the door. Among the acanthus leaves is the head and torso of a man wearing a beret. He looks worried and holds calipers that rest on a scroll. He is obviously an architect. Is it a likeness of *the* architect? (See page 168.)

The inclusion of a probable portrait of another architect as a signature is a mark of the O. T. Bassett Tower in El Paso. Above the entrance, there is a face resembling a medieval mason. Tradition identifies this face as that of Henry Trost. (See page 169.) The curling moustache and keen eyes bear a marked resemblance to those in photographs of the architect. The sixteen-story Bassett Tower, built 1929–1930, found Trost at age seventy

Public Market (1930), Fort Worth

trying his hand at Art Deco. (See page 170.) During the same time, he was occupied with the Luhrs Tower, a similar Art Deco project in Phoenix. The arrangement of setbacks and hipped roofs are closely related in both tall buildings. In Phoenix, beneath the attic story a Sullivanesque sequence of circular windows with Art Deco designs perpetuates the memories of the conquistadores. Helmeted heads and armored torsos in green terra cotta cap the piers. The smooth stucco finish of the Luhrs Tower accentuates the play of sunlight and shadow of the desert climate. In contrast, the Bassett Tower has a veneer of tan brick. Strong vertical piers increase the feeling of height. At the entrance, Greek borrowings are translated into Art Deco design. A sculptural frieze alternates triglyphs with metopes that are decorated with masks. The moldings beneath the frieze contain a

Public Market (1930), Fort Worth

Detail, Public Market, Fort Worth

O. T. Bassett Tower (1929–1930), northeast corner of East Texas Avenue and South Stanton, El Paso

repeated pattern of acanthus leaves. (See page 171.) The clever *moderne* disguise hides the identity of the motifs unless they are carefully studied. The Basset Tower may be Trost's finest monument. It is, in a sense, autobiographical: there are influences of the Classical Revival of the architect's youth, the powerful memory of lessons learned from Sullivan, and the vigorous pioneering effort in the use of reinforced concrete all synthesized with a grand gesture toward a new idiom—Art Deco. The Bassett Building was Trost's last work in El Paso; he died at age seventy-three on 19 September 1933.

The times had already gone awry. The stock market crash in 1929 cast a pall of gloom over the country. In West Texas, the Depression was worsened by years of drought that turned the landscape into the Dust Bowl of the 1930s. The exuberance and optimism of the Roaring Twenties faded and with it the glamour and excesses of Art Deco. On 16 June 1933, Franklin D. Roosevelt won approval for the National Industrial Recovery Act, and shortly afterward, the Public Works Administration came into being. West Texas, as well as the country generally, was the beneficiary of building programs that in-

cluded courthouses, post offices, schools, fire stations, police stations, and other public buildings. The architectural solutions, stripped of gaudy ornament, concentrated on dynamic functionalism, a product of the machine age. Everyday appliances were repackaged for more efficient performance. Architecture was stripped to achieve maximum utility. Corners were cut and replaced by flowing curves; glass block walls added a new look. Le Corbusier called the house "a machine for living in," though this phrase was never meant as it has been interpreted. Aerodynamic design allowed cars to move faster without the impediments of sharp angles and protruding fenders. Airflow trains gained momentum as did travel by plane and dirigible. The "good life of the future" was dramatized by Chicago's Century of Progress Exposition 1933-1934. Buzz words were function, utility, Buckminster Fuller, and Buck Rogers.

"FUNCTION determines form," "New materials for a new society," "Every age must free itself from the past"—these were the messages sent after 1930 from the German Bauhaus and the European International style. These ideas carried out in steel and concrete devoid of ornament began to filter into the awareness of Americans and to exert an influence on the curricula of the schools of architecture throughout the country. The Museum of Modern Art in New York extolled modern architecture. In 1932, Henry-Russell Hitchcock, Jr., with Philip Johnson published *The International Style: Architecture Since 1922.* After the Nazis closed the Bauhaus, in the early 1930s, important European architects, artists, and craftspersons sought asylum in the United States. Walter Gropius was invited to teach at the Harvard Graduate School of Architecture. Mies van der Rohe went to the Armour Institute in Chicago, which under Mies's guidance became the Illinois Institute of Technology. The belief he preached almost as an article of faith was that aesthetically satisfying products would be the result of designs dictated by function and mass produced by the machine. Everything from toothbrushes to architecture would become available to everyone at affordable prices. The corollary was that if the environment for work and play was improved by freeing people from inappropriate designs from the past and by substituting functional and, therefore, handsome spaces for living, people would become more civilized, more productive, and happier. Unfortunately, this idealistic experiment was interrupted by the disasters of war. When World War II ended, the world had changed.

A change that has taken place in the last few decades has been the rediscovery of the past—now called "finding one's roots." The new look at history has given a fresh exuberance to the work of some Post-Modern architects. This has not led to copying the past but to an artful reinterpretation of it often laced with humor. Another facet of the new respectability of historic architecture has been to increase the growing interest in the preservation and/or restoration of architecture of earlier generations—structures often in danger of being wantonly torn down to make space for parking lots and high-rise offices. Preservation in the best sense is not directed toward a building because it is old but because it is a good or memorable example of a style that can inform a community about its development and history. Many buildings are rehabilitated to serve useful functions as well as those that are preserved as cultural and historic landmarks.

Having come of age in little more than a century, West Texas architecture has only just reached the point of joining the ranks of bona fide antiques; therefore, its past is still on the surface for those who are willing to look, to perceive, and to discover. The historic process is fresh and vigorous and visible. The evidences of the rapid growth are marked in still-existing dugouts (an occasional one still inhabited); adobe, picket and sotol, and box-and-strip houses; in stores and railroad sta-

(Above and opposite) O. T. Bassett Tower (1929–1930), El Paso

tions; in white churches at a country crossroads; in stone on brick and concrete on Main Street, courthouse squares, and on boulevards of stately homes.

Human memory dims; records are destroyed; history is subject to the whims of revisionism. It is in the solidity of artifacts and in architecture that an answer is contained to the age old question, Where did we come from? Walls speak of protection, of the values held, the hopes dreamed; walls illustrate the rotation from function to fashion and back again. And nowhere do walls speak to the present more clearly than in West Texas, where the past is only a step away and waits to become a part of the future.

An old-timer on the High Plains allowed, "This country can promise less and deliver more than anywhere on earth." This fits West Texas like a handmade boot. It is not just the size, measured by the gigantic spread of acres or the spirit of the pioneers and their descendents; it is the unexpected richness imprinted on an architectural heritage that records the struggle to make a lonesome land a home.

Notes

Chapter 1
In the Beginning, the Open Range

2 *According to the U.S. Census* Della Tyler Key, *In Cattle Country: A History of Potter County* (Wichita Falls, Tex.: Nortex Offset Publications, 1972), p. 9.

2 *Five years later* T. R. Fehrenbach, *Lone Star* (New York: Collier Books, 1985), p. 554.

2 *In 1876, a law was passed* Key, *In Cattle Country*, p. 9.

2 *At the end of the next four years,* Ibid.

3 *This was later mis-translated* Herbert E. Bolton, *Coronado* (Albuquerque: University of New Mexico Press, 1990), p. 243.

3 *The country where* Ibid., pp. 253–254.

3 *Another member of the* Ibid., p. 254.

3 *The description resembles* See W. C. Holden, "Indians, Spaniards, and Anglos," in *A History of Lubbock,* ed. Lawrence Graves (Lubbock: West Texas Museum Association, Texas Technological College, 1959), pp. 23 25.

3 *During the two days we watched* W. C. Holden, *Rollie Burns* (College Station: A&M Univ. Press), pp. 21–22.

3 *Evidence of this approaching* Pauline D. Robertson and R. L. Robertson, *Cowman's Country* (Amarillo: Paramount Publishing, 1981), p. 19.

3 *A year later Thomas* Key, *In Cattle Country*, p. 15.

4 *In 1882, he sold* Robertson and Robertson, *Cowman's Country*, p. 71.

4 *Early in the winter* Key, *In Cattle Country*, p. 20.

4 *The property was held* Ibid., p. 22.

4 *It was stipulated* Robertson and Robertson, *Cowman's Country*, p. 157.

4 *It is not an exaggeration* Fehrenbach, *Lone Star*, p. 608.

4 *He writes, "Say Texas anywhere* Fehrenbach, *Lone Star*, p. 554.

4 *"A six-shooter and a fast* Robertson and Robertson, *Cowman's Country*, p. 45.

4 *The brief period of the open* Walter Prescott Webb, *The Great Plains*

(New York: Grosset and Dunlap, 1971), p. 222.

5 *It was 250 miles* Robertson and Robertson, *Cowman's Country*, p. 19.

5 *A Texas cowboy named* William H. Forbis, *The Cowboys* (New York: Time-Life Books, 1973), pp. 91-92.

6 *Rollie Burns, quoted earlier* Holden, *Rollie Burns*, p. 182.

6 *He added, "The rain* Ibid., p. 184.

6 *He wrote, "When the roof* Everett Dick, *The Sod-House Frontier (1854–1890)* (Lincoln: Johnsen Publishing, 1954), p. 115.

6 *The cost was as follows* Ibid., p. 112.

7 *On the Goodnight land* Robertson and Robertson, *Cowman's Country, p.* 19.

7 *The Adairs left after a few* Ibid., p. 24.

7 *The improvements at the* Ibid., p. 29.

11 *He read the north, south* Forbis, *The Cowboys*, p. 82.

11 *The amount may seem* Philip Ashton Rollins, *The Cowboy* (Albuquerque: Univ. of New Mexico Press, 1979), p. 168.

11 *Christian said, "The hoot* Forbis, *The Cowboys*, p. 92.

11 *Studebaker sold chuck* Ibid., p. 150.

12 *While on the trail* Andy Adams, *The Log of a Cowboy* (Lincoln: Univ. of Nebraska Press, 1964), pp. 23–24.

12 *They had to become familiar* John A. Kouwenhoven, *Made in America* (New York: Doubleday, 1962), p. 14.

12 *Rollins points out that the vest* Rollins, *The Cowboy*, p. 110.

12 *According to Rollins* Ibid., p. 129.

Chapter 2
Windmills, Barbed Wire, and Rails

15 *For homesteaders, gambling* Jan Blodgett, *Land of Bright Promise* (Austin: University of Texas Press, 1988), p. 4.

16 *The device that came* Pauline D. Robertson and R. L. Robertson, *Cowman's Country* (Amarillo: Paramount, 1981), p. 50.

16 *In 1882, such well-drilling* Ibid., p. 51.

16 *In 1883, he requested* Ibid.

16 *The plains would have never* George E. Hancock, *Go-Devils, Flies and Black-eyed Peas,* (Corsicana, Tex.: George E. Hancock, 1985), pp. 29–30.

18 *Even historians have grown* Walter Prescott Webb, *The Great Plains* (New York: Grosset and Dunlap, 1971), p. 319.

18 *In 1883, Goodnight installed* Robertson and Robertson, *Cowman's Country,* p. 50.

18 *During 1884–1885, he led* Ibid., p. 27. J. Evetts Haley in *Charles Goodnight* (Norman: University of Oklahoma Press, 1979) writes that "in 1881 and 1882, the T Anchor put up the first big enclosure, fencing in two hundred and forty acres of grass, with posts eighty feet apart, so that when mustangs and antelopes hit the fence full tilt, the wires would 'give' considerably instead of breaking" (p. 321).

18 *Goodnight's barbed wire* Ibid.

18 *The smooth wire was useless* Webb, *The Great Plains,* p. 299.

19 *Whatever the case may* Ibid., p. 300.

19 *The new concept in* Ibid., p. 301.

19 *The importance of barbed* J. Evetts Haley, *Charles Goodnight* (Norman: University of Oklahoma Press, 1979), p. 322.

19 *In his writing, Webb emphasized* Webb, *The Great Plains*, p. 317.

19 *Of all of the advantages* Haley, *Charles Goodnight*, p. 320.

20 *The first railroad to cross* Della Tyler Key, *In Cattle Country: A History of Potter County* (Wichita Falls: Nortex Offset Publications, 1972), p. 32.

20 *The tracks moved on* Ibid., p. 35.

20 *Land near the present city* Ibid.

20 *This raggle-taggle camp* Amarillo Historic Building Survey and Preservation Program Recommendations, compiled by Charles Page and Associates (Amarillo: N.p., 1981), p. 16.

20 *The article further enlightened* Della Tyler Key, *In Cattle Country,* pp. 42–43.

20 *Shortly after the votes* Ibid.

20 *At this point, the officials* Ibid., p. 46.

20 *She described with* Ibid., p. 50.

21 *Having taken this step* Ibid., p. 77.

21 *At the same time he pointed* Ibid.

21 *Some residents stubbornly* Ibid., p. 80.

21 *In June 1899 the new* Ibid., pp. 81–82.

21 *Another strong point* Ibid., p. 82.

21 *This was opened for* Ibid., p. 78.

21 *It was named, without benefit* Ibid.

21 *Sometime late in the fall* Ibid., p. 81.

21 *Finally late in the spring* Ibid.

21 *The parklike area* Ibid.

21 *The yellow brick Commercial* John C. Dawson, *High Plains Yesterdays* (Austin: Eakin Press, 1985), p. 58.

21 *hot water and baths* Ibid., pp. 60–61.

22 *This void was filled* Ibid., p. 58.

22 *Both stairways led* Ibid., pp. 58–59.

22 *Consider the ad* Ibid., p. 59.

22 *If intellectual fare was lacking* Ibid.

22 *Jan Blodgett observed in her* Blodgett, *Land of Bright Promise*, p. 1.

22 *Dr. W. C. Holden has* William C. Holden, "Immigration and Settlement in West Texas," *West Texas Historical Association Yearbook 5* (June 1920):72–73.

23 *A requirement, according to* Blodgett, *Land of Bright Promise*, p. 13.

23 *Readers were urged to* Ibid., p. 23.

23 *Hereford's Commercial Club* Ibid.

23 *Then, with an uncanny* Ibid., p. 28.

23 *Could this be the same land* Ibid., p. 7.

23 *With a respect for honesty* Ibid., p. 6.

24 *In the beginning, railroad stations* Carroll L. Meeks, *The Railroad Station: An Architectural History* (New Haven: Yale University Press, 1964), pp. 27–28.

24 *Although many changes* Lawrence Grow, *Waiting for the 5:05* (New York: Main Street/Universe Books, 1977), p. 11.

24 *Andrew Jackson Downing's best seller* Andrew Jackson Downing, *Victorian Cottage Residences* (1873; reprint, New York: Dover, 1981), p. 16.

24 *In the 1852 edition of his* Rural Grow, *Waiting for the 5:05*, p. 12.

24 *In warm weather* Ibid., p. 13.

24 *Displaying a typical* Ibid.

25 *The architect was Louis Curtiss* Fred T. Comee, "Louis Curtiss of Kansas City," *P/A*, (August 1963):132.

25 *He had gone to Paris* Ibid., p. 129.

25 *In 1906, Curtiss was* Ibid., p. 132.

25 *As Brendan Gill has phrased* Brendan Gill, *Many Masks* (New York: Ballantine Books, 1988), p. 161.

25 *A clear indication of the* Comee, "Louis Curtiss," p. 132.

25 *On the upper part of the west* The *History of the Achison, Topeka, & Santa Fe*, ed. Pamela Berkman (Greenwich, Ct.: Brompton Books, 1988), pp. 29–30.

25 *It reads, "I will go* Comee, "Louis Curtiss," p. 128.

25 *It was the offshoot* John Leeds Kerr, *Destination Topolobampo* (San Marino, Calif.: Golden West Books, 1986), p. 50.

25 *In 1900, at a banquet* Ibid., p. 48.

25 *San Angelo, hoping to* Ibid., p. 69.

27 *Albert T. Camfield* Craig Alan Drone, "The Station at San Angelo," (Master's thesis, College of Architecture, Texas Tech University, 1989), p. 94.

27 *The second floor* Ibid., pp. 117–118.

27 *Completed in 1910, the* Ibid., p. 112.

27 *The tower was capped* Ibid., p. 106.

27 *The KCM & O passed* Ibid., p. 119.

27 *Craig Drone in his study* Ibid., p. 169.

27 *A typical station of this type* Meeks, *The Railroad Station*, p. 73.

27 *Carroll Meeks has observed* Ibid.

28 *Unlike the landing at which* Grow, *Waiting for the 5:05*, p. 8.

Chapter 3
Box-and-Strip: West Texas Vernacular

32 *The term* vernacular Bernard Rudofsky, *Architecture without Architects* (New York: Museum of Modern Art, 1965).

32 *John Deodat Taylor changed* John A. Kouwenhoven, *Made in America* (New York: Anchor Books, 1962), p. 50.

32 *The label was so apt that* Ibid.

32 *He pointed out that* Ibid., p. 49.

32 *On 17 August 1889, the paper* John L. McCarty, *Maverick Town* (Norman: University of Oklahoma Press, 1988), p. 232.

33 *A few months later* Ibid., p. 233.

33 *There was something about* A. C. Greene, *A Personal Country* (College Station: Texas A&M University Press, 1979), pp. 117–118.

34 *Mary Hampton Clack, who* Pioneer *Days—Two Views* (Abilene, Tex.: Zachry Associates, 1979), from "Miss Tommie's Recollections," presented by Kathryn Duff and Betty Kay Seibt, p. 72.

34 *A year later she saw* Ibid.

34 *He recalled, "Mother took* King County: *Windmills and Barbed Wire*, compiled and edited by the King County Historical Society (Quanah, Tex.: Nortex Press, 1976), p. 216.

34 *Miss Tommie Clack's Pioneer Days*, p. 151.

35 *Miss Tommie also* Ibid.

35 *They were sometimes mounted* See Seymour V. Connor, "The New Century," in *A History of Lubbock, part 1*, ed. Lawrence Graves (Lubbock: West Texas Museum Association, Texas Technological College, 1959), p. 100.

35 *Covering a window* Glenda Riley, *The Female Frontier* (Lawrence: University of Kansas Press, 1988), p. 88.

35 *A lack of insulation* Joe Pickle, *Gettin' Started: Howard County's First Twenty-Five Years* (Burnet, Tex.: Nortex Press, 1980), p. 254.

35 *Then, all that was necessary* Ross Edwards, *Fiddle Dust* (Denver: Big Mountain Press, 1965), p. 27.

36 *There were usually three tubs* George Hancock, *Go-Devils, Flies and Black-eyed Peas* (Corsicana, Tex.: Private Printing, 1985), p. 67.

36 *(Interestingly, Joe Pickle* Pickle, *Gettin' Started*, p. 254.

36 *The house was 'L' shaped* David L. Caffey, *The Old Home Place: Farming on the West Texas Frontier* (Burnet, Tex.: Eakin Press, 1981), p. 57.

39 *The trouble was* Ibid., pp. 58–59.

41 *The outhouses I have* Jim W. Corder, *Lost in West Texas* (College Station: Texas A&M Press, 1988), pp. 21–22.

42 *Caffey described adolescent* Caffey, *The Old Home Place*, p. 28.

42 *In the period after it was completed* See Seymour V. Connor, "The Founding of Lubbock," in *A History of Lubbock*, part 1, ed. Lawrence Graves, (Lubbock: West Texas Museum Association, Texas Technological College, 1959), p. 85.

42 *A society notice informed* Ibid.

43 *Plans were submitted to* Ibid., p. 82.

43 *From it a cupola rose* Ibid., p. 86.

43 *The walls were resquared* Gary Wesner, "Courthouse Changes Reflect County's Growth, Economy," *Lubbock Avalanche-Journal,* 10 March 1991, 2C.

43 *On Saturday night* Connor, "The Founding of Lubbock," p. 86.

43   *Mrs. Nonnie Rogers* Charles Didway, ed., *Wagon Wheels: A History of Garza County* (Seagraves, Tex.: Pioneer Book Publisher, 1973), p. 98.

43   *By the last years of the 1890s* Connor, "The Founding of Lubbock," p. 86.

44   *One participant in a group* Virginia Browder, *Hall County Heritage Trails* (Canyon, Tex.: Staked Plains Press, 1984), 2:11.

44   *Two sources of local* Connor, "The Founding of Lubbock," p. 84.

44   *This was a subscription school* Pioneer *Days*, p. 174.

44   *Miss Tommy explained* Ibid., p. 205.

44   *Children were often told* Didway, *Wagon Wheels*, p. 139.

44   *Merchandise boxes provided* Lore and Legend Mitchell County, (Colorado City, Tex.: *Colorado Record*. 1976), 1:49.

47   *They may have been top-string* Didway, *Wagon Wheels*, p. 77.

47   *Desks had been ordered* King County, p. 105.

47   *But before there were schools* Bill Neal, *The Last Frontier: The Story of Hardeman County* (Quanah, Tex.: Quanah Tribune-Chief, 1966), p. 57.

47   *The first sermon was* Lore and Legend, p. 50.

47   *Next morning, sure enough* Neal, *The Last Frontier*, p. 61.

48   *Her son wrote of his* Max Coleman, *From Mustanger to Lawyer*, (Lubbock, Tex.: Max Coleman, 1960), 1:126.

48   *Sad to say, Sallie Coleman died* "A historic structures report on St. Paul's on the Plains Episcopal Church" was assembled and written by a class in architectural preservation under the guidance of visiting professor S. Elizabeth Sasser, AIA, during the fall of 1989. See p. 23.

48   *Although the building was not* Ibid.

48   *It was noted that a member* Ibid. pp. 23–24.

48   *Mary Elizabeth Randal* Ibid., p. 32.

48   *Joe Pickle reminds a younger* Pickle, *Gettin' Started*, p. 225.

49   *In the evenings, "lanterns* Ibid.

51   *If there was a podium* Ibid., p. 223.

51   *He continued, "Music* Ibid.

51   *Henrietta Nichols called* Didway, *Wagon Wheels*, pp. 52–53.

51   *According to David Caffey* Caffey, *The Old Home Place*, pp. 28–29.

51   *Where brush was needed* Didway, *Wagon Wheels*, p. 53.

51   *West Texas is like the Biblical* Greene, *A Personal Country*, pp. 127–128.

Chapter 4
Box and Strip Meets Queen Anne

53   *Four decades later, however* Andrew Jackson Downing, *Victorian Cottage Residences* (1873; rpt. New York: Dover, 1981), pp. 1–2.

53   *To West Texans living* Ibid., pp. 4–5.

53   *Russell Lynes, in* Russell Lynes, *The Tastemakers* (New York: Harper & Brothers, 1955), pp. 108–109.

54   *The result was a legacy* John Maass, *The Victorian Home in America* (New York: Hawthorn Books, 1972), pp. 140–141.

54   *Maass, reassessing what* Ibid., p. 141.

55   *When translated into English* John Maass, *The Gingerbread Age* (New York: Bramhall House, 1967), p. 64.

55   *In Switzerland, fretwork* Ibid., p. 65.

55   *At the Philadelphia* Maass, *Victorian Home*, p. 141.

56   *One ad announced* Maass, *The Gingerbread Age*, p. 101.

56   *A few examples include* Elizabeth Pomada and Michael Larsen, *Daughters of Painted Ladies* (New York: E. P. Dutton, 1987), p. 144.

62   *The 1907 footed bathtub* Jane Knapik, *Uvalde Heritage Homes* (Uvalde, Tex.: N.p., 1976), p. 58.

62   *The new generation of* Ibid., p. 54.

62   *Perhaps to unnerve his* Ibid., p. 52.

62   *One account relates that* Ibid.

62   *Reception rooms, hall and* Ibid., pp. 30–31.

63   *Alexis de Tocqueville* Alexis de Tocqueville, *Democracy in America*, trans. Henry Reeve (London: Oxford University Press, 1952), p. 325.

63   *The color of buildings may* Downing, *Victorian Cottage Residences*, pp. 13–14.

64   *He favored the picturesque* Roger W. Moss and Gail Caskey Winkler, *Victorian Exterior Decoration* (New York: Henry Holt, 1987), p. 19.

64   *These ready-mixed colors* Ibid., p. 15.

64   *As early as 1861* Ibid., p. 20.

64   *By the 1880s, Wadsworth* Ibid., p. 23.

67   *A comment on the Fretwell's* History of Erath County, comp. Erath County Historical Commission (Dallas: Taylor Publishing, 1980.), p. 45.

69   *Louis Sullivan, Chicago's* Louis H. Sullivan, *The Autobiography of an Idea* (New York: Peter Smith, 1949), pp. 324–325.

69   *One of the first concrete* A Time to Purpose, ed. Mrs. Ralph E. Randall and the Carson County Historical Survey Committee (Carson County: Pioneer Publishers, 1966), 2:258–259.

70   *The ground floor* Ibid., p. 259.

70   *Above the date, there* Jon Irwin, "The Hayden [Potton] House," *Texas Architect*, 21 (September 1971):18–19.

71   *In 1904, five years* Ann Ruff and Henri Farmer, *Historic Homes of Texas* (Houston: Lone Star Books, 1987), p. 10.

71   *It is reported that a sign* Ibid.

71   *The part played by electric* Carl L. Avera, *Wind Swept Land* (San Antonio: Naylor, 1964), p. 35.

72   *The streets for two* Ibid., pp. 46–47.

72   *The crowning feature* Ibid., p. 54.

74   *A veranda reaches* Herbert Gottfried and Jan Jennings, *American Vernacular Design—1870–1940* (New York: Van Nostrand Reinhold, 1985), pp. 112–113.

Chapter 5
Main Street: From Hitching Post
to Horseless Carriage

77   *I walked up town* A Time to Purpose: Carson County, ed. Mrs. Ralph E. Randel (Panhandle: Pioneer Publishers, 1966), 2:306–307.

78   *A. Richard Williams* A. Richard Williams, *The Urban Stage: A Reflection of Architecture and Urban Design* (Champaign, Ill.: Superior Printing, 1980), p. 83.

79   *You can come into Albany* A. C. Greene, *A Personal Country* (College Station: Texas A&M University Press, 1979), pp. 166–167.

81   *He wrote that people* A History of Erath County (Lubbock: Craftsman Printers, 1980), p. 108.

81   *The district courtroom might* Willard B. Robinson, *The People's Architecture* (Austin: University of Texas, 1983), pp. 102–133.

83   *The cornerstone was a symbol* Ibid., pp. 152–153.

84 *In Weatherford, a brother* Greene, *A Personal County*, p. 39.

84 *"Nowhere outside of the* Marcus Whiffen, *American Architecture Since 1780: As Guide to the Styles* (Cambridge: MIT Press, 1969), p. 167.

88 *A fifty piece orchestra* Lore and Legend: *Mitchell County* (Colorado City: *Colorado City Record*, 1976), pp. 84–85.

88 *Add to these libations* Ibid.

88 *An enthusiastic Memphis* Virginia Browder, *Hall County, Heritage Trails*, (Canyon: Staked Plains Press, 1984), 1:355.

89 *One reason for the change* Virginia and Lee McAlester, *A Field Guide to American Houses* (New York: Alfred A. Knopf, 1986), p. 345.

92 *The house begun in 1903* Judy Alter, *Thistle Hill* (Fort Worth: Texas Christian University Press, 1988), p. 2.

92 *This "honeymoon cottage,"* Ibid., p. 3.

92 *The decorations were* Ibid., pp. 10–11.

95 *As soon as Thistle Hill* Ibid., p. 17.

96 *To preserve the city's sanity* Ibid., p. 12.

96 *When encountering a vehicle* Inez Baker, *Yesterday in Hall County, Texas* (Memphis, Tex.: N.p., 1940), p. 61.

96 *Colorado City issued* Lore and Legend, p. 153.

96 *(The first licensing of a car* Ibid.

96 *A native, living near Post,* Charles Didway, ed., *Wagon Wheels: A History of Garza County* (Seagraves, Tex.: Pioneer Book Publishing, 1973), p. 130.

97 *If the numerous shootings* Bill Neal, *The Last Frontier: The Story of Hardeman County* (Quanah: *Quanah Tribune-Chief*, 1966), p. 207.

97 *The tower, which was open* Robinson, *The People's Architecture*, pp. 141, 144.

98 *A child would have* A Time to Purpose, p. 259.

98 *One customer, remembering* Ibid.

99 *In Hall County in the spring* Baker, *Yesterday*, p. 68

99 *The county's first cotton gin* Ibid.

99 *In those days the "seed* Ibid.

99 *A machine shop, hotel* Didway, *Wagon Wheels, p. 7.*

100 *Gasoline engines were* Ibid., p. 9.

100 *This was the first plant* Ibid., p. 8.

100 *Post, until the end of his life,* Jack Maguire, "The Cereal That Won the West" (photocopy distributed by Post Chamber of Commerce; N.p., n.d.).

100 *According to the account* Neal, *Last Frontier*, p. 205.

100 *"The theatre was open week-day* Ibid.

100 *He said, "I got scared* King County: *Windmills and Barbed Wire* (Quanah: Nortex Press, 1976), p. 203.

100 *Another moviegoer in those* H. G. (Grady) Perry, *Grand Ol' Erath,* (Dublin, Tex.: N.p., 1974), p. 174.

101 *This was "sometime before* Virginia Browder, *Donley County* (Clarendon, Tex.: Nortex Press, 1975), p. 260.

101 *Admission to a one-reel* Oliver Knight, *Fort Worth* (Fort Worth: Texas Christian University Press, 1990), p. 157.

101 *new brick buildings* Lore and Legend, op. cit., p. 85.

101 *"Long tents were the only* Neal, *Last Frontier*, p. 109.

101 *One who saw the parades* Browder, *Donley County*, p. 250.

101 *The one and only hotel* Neal, *Last Frontier, p. 196.*

102 *He prepared his white elephant* M. R. Werner, *P. T. Barnum* (London: Jonathan Cape, 1923), p. 354.

102 *James J. Corbett and John L.* Knight, *Fort Worth*, p. 157.

102 *It goes like this: "One of the* V. Browder, *Donley County*, p. 250.

Chapter 6
South to the Rio Grande

105 *He observed, "A bush of ocotillo* Paul Horgan, *The Heroic Triad* (Austin: Texas Monthly Press, 1987), p. 13.

107 *In Langford's words* J. O. Langford with Fred Gipson, *Big Bend* (Austin: University of Texas Press, 1986), p. 51.

107 *For ten dollars, Cleofas* Ibid., p. 63.

107 *Such stones were also* Ibid., pp. 64–65.

107 *This was the total outlay* Ibid., p. 65.

107 *Langford explained* Ibid., p. 78.

107 *As in the earlier room* Ibid., p. 106.

108 *For him, the sotol plant* Ibid., p. 27.

108 *When the picket and sotol* The Ranching Heritage Center: The Museum of Texas Tech University (Lubbock: Texas Tech University Press, 1976), p. 24.

108 *In Carson County in 1880* A Time to Purpose: Carson County, ed. Mrs. Ralph E. Randel (Panhandle: Pioneer Publishers, 1966), 2:60.

109 *When Mary Hampton* Mary Hampton Clack, "Early Days in West Texas," in *Pioneer Days . . . Two Views* (Abilene: Zachry Associates, 1979), p. 82.

109 *Langford, upon arriving* Langford, *Big Bend*, p. 34.

111 *Susan Magoffin continued* Susan Shelby Magoffin, *Down the Santa Fe Trail and into Mexico*, ed. Stella M. Drumm (Lincoln: University of Nebraska Press, 1982), p. 104.

111 *In 1850, James Wiley Magoffin* Lenore Harris Hughes, *Adobe Adobes* (El Paso: Hughes Publishing, 1985), p. 69.

111 *Instead of selecting the* Ibid., p. 70.

113 *Today, the scoring* Portals at the Pass, ed. Evan H. Antone (El Paso: El Paso Chapter of the American Institute of Architects, 1984), p. 12.

113 *The work was done by* Ysleta del Sur Pueblo Community Building, from *Texas Architect* (October 1971): 7–8.

113 *The present church* A Catalogue of Texas Properties in the National Register of Historic Places, comp. James Wright Steely (Austin: Texas Historical Commission, 1984), p. 56.

113 *To add to the confusion* Lenore Harris Hughes, *Holy Adobe* (El Paso: Hughes Publishing, 1982), p. 96.

113 *The death of Saint Anthony* Ibid.

113 *The dance is led by the Tribe's* Ibid.

114 *Reconstructed in the nineteenth* Portals at the Pass, p. 3.

114 *An early guidebook, which* Texas: A Guide to the Lone Star State (New York: Hasting House, 1940), p. 563.

114 *Persuaded that the saint* Hughes, *Holy Adobe*, p. 93.

117 *There is an unusual graveyard* Ibid.

117 *The town of San Elizario was* Ibid., p. 99.

117 *San Elizario as it appears* Portals at the Pass, p. 7.

118 *The "Queen of Gingerbread"* For further information, see *From Hacienda to Bungalow* by Agnes Lufkin Reeve (Albuquerque: University of New Mexico Press, 1988), pp. 126–130.

122 *Designed by John J. Stewart* Portals at the Pass, p. 15.

124 *Many of El Paso's most gracious* Lloyd C. and June-Marie Engelbrecht, *Henry C. Trost: Architect of the Southwest* (El Paso: El Paso Public Library Association, 1981), p. 3.

124 *The elder Trost kept a grocery* Ibid.

125 *After attending classes* Ibid.

125 *At the age of twenty* Ibid., p. 4.

125 *The eight years that Trost* Ibid., pp. 4–8. These pages provide a discussion of Trost's career in Colorado, Texas, and Kansas and his return to Chicago.

126 *Marcus Whiffen accepts this American Architecture since 1780* (Cambridge: MIT Press, 1969), p. 206.

126 *The account observed* Englebrect and Engelbrecht, *Trost*, p. 11

126 *One of his sketches, published* Englebrecht and Engelbrecht, Ibid.

126 *The sketch was for a "wrot* Ibid.

126 *Back of this Spanish mission style* Ibid., pp. 117–118.

127 *After a brief and productive* Ibid., p. 32.

127 *Brown refused to bow* Whiffen, *American Architecture*, p. 214.

127 *The smoothly plastered* Ibid., p. 213.

129 *Turney was born in Marshall* Englebrecht and Engelbrecht, *Trost*, p. 39.

130 *The Engelbrechts were* Ibid., p. 44.

132 *The story is told that* Portals at the *Pass*, p. 25.

132 *To make this possible, the city's* Englebrecht and Engelbrecht, *Trost*, p. 50.

132 *The interest of the public* Ibid., p. 51.

132 *With silent films in mind* Ibid., p. 61.

132 *After the fire, she conceived* Ibid., p. 64.

132 *This might have remained* Ibid.

133 *But insisting on the last* Ibid., p. 67.

133 *These include, "the low* Ibid., p.68.

133 *El Paso American Institute* Portals at the *Pass*, p. 48.

Chapter 7
The 1920s: Bungalows and Eclectic Borrowings

136 *Just as cattle and grain* Roger M. Olien and Diana Davids Olien, *Life in the Oil Fields* (Austin: Texas Monthly Press, 1986), p. 35.

137 *As Judge Orland L. Sims put it* Judge Orland L. Sims, *Cowpokes, Nesters, and So Forth* (Austin: Encino Press, 1970), p. 202. A slightly different account is given on a historic marker located beside Santa Rita #2.

137 *They were a hard-working* Ibid., p. 206.

137 *"Bing" Moddox, who* Olien and Olien, *Oil Fields*, p. 6.

137 *They respected self-reliance* Ibid., p. 35.

137 *In seventeenth-century India* Anthony D. King, *The Bungalow* (London: Routledge & Kegan Paul, 1984), p. 9.

137 *The rooms were surrounded* Ibid., p. 14.

137 *The title* bungalow *was* Ibid., p. 34.

137 *Anthony King referred to* Ibid., p. 65.

138 *The morbid thought* Ibid., p. 95.

138 *An early bungalow was* Marcus Whiffen, *American Architecture since 1789* (Cambridge: MIT Press, 1981), p. 219.

138 *It was the well-known California* Ibid., pp. 218, 219.

138 *Frederick Hodgson wrote in 1906* King, *The Bungalow*, p. 154.

138 *Marcus Whiffen has said* Whiffen, *American Architecture*, p. 217.

139 *Far from the city* King, *The Bungalow*, p. 127.

141 *Some stones project* Herbert Gottfried and Jan Jennings, *American Vernacular Design—1870–1940* (New York: Van Nostrand/Reinhold, 1985), p. 29.

141 *The kind doctor appears to have* Gloria Canseco provided the information on the Canseco House in an interview 6 May 1991 in Laredo.

143 *An interesting feature* Lloyd C. and June-Marie Engelbrecht, *Henry C. Trost: Architect of the Southwest* (El Paso: El Paso Public Library Association, 1981), p. 63.

143 *In retrospect the hotel seems* Ibid.

143 *Goodhue was chief* Ibid., p. 71.

145 *The hotel was known, when* Ibid., p. 72.

146 *Far from Renaissance Spain* Ibid.

146 *Brendan Gill has suggested that* Brendan Gill, Many Masks: *A Life of Frank Lloyd Wright* (New York: Ballantine Books, 1987), p. 107.

146 *Trost was listed* Engelbrecht and Engelbrecht, *Trost*, p. 11.

146 *William Ward Watkin* Nolan E. Barrick, *Texas Tech: The Unobserved Heritage* (Lubbock: Texas Tech Press, 1985), p. 10.

146 *In its architecture* Ibid., pp. 18, 19.

146 *The concept for the* Ibid., p. 29.

146 *Where stone was subjected to* Ibid., pp. 19, 20.

149 *A phrase of Mirabeau B.* Ibid., p. 23.

149 *These heroes ranged* Ibid., pp. 24, 25.

149 *It is also claimed that* Ibid., p. 28.

149 *At the upper level above* Ibid., p. 35.

153 *Five additional stories* From information recorded about the Hamilton Hotel history by Gale Alder (1981) for the Webb County Heritage Foundation, Laredo, Texas.

155 *The wanderers had been* Elinor Lander Horwitz, *The Bird, the Banner, and Uncle Sam* (Philadelphia: J. B. Lippincott, 1976), p. 50.

Chapter 8
Art Deco in West Texas

157 *Concrete was already a part* Judith Singer Cohen, *Cowtown Moderne* (College Station: Texas A&M Press, 1988), pp. 8–10.

157 *The following year, in 1926* Ibid., p. 10.

157 *For the Metropolitan show* Alastair Duncan, *American Art Deco* (New York: Harry N. Abrams, 1986), p. 25.

158 *It was not until the late 1960s* Ibid., p. 7.

158 *The setbacks associated* Ibid., p. 14.

158 *Henry the Eighth* Barrington Boardman, *Flappers, Bootleggers, "Typhoid Mary" and the Bomb* (New York: Harper and Row, 1989), p. 45.

159 *The glazed and fired clay* Duncan, *American Art Deco*, p. 148.

159 *Carla Breeze writes* Carla Breeze, *Pueblo Deco* (New York: Rizzoli, 1990), p. 95.

159 *It seems to relate to* Ibid.

160 *One of the more amusing* Ibid., p. 89.

160 *Its boards supported the oratory* From the historic marker in front of the theater in Wichita Falls.

160 *As early as 1900 in New* Rudi Stern, *Let There Be Neon* (New York: Harry N. Abrams, 1979), p. 16.

160 *Like Art Deco, neon* Ibid.

164 *He noted, "Neon ... became* Ibid.

165 *Not only were eagle "gargoyles"* Duncan, *American Art Deco*, p. 170.

165 *"For my part I wish that* Elinor Lander Horwitz, *The Bird, the Banner, and Uncle Sam* (Philadelphia: J. B. Lippincott, 1976), pp. 37 38.

167 *The carvings were the work* Breeze, *Pueblo Deco*, p. 51.

167 *It was built in 1930* Willard Robinson, *The People's Architecture* (Austin: Univ. of Texas at Austin, 1983), p. 257.

167 *The curling moustache* Loyd C. and June-Marie Engelbrecht, *Henry C. Trost,* (El Paso: El Paso Public Library Association, 1981), p. 74.

169 *The Bassett Building* Ibid., p. 111.

170 *An old-timer on the High Plains* Joe Pickle, *Gettin' Started, Howard County's First Twenty-five Years* (Big Springs: Howard County Heritage Museum, 1980), p. 9.

Bibliography

Adams, Andy. *The Log of a Cowboy*. Lincoln: University of Nebraska Press, 1964.

Alter, Judy. *Thistle Hill*. Fort Worth: Texas Christian University Press, 1988.

Amarillo Historic Building Survey and Preservation Program Recommendations. Compiled by Charles Page and Associates. Amarillo: N.p., 1981.

Avera, Carl L. *Wind Swept Land*. San Antonio: Naylor, 1964.

Baker, Inez. *Yesterday in Hall County, Texas*. Memphis, Tex.: N.p., 1940.

Barrick, Nolan E. *Texas Tech: The Unobserved Heritage*. Lubbock: Texas Tech University Press, 1985.

Blodgett, Jan. *Land of Bright Promise*. Austin: University of Texas Press, 1988.

Boardman, Barrington. *Flappers, Bootleggers, "Typhoid Mary" and the Bomb*. New York: Harper and Row, 1989.

Bolton, Herbert E. *Coronado*. Albuquerque: University of New Mexico Press, 1990.

Breeze, Carla. *Pueblo Deco*. New York: Rizzoli, 1990.

Browder, Virginia. *Donley County: Land o' Promise*. Clarendon: Nortex Press, 1975.

———. *Hall County: Heritage Trails*. 2 vols. Canyon: Staked Plains Press, 1984.

Caffey, David L. *The Old Home Place: Farming on the West Texas Frontier*. Burnet, Tex.: Eakin Press, 1981.

A Catalogue of Texas Properties in the National Register of Historic Places. Compiled by James Wright Steely. Austin: Texas Historical Commission, 1984.

Coleman, Max. *From Mustanger to Lawyer*. Vol. 1. Lubbock: Max Coleman, 1960.

Comee, Fred T. "Louis Curtiss of Kansas City." P/A, August 1963.

Connor, Seymour V. "The Founding of Lubbock." In *A History of Lubbock*. edited by Lawrence Graves, pp. 68–97. Lubbock: West Texas Museum Association, Texas Technological College, 1959.

———. "The New Century." In *A History of Lubbock*, edited by Lawrence Graves, pp. 98–126. Lubbock: West Texas Museum Association, Texas Technological College, 1959.

Corder, Jim W. *Lost in West Texas*. College Station: Texas A&M Press, 1988.

Dawson, John C. *High Plains Yesterdays*. Austin: Eakin Press, 1985.

Dick, Everett. *The Sod-House Frontier* (1854–1890). Lincoln: Johnsen Publishing, 1954.

Downing, Andrew Jackson. Victorian Cottage Residences. 1873. Reprint. New York: Dover Press, 1981.

Drone, Craig Alan. "The Station at San Angelo." Master's thesis, Texas Tech University, 1989.

Duncan, Alastair. *American Art Deco*. New York: Harry N. Abrams, 1986.

Edwards, Ross. *Fiddle Dust*. Denver: Big Mountain Press, 1965.

Engelbrecht, Lloyd C. and June-Marie. *Henry C. Trost: Architect of the Southwest*. El Paso: El Paso Public Library Association, 1981.

Fehrenbach, T. R. *Lone Star*. New York: Collier Books, 1985.

Forbis, William H. *The Cowboys*. New York: Time-Life Books, 1973.

Gill, Brendan. *Many Masks: A Life of Frank Lloyd Wright*. New York: Ballantine Books, 1988.

Gottfried, Herbert, and Jan Jennings. *American Vernacular Design—1870–1940*. New York: Van Nostrand/Reinhold, 1985.

Greene, A. C. *A Personal Country*. College Station: Texas A&M University Press, 1979.

Grow, Lawrence. *Waiting for the 5:05*. New York: Main Street/Universe Books, 1977.

Haley, J. Evetts. *Charles Goodnight*. Norman: University of Oklahoma Press, 1979.

Hancock, George E. *Go-Devils, Flies and Black-eyed Peas*. Corsicana, Tex.: George E. Hancock, 1985.

History of the Achison, Topeka, & Santa Fe. Edited by Pamela Berkman. Greenwich, Conn.: Brompton Books, 1988.

History of Erath County. Compiled by Erath County Historical Commission. Dallas: Taylor Publishing, 1980.

"A Historic Structures Report on St. Paul's on-the-Plains, Episcopal Church." Edited by S. Elizabeth Sasser. Lubbock: College of Architecture, Texas Tech University, 1989. Photocopy.

Holden, W. C. "Immigration and Settlement in West Texas." *West Texas Historical Association Yearbook* 5 (June 1920).

———. *Rollie Burns*. 1932. Reprint. College Station: A&M University Press, 1986.

———. "Indians, Spaniards, and Anglos." In *A History of Lubbock*, edited by Lawrence Graves, pp. 17–44. Lubbock: West Texas Museum Association, Texas Technological College, 1959.

Horgan, Paul. *The Heroic Triad*. Austin: Texas Monthly Press, 1987.

Horwitz, Elinor Lander. *The Bird, the Banner, and Uncle Sam*. Philadelphia: J. B. Lippincott, 1976.

Hughes, Lenore Harris. *Holy Adobe*. El Paso: Hughes Publishing, 1982.

———. *Adobe Adobes*. El Paso: Hughes Publishing, 1985.

Jon Irwin. "The Haydon [Potton] House." Texas Architect 21 (September 1971): 17–19.

Kerr, John Leeds. *Destination Topolobampo*. San Marino: Golden West Books, 1986.

Key, Della Tyler. *In Cattle Country: A History of Potter County*. Wichita Falls, Tex.: Nortex, 1972.

King County: Windmills and Barbed Wire. Comp. and ed. by the King County Historical Society. Quanah, Tex.: Nortex Press, 1976.

Knapik, Jane. *Uvalde Heritage Homes*. Uvalde, Tex.: N.p., 1976.

Knight, Oliver. *Fort Worth*. Fort Worth: Texas Christian University Press, 1990.

Kouwenhoven, John A. *Made in America*. New York: Doubleday, 1962.

Langford, J. O. *Big Bend: A Homesteader's Story*. Austin: University of Texas Press, 1986.

Lore and Legend: Mitchell County, Vol. 1. Colorado City, Tex.: *Colorado Record*, 1976.

Lynes, Russell. *The Tastemakers*. New York: Harper & Brothers, 1955.

McCarty, John L. *Maverick Town.* Norman: University of Oklahoma Press, 1988.

McAlester, Virginia and Lee. *A Field Guide to American Houses.* New York: Alfred A. Knopf, 1986.

Maass, John. *The Gingerbread Age.* New York: Bramhall House, 1967.

———. *The Victorian Home in America.* New York: Hawthorn Books, 1972.

Magoffin, Susan Shelby. *Down the Santa Fe Trail and into New Mexico.* Edited by Stella M. Drumm. Lincoln: University of Nebraska Press, 1982.

Maguire, Jack. "The Cereal That Won The West." Photocopy distributed by Post Chamber of Commerce. N.p., nd.

Matthews, Sallie Reynolds. *Interwoven.* College Station: Texas A&M University Press, 1988.

Meeks, Carroll L. *The Railroad Station: An Architectural History.* New Haven: Yale University Press, 1964.

Moss, Roger W., and Gail Caskey Winkler. *Victorian Exterior Decoration.* New York: Henry Holt, 1987.

Neal, Bill. *The Last Frontier: The Story of Hardeman County.* Quanah, Tex.: *Quanah Tribune-Chief,* 1966.

Olien, Roger M., and Diana Davids Olien. *Life in the Oil Fields.* Austin: Texas Monthly Press, 1986.

Perry, H. G. (Grady). *Grand Ol' Erath,* Vol. 1. Dublin, Tex.: N.p., 1974.

Pickle, Joe. *Gettin' Started: Howard County's First Twenty-Five Years.* Burnet, Tex.: Nortex Press, 1980.

Pioneer Days—Two Views. Edited by Kathryn Duff and Betty Kay Seibt. Abilene: Zachry Associates, 1876.

Pomada, Elizabeth, and Michael Larsen. *Daughters of Painted Ladies.* New York: E. P. Dutton, 1987.

Portals at the Pass. Edited by Evan H. Antone. El Paso: El Paso Chapter of the American Institute of the Architects, 1984.

The Ranching Heritage Center: The Museum of Texas Tech University. Lubbock: Texas Tech University Press, 1976.

Reeves, Agnes Lufkin. *From Hacienda to Bungalow.* Albuquerque: University of New Mexico Press, 1988.

Riley, Glenda. *The Female Frontier.* Lawrence: University of Kansas Press, 1988.

Robertson, Pauline D. and R. L. *Cowman's Country.* Amarillo: Paramount Publishing, 1981.

Robinson, Willard B. *The People's Architecture.* Austin: University of Texas, 1983.

Rollins, Philip Ashton. *The Cowboy.* Albuquerque: University of New Mexico Press, 1979.

Rudofsky, Bernard. *Architecture without Architects.* New York: Museum of Modern Art, 1965.

Ruff, Ann, and Henri Farmer. *Historic Homes of Texas.* Houston: Lone Star Books, 1987.

Sims, Judge Orland L. *Cowpokes, Nesters, and So Forth.* Austin: Encino Press, 1970.

Stern, Rudi. *Let There Be Neon.* New York: Harry N. Abrams, 1979.

Sullivan, Louis H. *The Autobiography of an Idea.* New York: Peter Smith, 1949.

Texas: A Guide to the Lone Star State. Compiled by the Workers of the Writers' Program of the Work Projects Administration in the State of Texas. New York: Hastings House, 1940.

A Time to Purpose. Vol. 2. Edited by Mrs. Ralph E. Randall and the Carson County Historical Survey Committee. Carson County, Tex.: Pioneer Publishers, 1966.

Tocqueville, Alexis de. *Democracy in America.* Translated by Henry Reeve. London: Oxford University Press, 1952.

Wagon Wheels: A History of Garza County. edited by Charles Didway, Seagraves, Tex.: Pioneer Book Publisher, 1973.

Webb, Walter Prescott. *The Great Plains.* New York: Grosset and Dunlap, 1971.

Werner, M. R. *P. T. Barnum.* London: Jonathan Cape, 1923.

Whiffen, Marcus. *American Architecture since 1780: A Guide to Styles.* Cambridge: MIT Press, 1969.

Williams, A. Richard. *The Urban Stage: A Reflection of Architecture and Urban Design.* Champaign, Ill.: Superior Printing, 1980.

"Ysleta del Sur Pueblo Community Building." *Texas Architect* 23 (October 1971): 7–9.

Glossary of Architectural Terms

Abacus A square slab forming the upper part of the capital of a column.

Architrave The beam that connects columns and is placed below the frieze in the **entablature**.

Ashlar Rectilinear stones laid in a regular course.

Assemblage A surface covered by a variety of materials, usually forming an abstract pattern.

Balloon Framing A system of light wood framing using thin plates and studs secured with nails and rising the entire height of the building. This system, originating in Chicago during the 1830s, superceded timber- and brace-framed construction. The principal characteristics are the use of small-dimension sawn lumber and nailed connections. Closely placed vertical studs are covered by wood sheathing.

Balustrade A handrail supported by small pillars, each referred to as a *baluster*.

Bargeboard or **Verge Board** A board attached to the edge of a gabled roof.

Batter A term applied to a wall with a slanting face. (*See* illustration.)

Bay Units measuring the spaces between columns or wall segments; also used to identify projecting windows.

Board-and-Batten A wall system composed of wide vertical boards covered by narrow strips over the cracks between boards. The boards are nailed to a plate and sill at top and bottom.

Box-and-Strip A vernacular term used in West Texas for **Board and Batten.**

Bracket A support for an overhang; when supporting the upper portion of a cornice, brackets are often termed *modillions* or *consoles.*

Canales Wooden gutter spouts used for carrying rainwater from the adobe roofs of homes and churches in southern Texas and in the pueblos and Spanish villages of New Mexico.

Canted Bay A three sided bay window with two canted (slanted) sides and one parallel to the main wall of the house. This type occurs frequently in the Queen Anne style. The canted sides may be covered with decorative hoods. (*See* illustration.)

Battered wall, Cottle County Courthouse, Paducah

Canted bay with hood, 206 South Elm, Weatherford

Crenellation (crenels and merlons), Brownwood jail

"Jigsaw" gingerbread, Historical Museum, Seymour

Capital The crowning feature of a column.

Captain's Walk A square platform at the top of a hipped roof surrounded by a balustrade. Also called the *widow's walk* .

Colonnade A series of columns.

Cornice The topmost part of the classical entablature, or any horizontal part projecting from the top of a wall. The *raking cornice* frames the triangular lines of a pediment rising from the horizontal base.

Crenellation The upper feature or battlement placed on a fortified wall. The notched openings are *crenels* and the solid masonry sections are *merlons*. (*See* illustration.)

Cresting An ornament placed along the roof ridge.

Cupola A small domed structure placed above a roof or tower.

Dormer A window projecting from a pitched roof.

Echinus Molding The rounded molding placed beneath the abacus block of the Doric order.

Entablature The upper portion of an architectural order supported on columns and consisting of the architrave, the frieze and the cornice.

Facade The principal face of a building or any one of its sides.

Fanlight A semicircular window, often over a door.

Finial The decorative ornament at the apex of an architectural feature, for example, a spire or roof.

Fluting Vertical channeling of a column shaft.

Frieze The portion of the entablature between the architrave and the cornice. This is often decorated with sculpture in relief.

Gable A triangular wall defined by the enclosing lines of a pitched roof.

Gazebo A pavilion or small garden house.

Gingerbread Elaborate ornament, usually of wood, applied to Victorian architecture.

Hipped Roof A roof with inclining planes sloping up from four sides.

Intaglio A design incised in stone or a like medium that is cut below the surface.

Jacal A method of construction using vertical poles set in the ground and then daubed with mud as filling and insulation.

Jigsaw Work Decorative moldings and bargeboards cut in patterns with a jigsaw, particularly popular during the Gothic Revival in the nineteenth century. (*See* illustration.)

Keystone The central stone of an arch.

Latias Peeled branches or poles laid diagonally or at right angles across the beams, or *vigas*, forming a ceiling. Also called *savinos*. (*See* illustration.)

Medallion A medallike design with a figure in relief.

Metope In the frieze of the Greek Doric order, the slabs placed between the triglyphs, usually carved or relief.

Mirador A small room on the roof of a Spanish house commanding a wide view.

Modillion *See* **Bracket**.

Neoclassic (1900–1940) An architectural development, or style, characterized by a two-story porch supported by colossal columns in most instances of the Corinthian, Composite, or Ionic Orders.

Oriel The oriel window projects out from a wall of an upper story. It may be two or three sided and have its own roof, a tent form, or half dome.

Palladian A design adapted from the work of the late Italian Renaissance architect Andrea Palladio (b. 1508–d. 1580).

Parapet A wall rising above the roof, sometimes battlemented.

Pavilion A summer house or a structure connected to a larger building.

Pediment A triangular wall that fills in between the slopes of a gabled roof. In classical architecture it is above the entablature and is usually ornamented with sculptured figures.

Pergola An arbor often roofed with vines. Also a small summer house.

Pilaster A strip partially set into a wall often having the characteristics of a Classical order. It may function structurally, but it is often purely decorative.

Placita A courtyard surrounded by the wings of a house. *Patio* is a term used frequently for a roofless inner room. The *placita* may be defined by three wings of the house and thus be more open.

Polychrome Having many and varied colors.

Portal an open porch that is covered by a roof.

Port Cochere A side porch and entry arranged as a roofed space to permit passengers to get out of carriages (and later cars) in a protected area.

Vigas and *latias*, Nuestra Senora de la Concepción del Pueblo Socorro at Socorro

Quoins, Eddelman-McFarland House, Fort Worth

Spindlework, 206 South Elm, Weatherford

Portico An entry porch with the roof supported on at least one side by columns.

Prefabrication Factory manufacture of standardized parts to be shipped to and assembled at the building site.

Puddled Adobe A method used by the pre-Columbian Indians in the Southwest for building up walls by adding successive layers of hand-shaped adobe, each course drying before the next application.

Puzzle Rubble Broken stone put together in one large surface of uncoursed stonework.

Quoins Stones at the corners of buildings, distinguished by a texture in contrast with the masonry wall treatment. (*See* illustration.)

Relief Carving Sculpture created by carving the design so that it is raised above the background. Also called *bas-relief.*

Rondel A small circle usually filled with sculpture in relief.

Rubble Undressed stones that may be coursed or laid in a random fashion.

Rustication Stonework with a roughened surface and beveled edges.

Savinos *See* **Latias.**

Semiattached Column A portion of a column embedded in a wall, usually as a decorative device but sometimes as reinforcement. The column may have the characteristics of one of the Classical orders.

Spindlework Slender wood designs turned on a lathe; an identifying feature of the Queen Anne style. (*See* illustration.)

Spire The tapering termination of a tower. (*See* illustration, p. 185.)

Stickwork The ornamental placement of pieces of millwork, often found in gable ends.

String Course A molding that projects and runs horizontally along the face of a building. This is a method of emphasizing the stories.

Tequitqui A Nahuatl term that means "tributary"; it is used to designate a new quality of style, found after the Spanish Conquest of Mexico. This resulted from the interpenetration of indigenous elements with European art.

Terra Cotta Baked clay building material that may be glazed in multiple colors. Architecturally, it may be used as a veneer and is often set in decorative patterns.

Transom A hinged window placed above a door and used for ventilation.

Triglyph A block with vertical channels alternating with the metope in the frieze of a Doric entablature.

Turret A small tower.

Veneer A surface layer.

Veranda A porch characterized by openess and having the characteristics of a gallery intended for walking and social activities. There is a strong link with the grounds or yard.

Vernacular As the term pertains to building, it implies the use of traditional methods handed down from one generation to another: traditional methods of construction that do not rely on professionally trained architects.

Viga A log that is used as a primary ceiling beam. *See* ***Latias.*** (See illustration, p. 183.)

Volute A spiral ornament.

Zaguan A covered passage leading into a courtyard.

Ziggurat A structure built of stepped terraces each smaller than the one on which it rests; the walls slant from the base upward. Used to describe mud pyramids built in Mesopotamia.

Spire, depot at El Paso

Index

Dugout to Deco: Building in West Texas, 1880–1930

was supported generously by the <u>CH</u> Foundation and

the Helen Jones Foundation

in honor of the sisters

Christine DeVitt and Helen DeVitt Jones.